Five
Last
Acts

The safe and dignified ways that people use
to end their own lives when faced with
unbearable and unrelievable suffering

2nd edition, expanded and revised

Chris Docker

First edition 2007
published by Exit,
17 Hart Street
Edinburgh EH1
3RN
Scotland U.K.

Second edition
2010
© Chris Docker

Dedicated to Virginia Woolf, (1882 – 1941)

Contents

Foreword

By David Donnison and Kay Carmichael

Readers in the pride of their youth may wonder why anyone would write a book about methods for killing oneself. Well, here's why.

A hundred years ago, when death approached, three-quarters of our people would be lying in their own beds, close relatives nearby, and visited occasionally by friends, a nurse or a doctor who could do little more than make the patient as comfortable as possible. Later, their bodies would be laid out and the neighbours would come to pay their last respects. Death was a domestic event; its timing decided by nature.

Today, three-quarters of us will die in hospitals or other institutions, surrounded by strangers and tended by people in white coats with the technology to keep us alive for long periods. Death has become – and will increasingly become – a medical event; its timing often decided by doctors.

Patients are increasingly demanding that their voices be heard when that decision is made. Armed with information from the Internet about the likely course of their diseases, supported by pressure groups speaking for the people who suffer from these diseases, and more prepared than their grandparents were to take legal action to enforce their rights, their voices are indeed more often heard. Doctors are less tempted to act as 'sage on the stage', seeing themselves more as 'guide on the side', helping patients to make their own decisions so far as nature permits.

If you want your life prolonged as far as possible, the doctors can do their best for you. But if you ask them to help you bring it to a decent end you will run into all sorts of legal and professional obstacles. Assisting a suicide is a crime in the UK which may get professionals struck off. Middle-class patients, with doctors among their close friends and relatives, often get help in drawing things to a close. But too many people find themselves helpless victims of pain or humiliating dependence on strangers, watching their loved ones buckle under the burdens they unwillingly lay on them. Meanwhile many more fear this may become their fate.

So it's not surprising that, for years, every survey of the British has shown that large and growing majorities of our fellow citizens – now about 80 per cent – would support the legalisation of voluntary euthanasia in the kinds of cases most of us would regard as reasonable – subject to the safeguards that more civilised nations like the Dutch have worked out to protect us from unscrupulous relatives and people like Dr. Shipman.

But politicians, who were prepared to introduce family allowances, abolish the death penalty, take us into Europe and into the Iraq disaster – all widely opposed by many of their people – are not prepared to accept the views of this massive majority. That's probably because well-funded and strident spokesmen of some faith groups oppose such a reform; and because the dead and dying have no votes.

Stuck in this impasse, a small but growing number of courageous patients, their carers and doctors, are going to the courts to seek permission for one form or another of assisted suicide. Some succeed and some fail – but all have to go through a ghastly process in a public arena that was never intended to deal with such complex, personal and painful issues. Eventually, one of the Parliaments or Assemblies of the United Kingdom will enable doctors to respond more humanely to patients approaching the end of their lives. Perhaps the Scottish Parliament, already innovative in so many ways, will give a lead?

The argument for a legal, civil right that enables people facing intolerable circumstances to gain professional help either to prolong life as far as possible or to bring it to an end has long been won. The opinion polls repeatedly show that. While we wait for our politicians to gain the courage to respond to that majority we are morally entitled to find an exit for ourselves in ways that are as secure, painless and dignified as possible.

For that, no-one is better equipped to help than Chris Docker who has won widespread respect for the work he has done on this question for over fifteen years. This book brings up to date his publications of earlier years for which many people have been grateful. Even if they never feel the need to use his advice, his readers will be better equipped to discuss in a relaxed and rational way the decisions that have to be taken towards the end of our lives.

David Donnison is Professor Emeritus in the University of Glasgow. He was Convener of the Voluntary Euthanasia Society of Scotland, and took a leading role in the biggest opinion survey on euthanasia yet made in Britain[1].

Dr. Kay Carmichael, writer, broadcaster and social worker, also played a leading part in the movement for legalising voluntary euthanasia.

---

[1]Donnison D, Bryson C, Matters of Life and Death: Attitudes to Euthanasia, in: Jowell R, Curtice J et al (eds), British Social Attitudes 13th Report, Dartmouth 1996:161-183

Introduction

Death is the big unknown. Some ancient civilisations based their whole culture on trying to be as certain as possible about death, to cover all the possibilities when the moment arrived. From this they developed a psychology of dying which also gave them insights into living.

The advance of medicine gave greater life expectancy but also, in many ways, made death a more complex affair. With prolongation of life came uncertainties about living on into an intolerable state during the period before dying. In a society where individuals are accustomed to be able to exert control over their lives, these very uncertainties are unwelcome. The sense of control is something we cherish as our power to do nearly everything else slips away. We may live to be a hundred or more, and die peacefully in our sleep, but if it should not go that smoothly we want to know what to do about it.

Why this book?
Firstly the demand. People want to feel empowered. They might never use the information, but they want to have some certainty at the end of life – in case medical promises of a peaceful, dignified death don't live up to expectation. We know *most* end-of-life suffering and indignity can be ade-quately controlled: we also know (especially from the many high profile cases) that not all of it can. 'Most' is of little comfort if it happens to be your suffering and indignity that is not adequately controlled. This book is to supply information. Facts that you can check and feel confident about. Not just relying on the Internet, or the reassurances of a colourful personality; and not even the increasingly uncertain prospect of help from abroad. This book offers the fruits of twenty years of research and also the sources – to enable you to see

how the conclusions are reached. This is particularly useful if, for instance, someone comes on the television and says it is 'easy' to just starve yourself (for instance) and you have to ask yourself, which claims are correct? You'll find two styles in this volume. There is the simple and straightforward description of what you need to know. Then there is the more detailed source reference material and analysis.

But firstly, what is the moral position? There is a consensus among ethicists and the law for exceptional cases that, when life starts and a child has no prospect of any enjoyment of life whatsoever, it would be cruel and inhuman to continue. (In all other cases we strive for life.) For instance, for an infant that cannot speak, taste, see, has zero chance of improvement or adulthood, and is entering a world where pain will be its only experience; we allow that life to end. A competent adult should be in an even stronger position. As their own life draws to a close, they are best placed to indicate the views of the most important person in the equation: their own. Whether one argues from a utilitarian point of view in order to maximize beneficial outcomes and minimize harm; or with Kantian arguments based on autonomy, dignity and individual rights, the same conclusion can be reached namely: that, as long as they do not interfere with the liberty of others, persons should be free to pursue their own good in their own way.

When death approaches in old age, things may not be as simple as logic would have them be. Palliative care is so advanced in the developed world that most pain can, given the right drugs and equipment, be controlled; but the ability to control pain is not 100%, neither is the ability to control distressing and degrading symptoms. Our right to life and desire for life is so strong, we need extreme circumstances to convince us it should end. The wonderful and persuasive benefits of modern palliative care are not to be minimized. But they should not be placed on such a pedestal as to overrule a person's free will completely.

When it is a child's life, a doctor has to decide, using the most stringent – if arbitrary – rules to make that decision. In the case of a competent adult, that individual is the only one who can decide, yet the law ties their doctor's hands. Simply stopping treatment will not necessarily result in death. The law in most countries does not allow a medical person to provide a kind, reassuring and safe injection, on request, to draw the final days to a close, even with suitable safeguards. This leaves the person with the more complex option of taking matters into their own hands. Failure can bring even more suffering to an already unbearable situation. If someone has rationally decided to end their life a little earlier, in the face of unbearable and unrelievable suffering, is it not a blessing if they can do so without further unnecessary pain? This book does not encourage anyone to take that final decision. But if the decision is taken, it aims to provide the most scientific knowledge available by which further unnecessary pain and indignity may be avoided. Experience has shown that having this knowledge will often give people the courage to face misfortune and even the will to live longer.

The 'least worst options' explored in this book should not be put into effect before all other possibilities have been examined. Palliative care is continuously changing and should not be discounted simply because you knew someone it failed to benefit some years ago, or with different ailments. On the other hand, it is counterproductive to leave all but a skimming through of the text until the last minute. The book holds an escape route, a key to a door marked 'exit', a way out. Like many journeys, considerable planning and familiarity with the route, the accessories you will need, back-up plans and so on, are all sensible precautions.

If you are in depression, please remember that some kinds of depression can be successfully treated. Depression becomes even more common as we get older, partly because there are often more reasons for unhappiness. But such depression sometimes responds to antidepressant drugs or psychological treatments, persevered with over a number of weeks. Impulsive suicide, even if very understandable, is to be discouraged. Not only later in life, but among young people whose feelings have been savagely hurt. Emotional wounds often heal, even if it doesn't seem so at the time. Help from loving friends and doctors may be there just around the corner.

Sometimes we hear from people who feel driven to suicide out of despair brought on by emotional turmoil that makes life too much to bear. Although we try to offer a sympathetic ear when possible, we would urge people who are in this category to turn to people who have more time and expertise in this area than we have – for example, the Samaritans (In the USA and other countries: Crisis Intervention Agencies or Suicide Prevention Agencies. You can also find a list of numbers outside the UK at www.befrienders.org) The Samaritans provide sympathetic, caring and completely confidential support by telephone. They are non-religious based and available to anyone. You can share you innermost feelings with volunteers without fear of judgement or criticism, and safe in the knowledge that they will not repeat anything to anyone else. Actually, you don't even need to tell them your name. They are emphatically *not* an 'anti-suicide' society – they simply provide an opportunity to talk when there is perhaps no-one else to talk to. You call will not be traced. Find out more at www.samaritans.org or you can call them on 08457 90 90 90 in the UK and Northern Ireland. You should be aware that there is a critical period immediately after the diagnosis of cancer during which the excess risk of ill-considered suicide is particularly high. Take your time.

Be very careful of the legal position if you are planning to end your life by your own hand or with the help of another. *The Suicide Act 1961* (England & Wales) is fairly broad in allowing prosecution of anyone that can be considered to have aided, abetted, counselled or procured the suicide or attempted suicide of another person. Suicide itself is not an offence, but the penalty for assisting can be up to fourteen years' imprisonment. There are indications that prosecutions will not be brought in compassionate cases where the Crown Prosecution Service feels that certain conditions have been met. But the details are far from being fully tested and certainly no guarantee can be held in advance. (Further details from the CPS website at www.cps.gov.uk under 'assisted suicide.') Even providing information or being present could be interpreted as an illegal act. I have sometimes heard people say that assisted suicide is 'not illegal' in Scotland. This is dangerously misleading. Scots law can pursue similar ends when prosecuting through the common law whereas English law uses a statutory provision.

Is this book illegal? If not, how does it differ from just giving the same information to a friend? The information provided by Exit, in this book and through workshops, is not directed at a specific person about to use it to end their life. In the legal parlance of Scotland, we say that there has to be a new action intervening to connect the information and a suicide (a *'novus actus interveniens'*). Only a tiny proportion of people reading this book, fortunately, will ever have to use it. Exit does not know who they are, and so is not connected to the suicide. If the law changes after this edition goes to press, you will find updates in the magazine we send to members or news of them on the Exit Euthanasia Blog: http://exiteuthanasia.wordpress.com/

One other thing you should know – it is not possible to pop over to the Netherlands or Belgium to be euthanized by a doctor. Those countries, and the one or two states in the USA that offer assistance in dying, have strict rules to prevent 'suicide tourism.' Switzerland has slightly more relaxed rules so far, and a different approach means doctors are not so directly involved; but the financial costs are very high, there is no guarantee of assistance, and the Swiss government may well outlaw such leniency if current proposals are passed. Similarly finding drugs in Mexico or exotic locations is fraught with pitfalls. For these many reasons, *Five Last Acts* is your best security with which to face an unknown future.

"What is the best method?"
This is a question the present author has been asked many times, especially at the workshops around the country where the techniques explained in these pages are demonstrated. My answer is always the same: "It depends." My preference is to have access and familiarity with *at least* two or three methods: it is much harder to learn how to use them successfully if you leave it until you are already ill, but the point often overlooked is that *your circumstances may change* before you seriously want to end your life. Your mobility may be affected; you may or may not be hospital- or nursing-home- bound; you might otherwise find yourself not at home with all the equipment you planned on using; or someone may have discovered your drugs cache and removed it.

Hopefully none of these things will happen, but do you want to chance your luck? Differing circumstances sometimes call for different methods, so the wise will prepare for a number of eventualities. To be as foolproof as possible, the best planning will take the unexpected into consideration – that way you are easily within your abilities, not stretching them or putting all your 'eggs in one basket.' Rather than just choose a method you like 'best' – you might decide the wisest course is to study them all and master as many as you can. Then you can practice (safely) until you *know* what you would do – and without referring to this book! Don't wait until you are ill. Make the knowledge your own now – think of it like carrying an umbrella in the car in case of a rainy day. When you have that secure knowledge, even if you never use it, you will have gained something that is of inestimable value: being in control.

Make it part of a big picture
Focussing on the act of ending one's life alone makes it all too easy to overlook essential details. You're driving a brand new car on a clear road at 70 miles an hour and everything's fine. Suddenly there's a downpour. You realise too late that the controls for the windscreen wipers are not where they were on your old car. You manage to get the car under control and onto the hard shoulder.

It might have been different. There might have been a passenger who could have pointed out the relevant switch. (They might also have felt traumatised until everything was ok!) Things don't always happen the way we plan them. The section on moral and legal issues is based on many case studies – real life examples. It highlights some of the not uncommon contingencies. Examples where all the planning, confidence and foresight has to be modified rapidly at the last minute with potentially serious consequences, either for the person ending their life or for their nearest and dearest. By taking the time to get into a habit of thinking through these and similar scenarios, you can avoid problems at the most critical time in your life – your death.

Making memories that matter
You might want to consider making it as if it were a memory, something you could imagine looking back on. For those that you leave behind, the memory of everything you did in your life (including how you died) is the most valuable thing you can give. In your own mind, write your own life story, continuing the story up to, including, and after your death. This is part of your legacy, more than in any material sense. The footprint you leave on the world before passing on. Fill in all the details you want, include all the wonderful things. From that vantage point, look back along your timeline at the various endings and possibilities, the possible causes of death, last chapters, conceivable last acts, how you handled it. Are there any details in the final scenario you want to change? The knowledge in this book, properly digested, will provide you with the calm assurance that you can be in control. Imagine that now, the calm confidence you will possess. A slight apprehension perhaps as you set sail on that final journey, but still the captain of your ship, a knowledgeable hand at the tiller. If loved ones grow anxious, it is your serenity that gives them strength. When all the details are as perfect in your own mind as you can make them, return to the present. Don't dwell morbidly on it. Give yourself a shake, maybe make a cup of tea. But you will be able to call on a clear picture of all the things you need to put in place so that, whatever eventuality should arise, you can take your last curtain call with dignity, in a way that fits your life story.

Individual memories, letters to loved ones
Although much of this book deals with the practicalities, using helium or drugs and so on, an issue that requires just as much thought is how we tidy up our affairs and ensure that any pain for those left behind is minimised. For some, their close friends and family will feel sympathetic to one's actions. Others may feel that it is better not to explain certain things in too much detail. Whichever your circumstances, it is very helpful to leave a clear statement explaining that your final act was your own carefully considered decision, and that nothing anyone else could have said would have changed anything.

Once you have made your own peace within yourself you can do the same with those close to you. Say in so many words how much you love them, how much you have valued the time shared together. Such a letter can both help to protect loved ones from blame and also stop them from blaming themselves (which is a frequent part of the grieving process). How should people remember you? At the time of death, it is easy to become overpowered by negative images of grief for the one departed.

Instead of writing one note to everyone, why not compose a different letter to each individual who is special to you? Special people are defined in our lives not so much by their name and background. Think about a special person for a moment. Probably there is some incident in the past. A word, a phrase, something they did or that you shared. It may have been something quite trivial, but there will be a point in time when you knew: knew how special they were. Recall the moment, then describe it in your letter to them. So they can recall it too.

The English language, for all its richness, doesn't really have a suitable word to denote suicide that is the result of a careful and rational choice in the face of unbearable suffering. The phrase 'self-deliverance' has long been used in Scotland, and is used frequently in this volume.

This second edition
The book has grown considerably from the original 186 pages. There are now over 40 illustrations and line drawings; and much of the text has been both expanded and simplified, to make it easier to follow and implement. Source material is even fuller; to assist other researchers and allow readers to have confidence in what is here put before them. An additional chapter on moral philosophy is included to put the ethical basis of publishing on a firmer footing: and researching it also turned up valuable information that will hopefully set readers' minds at ease on issues such as self-deliverance methods falling into the 'wrong hands,' statistical and psychological studies, and a philosophical analysis of self-deliverance as a 'heroic' and noble measure.

The helium chapter has been expanded and extra detail added to overcome slightest possibilities of discomfort or ill-ease. The starvation chapter has been greatly expanded to include new information of practical value. The compression chapter has been expanded to provide even greater safeguards. The guide to guides has been expanded to bring it up to date and cover more background. Alternative manuals are discussed. An index has been introduced. And the law has been given in much more explicit, accurate detail than was before possible, thanks to the guidelines of the Director of Public Prosecutions in England and Wales, and the evidence from the Solicitor General in Scotland. (While other jurisdictions worldwide are equally important, the position tends to be more straightforward and the main provisions, for instance in the Netherlands, Switzerland, Belgium and the USA are all mentioned.) The drugs chapter has been greatly enlarged to give further information on the possibilities of travelling to Mexico for drugs. The plastic bags chapter has been enlarged to include even more practical tips discovered at the workshop dress rehearsals.

The primary aim of this book is to give you the information that can increase your chances of a peaceful and dignified dying. Until the law is changed, it has its limitations – if you were completely paralysed, for instance, you sadly would not be able to use the information unaided. Finally, I have to ask readers' indulgence on matters of layout, including typographical errors or omissions. I have done my utmost to avoid the slightest factual error, including any references to people or other works mentioned. It would have been good to have another year to 'beautify' the book, produce a fuller index, and put all the references into an academically consistent format. But time and costs, as is so often the case, are most pressing. The highest concern is the need of people seeking a reliable manual with all the necessary instructions in one place. My own rules are: 1) it must be accurate, 2) it must be practical, 3) it must reach you with a minimum of danger to others. In these I am confident. I firmly believe it is probably the best source of such information you can obtain, anywhere in the world. And I hope it gives you both peace of mind and the essential knowledge you so earnestly require.

With every best wish,
Chris Docker, M.Phil (Law & Ethics in Medicine)

Director, Exit

Warning: In Britain and most countries, *it is perfectly legal* to buy and own this book. But, if you do pass it on or show it to someone who with your knowledge is at that point thinking of taking their life, you could, in certain circumstances, be open to prosecution.

Five Last Acts
is based on years of accumulated research up to the present day, both by the author and by others, and occasionally illuminated by fresh insights from the EXIT self-deliverance workshops.

My thanks go to all the people who helped directly or gave inspiration in the writing of this book, including:

Sarah Bailey, Dr Colin Brewer, Professor Robin Downie, Lindsay Friedman, Dr Stephen Jamison, John Hofsess, Derek Humphry, Ailsa Laing, Sheila Little, Marcelo Motta, Marilynne Seguin, Cheryl Smith, Professor Rex Whitehead. Also, the members of Exit, the participants at workshops, and the members of other right-to-die organisations worldwide, including people like Faye Girsh and Ruth von Fuchs, and people who have given time, effort, enthusiasm and money, and most importantly the heartfelt appreciation that makes this effort worthwhile. I in turn appreciate your patience, especially when other tasks such as the Exit magazine or speedy responses to emails have sometimes had to take a back seat as a result! My thanks go to all my tutors at Glasgow University for imbuing me with a grounding and sensitivity to many finer points of the law and medical ethics, for firmly sitting on my self-assurance with a strong dose of reality, and to those who checked my work and would prefer to remain anonymous for professional reasons. Finally, a special thank you to my dear friend Sarah Lewis, whose help and dedication in keeping the office running meant the organisation and the opportunity to produce this book were assured.

Is it all right to think about
. . . our own death . . . ?

Is it all right to think about ... our own death ...?

Since you have made the decision to obtain and read this book, it may come as no surprise that you are about to explore the last taboo. Surprisingly, many people who come to the workshops believe at first they do not need to do this. That if they get the necessary 'recipes' that they can leave any deeper consideration until later. Yet thinking about our own death is not so terrible once you start, and it is *absolutely essential* if you plan to cover as many eventualities as possible.

Perhaps you are glancing through this book while the TV is on or just before you have to do something else. That's fine, but the following section will require your full concentration, so make a mental note to come back to it again when you are not distracted, and with no pressing concerns.

First of all, given that it is going to happen one day, how would you like to die? Picture yourself in the future, shortly before death. What would be your ideal way to go? Probably lack of pain and suffering will feature highly. What else? Suddenly? In your sleep? Picture the circumstances – fill in as many details as possible – where you are, what you can see, hear, feel, touch, taste, even smell. At the end of your life, you are about to experience death the way that you would want. From that point in time, look back into the past, through all the time that has passed since the moment when you read this book. See the things that you did, the preparations that you made, that have put you now in this position of being in control, of knowing that your death will be in a manner of your choosing. It may include some initial periods of uncertainty, areas that you will explore using this book, doubts that you will put to rest.

When you have finished reading the book, you may choose to go back and do the exercise again, to check that there are no 'blank spots' in the knowledge that gave you this feeling of confidence near the end of your life.

Next, I would like to invite you to try imagining different circumstances, one at a time. If you were not, for some reason, to have your 'first choice' preferred death, what would the next choice be? Play the scene out in your mind's eye. Take a few minutes to do it, then clap your hands or stand up to bring you back fully alert to the present moment.

As you gain confidence in the methods outlined in this book, go over the scene carefully, adding difficulties of your own imagination to see how you cope with them. You might want to try imagining that you were hospitalised, or in pain and unable to concentrate well, if you had limited strength in your muscles or if you were taken very ill while away from home or in another country. What are the least worst options? Have you researched the methods outlined sufficiently to manage the situation? After each time you do this exercise, stand up or do something to shake yourself out of that frame of mind. The intention is not to dwell on these things in a morbid kind of way, but simply to picture the situation fully enough to test your plans of action. After learning the techniques in this book, picture the situation again until you are sure you can cope if all else fails and things are pretty bad. Your plan should include all traditional options, including getting a full and balanced idea of your condition (not rushing off at the first diagnosis). Also knowing how to find (and even demand) the best possible palliative care, but, after due reflection, making sure you can 'pull the plug' and end things yourself peacefully and competently should you decide to do so.

Once you have become practiced at this, it loses its power to shock and it is not in the least morbid. (People attending the Exit workshops are often surprised at how much good cheer and laughter there is as we get to grips with such serious issues.) More importantly, your sense of confidence grows, and death becomes less frightening.

Death has been called many things – including a journey or an adventure – and if these images or metaphors appeal to you, maybe think of this book as your travel guide . . .

Further reading
- How We Die, by Sherwin B. Nuland (Chatto & Windus 1994) contains detailed descriptions of the stages of various common fatal diseases.
- Handbook for Mortals, by Joanne Lynne and Joan Harrold OUP 1999), although written from a point of view more sympathetic to the palliative care movement than the self-deliverance movement, is a very readable book packed with much information of interest and help to people about to die, whether by their own hand or not.
- Final Acts of Love, by Stephen Jamison (Putnam Books, 1995) covers similar emotional territory but as a psychologist and former regional director for the Hemlock Society USA, and also as someone who facilitates workshops on living and dying.
- The Natural Death Handbook. Rider & Co; 3rd Revised edition (6 Nov 2003) by Josefine Speyer and the Natural Death Centre, edited by Stephanie Wienrich. Includes inspirational and practical ideas for preparing for death, including simplifying your affairs and knowing what to say to people.
- Creative Endings – designer Dying & Celebratory Funerals by Nicholas Albury, Lindesay Irvine, Philip Buckley & Stephanie Pieau (eds).

Moral and legal issues

What you need to know in advance . . .

We tend to think that knowing how to end one's life with dignity, to achieve a 'self-deliverance' is all about having the correct formula or technique.

Experience shows that not only do the best laid plans sometimes have to be modified unexpectedly, but often that the idea of acting just on one's own frequently runs into unchartered waters. Self-deliverance can be a fulfilling and very special act, a lasting testament to one's life, or it can be a traumatic experience both for the person at the centre of it and for those left behind.

Wrestling with complicated moral, emotional and legal questions at a time when intense feelings are pressing down on us is not only distressing but can interfere with our concentration and ability to do all that is necessary, especially if one is very ill.

What began as an add-on in the workshops soon proved one of the most popular devices, bringing self-awareness and dramatically improved perspectives. There follows three scenarios. Each one is a composite based on real-life events and draws together key points. If you are skimming through the book at this time, or are otherwise distracted, please make a point of coming back to this chapter to do the exercises with your full attention.

Read through each scenario carefully; then take a few minutes - perhaps with a pen and paper - to write down your thoughts. There are no trick questions about the methods or drugs used

- this is purely to focus on the legal and moral problems raised. What should the people involved have been asking themselves and each other? What are the moral dilemmas? The legal problems? List the key, or underlying, factors as you perceive them, write down the possible courses of action. Who is affected and how? If you need more time, just put your bookmark where you are in the chapter and come back to it.

Scenario One

A woman is desperately ill. She has a terminal illness, her suffering is increasing and it cannot be relieved. She is bedridden and too weak to effect her own self-deliverance. At first she persuades her ten-year old child to fetch pills for her and help to grind them up but she spilt them and was unable to end her life.

Now she has asked her husband to help. He does not know what to do. He is a prominent person in a small town where questions are likely to be asked. She says to him, "I would do it for you . . ."

You may want to use the space below to jot down your thoughts or maybe use a separate piece of paper.

When you have resolved the problems in your own mind (and bear in mind not everyone's analysis will be the same, and there may be more than one 'right answer'), turn to the notes at the end of the chapter for further questions that may come up.

....

....

....

....

....

....

Scenario Two

A gay man has decided to help with the suicide of his partner (who is terminally ill, with unbearable and unrelievable suffering) to make sure 'nothing goes wrong.' He knows he is breaking the law but plans to leave the country before anyone finds out.

1) He helps him study the literature and grind up some tablets and promises to stay with him 'till the end.'

2) After taking the tablets, his partner has difficulty positioning the elastic bands to hold a plastic bag in place. Reluctantly, he goes one step further and offers a second pair of hands. All seems to have gone well.

3) After a short period however, the now unconscious man starts struggling wildly. In tears, his partner tries to restrain his arms, but the unconscious man claws at the bag and breaks it. His partner realises that the only way to complete the act in time will be to suffocate him using a pillow.

You may want to use the space below to jot down thoughts or even use a separate sheet. When you have resolved the problems in your own mind, turn to the notes at the end of the chapter for further questions that may come up.

Scenario Three

A close friend has a terminal illness with only weeks to live. They are not able to obtain the self-deliverance literature in time. They know you have a copy of this book and ask you to let them use it.

You may want to use the space below to jot down your thoughts or maybe use a separate piece of paper. When you have resolved the problems in your own mind, turn to the notes at the end of the chapter for further questions that may come up.

....

....

....

....

....

....

....

....

....

....

....

....

Notes on the moral and legal dilemmas

Scenario One – some points to consider

Presumably she has asked the child thinking that she is too young to be prosecuted. But what of the lasting psychological effects on that child? Is it fair for her to grow up realising that she was the one who unknowingly gave her mother the means to end her life?

How is this different from a knowledgeable decision taken by a competent adult? The presumption about criminal responsibility may also be flawed. In Scotland, for instance, the age of criminal responsibility is eight, currently being reviewed to raise it (probably to ten, in line with England, Wales, and Northern Ireland).

She says to her husband, "I would do it for you", yet it seems they have not discussed it in times of health - is this emotional blackmail? If the husband is pressured into it, how will that affect him? Are the wishes of the dying person the only ones to consider? What about the feelings of the surviving relatives, who must live with their actions for the rest of their lives. Quite separately from how you judge the action to be right or wrong, how will it affect that surviving person psychologically and emotionally if it was *not* a decision entirely of their own choosing or one that they feel comfortable with.

It is quite possible that he will not escape detection. If he is charged and convicted, it may also affect the child, who could be left parentless. Does this affect the rights and wrongs of the mother's request? Does it affect how he should respond? Who should be responsible for making the final decision on whether to assist, the mother or the husband? Should we view the rights of all the persons concerned equally?

Could the couple have avoided heartache by sounding out each other's views on such a situation at a time when they were in good health? Could it have resulted in them acting differently when the situation arose? Even if it did not affect the outcome, would it make their emotional relationship different, would it make the decision easier to make, and would it make the decision easier to accept (and for the husband to live with)?

Not all couples share the same views on assisted suicide – some, even when they love each other very much, agree to differ on key issues and having different beliefs is not any indication of less affection felt. How does discussing feelings in advance make a difference? Does it allow a space to 'agree to differ'? Does it also perhaps increase confidence in the future, knowing how one's partner feels and might react, and make plans accordingly?

Over and above the moral question, some couples would be prepared to break the law for each other, some would not. How important is this?

The dying woman had also failed to plan properly – the method she had kept in reserve had its shortcomings and there was no back-up plan. Her 'dress rehearsals' had also been inadequate.

Does this perhaps affect your feelings about mastering several techniques, rather than just relying on one?

Scenario Two – some points to consider

Does the fact that the couple are gay make a difference and, if so, what difference? If they were not openly gay and in a less than tolerant community, could the threat of exposure and the emotional fall-out be a factor? Some gay networks, especially among people with HIV, exchange information on drugs for suicide or even pass on drugs illegally. Could they have relied on unverified information from sources that do not evaluate their recommendations rigorously?

How are the three acts different emotionally? Legally? Is agreeing to grinding up tablets and agreeing to stay with a person while they take them very different to actually taking part physically with the apparatus (the bag and elastic bands) that directly cause the death? The assistance has moved from preparation and passive presence to actively helping to cause death. If it goes as far as holding a pillow over the person's head, the survivor has been the main agent – not in assisted suicide but in euthanasia in the commonly accepted senses. Assisted suicide tends to imply the person ending their life takes the final action themself, whereas voluntary euthanasia means the final action is taken by someone else, usually a doctor, at the request of the person wanting to die. Legally, the difference is much harder to make, since there is no UK law relating to voluntary euthanasia, such as the Suicide Act 1961, and which only relates to England & Wales.

In view of the developments, how competent was the decision to help and how much of it was due to pressure of circumstances? Does the intention to leave the country before discovery indicate a willingness to go as far as necessary or not?

Scenario Three – some points to consider

If you have obtained this book from Exit, it is on the understanding that it is for private and personal use, and so you would be breaking your agreement with the organisation that supplied it – not very important perhaps, you might think, in view of the circumstances. But the agreement is not just there to protect *Exit*. What other reasons could there be?

How long did it take you to absorb the information in the book, and practice it until you were confident. Several readings? Days? Weeks? Perhaps attending a workshop and reading through the newsletter literature as well. Stockpiling drugs. Did you do this in good health when your mind was alert? How will the terminally ill person fare by comparison? Will they take the information in and be able to use it? Or is there a chance that they will make mistakes? If it goes wrong, how will you feel about that?

What about if you help them and it turns out that they were not as ill as they thought they were, but ended their life anyway?

If you give them the book, will they be building up their hopes, as if it will give them a simple 'answer' at first glance? If their hopes are then dashed because they cannot apply the information, will they be in a better or worse state?

People's dying experience varies greatly – often depending on the quality of palliative care they manage to receive. The degree of pain and symptom relief can, unfortunately, often depend on how

much fuss someone makes and how loudly they make it
(ironically, having a television crew on hand, if possible,
often guarantees a prompt and high quality response!) If a
person puts all their energies into finding a perfect method
of self-deliverance – and fails – have they used up valuable
time with which they could have been helping themselves in
other ways?

The main rationale behind the delays often built into Exit
providing self-deliverance information (based on information from several top consultant psychiatrists) is that acute
suicidal intentions become less within that time. These are
those that come suddenly, usually due to something like the
loss of a job or spouse or exam failure – or an initial
diagnosis of a disease which may be fatal (but often isn't). If
a person is very depressed, they may still feel 'suicidal' after
three months but they will probably be less inclined to put
the idea into practice. So a wait of a few months is a
safeguard – not a perfect one, but better than nothing. It is
a legally binding condition that was written into contract at
the time Exit's earlier manual *Departing Drugs* was published.

Exit's books are purchased without any screening, but the
minute that you make a personal decision to give the
information to someone who wants to use it, you become
personally involved. You also become involved legally. The
books are supplied generally without breaking the law. Of
the many thousands sold, only a tiny percentage of pur-
chasers use the information to commit suicide. Most people
want the book as a sort of insurance. There has to be
something else that happens between the sale and the
suicide that causes the latter event. In Scots Law this
principle is called *novus actus interveniens* (a 'new act intervening'). If you give the book to someone who specifically asks

for it in order to end their life, on the other hand, you are directly participating in assisting their suicide and far more culpable legally. You might infer that you are also more liable morally. A similar principle was upheld in England & Wales Justice Woolf refused a declaration sought by the Attorney General to stop sales of an English self-deliverance manual, holding that a crime under the Suicide Act would only be committed where an accused knew the purchaser of the book was intending to commit suicide, and that this person was assisted and encouraged by the advice in the book. A causal link is requitred.

The main rationale behind selling *Five Last Acts* without the three months' wait is that, due in part to the restricted nature of sales that applied to *Departing Drugs,* there are many books more readily available that do not give the same information with the same scrutiny and checks. People following poor information are more likely to suffer failed attempts and serious complications. *Five Last Acts* is therefore available without a waiting period. The same considerations apply if you think of passing the book on however. And if you give it to someone with the express knowledge that they intend to use it to end their life in the coming period you have similar legal and moral liability.

Further reading on dilemmas involved in relating to a person who is dying:

- Jamison S, Final Acts of Love – Families, Friends, and Assisted Dying, Tarcher/Putnam Books, NY 1995.
- Jamison S, Assisted Suicide – A Decision-Making Guide for Health Professionals, Jossey-Bass, California 1997.

For an introduction to decision-making analysis using philosophical ethics in everyday settings (without complex philosophical terms!):

- Kallman E, Grillo J, Ethical Decision Making and Information Technology, McGraw-Hill USA 1996.

Practical aspects of dying, for patients, families, caregivers and professionals, including case studies, useful conversations and a decision to stop eating and drinking:

- Lynn J, Harrold J, Handbook for Mortals – Guidance for People Facing Serious Illness, OUP 1999.

For further case studies:

- Battin M, Lipman A (eds). Drug Use and Assisted Suicide, Haworth Press 1966:291-342.
- Ogden R, Euthanasia Assisted Suicide & AIDS, Peroglyphics Publishing, Canada 1994.
- Cases in Biomedical Ethics in: Beauchamp T, Childress J, Principles of Biomedical Ethics (4th ed), OUP 1994.
- Crigger B (ed), Cases in Bioethics, St Martin's Press 1988.
- McLean S, Britton A, The Case for Assisted Suicide 1997 Harper Collins.

Understanding health and dying through the arts:

- Downie R, The Healing Arts - An Oxford Illustrated Anthology OUP 2002. *See also:* references to Downie's work in the Ethics appendix.

For an insight into managing dying by a registered nurse who worked in both the right-to-die movement and palliative care:

- Seguin M, A Gentle Death, Key Porter Books, Toronto 1994.

Other useful references:

- Docker C, Smith C, et al, Departing Drugs, Exit 1993.

- Huxtable R, Euthanasia, Ethics and the Law, Routledge-Cavendish 2007.

- Seinberg A, Youngner S, End-Of-Life Decisions – A Psychosocial Perspective, American Psychiatric Press 1998.

- Ferguson P, Killing "Without Getting Into Trouble"? Assisted Suicide and Scots Criminal Law. ELR 2(3):288-314.

The Suicide Act 1961
(Main text)

An Act to amend the law of England and Wales relating to suicide, and for purposes connected therewith.

1. Suicide to cease to be a crime

The rule of law whereby it is a crime for a person to commit suicide is hereby abrogated.

2. Criminal liability for complicity in another's suicide

(1) A person who aids, abets, counsels or procures the suicide of another, or an attempt by another to commit suicide, shall be liable on conviction on indictment to imprisonment for a term not exceeding fourteen years.

(2) If on the trial of an indictment for murder or manslaughter it is proved that the accused aided, abetted, counselled or procured the suicide of the person in question, the jury may find him guilty of that offence.

(3) The enactments mentioned in the first column of the First Schedule to this Act shall have effect subject to the amendments provided for in the second column (which preserve in relation to offences under this section the previous operation of those enactments in relation to murder or manslaughter).

(4) No proceedings shall be instituted for an offence under this section except by or with the consent of the Director of Public Prosecutions.

Further legal notes on 'having someone present'

The desirability of having someone with you when achieving self-deliverance is clear – both for comfort and as a safeguard should anything go wrong. But the legal consequences of such a situation varies considerably from country to country. In many countries, having someone with you, as long as their role is completely passive – not helping you in any way – is acceptable, but this is not the case in certain jurisdictions, including the UK. In Britain, anyone being present during a deliberate suicide may risk prosecution (even if the final act is committed abroad). That is not to say that prosecution will automatically follow, or that the person will receive a custodial sentence if convicted, but the possibility is definitely there and should be taken into consideration.

On the question of aiding and abetting a suicide (which in England and Wales carries a custodial sentence of up to fourteen years), the Crown Prosecution Service says: "The mental element that has to be proved is an intention to do the acts which the individual in question knew to be capable of helping, supporting or assisting suicide." For instance, a Mrs Charlotte Hough[1] sat with her friend until she died, probably from using a plastic bag and sleeping tablets supplied by Mrs Hough. Mrs Hough was charged with attempted murder and sentenced to nine months in prison. Persons assisting the suicide of an individual with a mental disorder may be viewed even less sympathetically by judges. Mr Wallis[2] had a one year prison sentence upheld for his part in the death of someone who was suffering from depression.

Commenting on Mrs Hough, and bearing in mind section 2(1) of the 1961 Suicide Act, Lord Lane said that, "Parliament had in mind the potential scope for disaster and malpractice in circumstances where elderly, infirm and easily suggestible people are sometimes minded to wish themselves dead." The Act states that, "A person who aids, abets, counsels or procures the suicide of another, or attempt by another to commit suicide shall be liable on conviction on indictment to imprisonment for a term not exceeding fourteen years."

General principles of accomplice liability require more than mere presence for aiding and abetting to occur. But even if there were no physical assistance with the act, a court might decide that there was agreement or encouragement.[3] To suggest that a person 'counselled' the suicide, consensus and mere contact might be enough.[4] For instance, if you have bought some pills and another person advises you of how many to take to commit suicide, that might be considered counselling. Procuring, on the other hand, requires a causal link such as buying the pills for you that you intend to use.[5] In all these cases, the involvement of another person, even something as simple as their presence while you end your life, could result in their prosecution after your death.

There remain cases where the legality or illegality of an action not only remains unclear, but it is unclear whether, even if there is enough evidence to bring a prosecution, that a prosecution will follow. Something may be illegal but there may, simultaneously, be a disinclination to prosecute. This has been demonstrated by the numerous cases of people going to assisted suicide clinics in Switzerland where someone falls foul of the law merely by accompanying them. The House of Lords have confirmed (in the case of Debbie Purdy) that someone cannot escape prosecution simply because the final act occurred in another jurisdiction or even on the high seas. It is an offence to assist someone to travel to Switzerland or anywhere else where assisted suicide is lawful. Anyone who does that is liable to be prosecuted.

There are also cases, such as that of Sue Lawson, where a second person (in this case, her brother) did nothing more than watch. Charges were brought against her brother, but dismissed five months later. In some cases where persons have failed to intervene but sat with a person after finding them unconscious, they have served probationary sentences. Although there should perhaps not be an assumption of complicity for merely being present, such cases are difficult. The situation can be further complicated if there is perceived to be a duty of care, whether that of a nurse or the sort of *de facto* duty that exists when an ailing person is cared for by relatives, or if an inheritance is involved. (In Scotland, the legal concept of the 'unworthy heir' also comes into play.)

In 2005, Jill Anderson came home and found her chronically-ill husband dying after taking an overdose – the latest of a number of apparently attempted suicides. On this occasion she sat with him until he died rather than calling an ambulance. Mrs Anderson was eventually acquitted, but not before the prosecution had argued that she had breached what amounted to a duty of care owed to her husband.[6]

The possibility that what amounts to a breach of a duty of care is a worrying one, although the courts can be seen to distinguish between the situation with *Anderson* and the more blameworthy case that involved allowing an anorexic to die. In 1977, a man and his mistress agreed to care for his sister who was suffering from anorexia. As her condition deteriorated, she became bed-ridden but no help was summoned and she died. They were convicted of her manslaughter because they had accepted her into their home and so assumed a duty of care for her,[7] and additionally we can see that she arguably could have been of reduced capacity due to the nature of her illness.

There has also been a successful prosecutions against someone (a Mr Cooper) who knowingly turned away a district nurse who might have intervened in an assisted suicide; and also, on another occasion, a couple who sat with their daughter (Sara Johnson), a multiple sclerosis sufferer, for eight hours after they came home and discovered her unconscious after taking pills in the latest of a succession of suicide attempts. Both these cases[8] were in the 1980's and only resulted in probation. It could be argued that they would be dealt with more leniently now, although the trauma of being taken to court and not knowing the outcome for some time can be very considerable. Even at the time, such cases were equivocal and convictions didn't always seem consistent.[9]

England and Wales

The Director of Public Prosecutions (DPP) has given a number of indications as to how guidelines will be applied in the case of charges of assisting a suicide being brought. The latest being in February 2010.[10] There is first an *evidential test*, to see if there is sufficient evidence to have a reasonable chance of securing a conviction. Secondly there is a *public interest test*, to decide whether it is in the public interest, once all the factors (including the severity of a likely sentence) have been considered. In cases where the only motive was compassion, and the person dying had both capacity and a clear and fixed intention, prosecution seems increasingly unlikely (at the time of going to print). But the crux is that, until parliament changes the law, such things cannot be known in advance. A person may even go through a long period of worry and emotional pain waiting to see whether charges will result in a court action. Moreover, the DPP's guidelines were issued in the first instance in relation to persons facilitating someone going abroad to end their life and are an indication of interpretation, not a change in the law. Three years previous to the

DPP's guidelines, an apparently contrary decision was reached in May 2007 when 58-year-old Frank Lund[11] was found guilty of murdering his wife by suffocating her with a plastic bag and a pillow. He was ordered to spend at least three years in prison, even though the judge recognised that, "This was a killing which took place at the express request and insistence of your wife who wished to die." He added, "It is the duty of citizens in this country not to take any steps which might lead to the death of another citizen." Only a year earlier, in a case with many similarities, Robert Cook, 60, was given a suspended sentence at Lewes Crown Court after admitting suffocating his wife with a plastic bag after she had taken an overdose. The exact process by which an assisted suicide could be prosecuted is slightly different in Scotland.

Scotland
The DPP guidance applies to England and Wales. In Scotland, assisting suicide is covered by the common law rather than by statute.[12] At the time of going to press, Scotland was considering a bill on assisted dying[13] and the situation also was outlined in oral evidence by the Solicitor General for Scotland (published on the Scottish Parliament website). The High Court in Scotland used to have a declaratory power where it could assert that a particular action was a crime, but that power no longer exists. It has been suggested that the only relevant difference between the position in England and Scotland is that the Director of Public Prosecutions has been obliged by court order to produce guidelines on the prosecution of assisted suicide, and the Lord Advocate has not.

The step by step procedure for determining whether to prosecute (when a report is made by the police to the Procurator Fiscal) holds many similarities with England and Wales. In Scotland, assisting a suicide would most probably fall under the general heading of the crime of homicide. There must first be sufficient admissible, credible, reliable evidence that a crime has been committed. Where homicide is concerned, one has to ask if the criminal act caused death; was it done with intent to kill – or done with such wicked recklessness as to be regardless of the consequences (a 'wicked disregard for life'). Establishing provocation reduces the crime from murder to culpable homicide, as can diminished responsibility.

If the first stage (evidential test) is satisfied, the second stage is the public interest test. The factors taken into consideration in determining the public interest from a prosecutor's perspective in Scotland are laid out in the Prosecution Code for Scotland (which is readily available online). In assessing public interest, the prosecutor considers the nature and gravity of the crime,[14] the age, circumstances and background of the person committing the crime, the age and personal circumstances of the person who died, the attitude of the person before they died and also that of their family, the motive, and any mitigating circumstances. The risk, if any, of 're-offending' is also taken into account.

The consent of a person who is assisted in their suicide is no defence in law in Scotland, just as it is no defence in England and Wales. The state of health of the person who is assisted to die doesn't matter either. With causation, a specific example used by the Solicitor General in explaining this to parliament, was that if a person supplies a lethal cocktail of drugs to a person who then ingests them, the chain of causation is not broken. And while motive is relevant in terms of proof, it is irrelevant in terms of criminal liability.

In summary, there are two main offences of relevance in Scots law: murder and culpable homicide.[15] The offences of murder and culpable homicide in Scotland are close equivalents of the offences of murder and manslaughter in England and Wales. Acts involving assisted dying may also, however, be relevant to other offences under common law or statute in Scotland. For example, the common law offences of assault, reckless endangerment and breach of the peace may be applicable, as well as various statutory offences under the Misuse of Drugs Act 1971 (c 38). Reckless endangerment can be charged when the accused has recklessly exposed another to the risk of harm, even if no harm has actually resulted.

A person surviving a suicide pact may also face prosecution for culpable homicide in Scots law. At very least, the parties in a suicide pact will have provided encouragement to one another.

Reckless encouragement may also form the basis of a prosecution in cases where, for instance, a letter was sent from one person to another, and a 'reasonable person' would realise that letter was likely to precipitate the recipient's suicide.[16]

Any involvement of another person, even passive, raises many moral and legal questions, and the answers to some of these may seem little more than a lottery. Such risks, problems and even unknown quantities should be discussed well in advance with any third party offering to be involved.

Cases and references:

1. (1984) 6 Cr App Rep (S) 406
2. (1983) 5 Cr App R (S) 342
3. See Huxtable R, Euthanasia, Ethics and the Law, Routledge-Cavendish 2007 p.59, for a discussion of these fine differences, and who in this aspect cites Clarkson [1971] 1 WLR 1402, and *Wilcox v Jeffrey* [1951] 1 All ER 464.
4. Ibid, *Giannetto* [1971] 1 Cr App Rep 1.

5. Ibid. *Attorney General's Reference (No 1 of 1975)* [1975] 2 All ER 684, at 687).
6. R *v Anderson,* 2005, unreported.
7. R *v Stone & Dobinson* (1977) QB 354.
8. These two cases are quoted and discussed in Huxtable R, Euthanasia, Ethics and the Law, Routledge-Cavendish 2007: 69-70.
9. See for instance, no conviction for failure to revive after a deliberate overdose, or turning away an ambulance after a husband's overdose. Ibid. P.69.
10. *Policy for Prosecutors in Respect of Cases of Encouraging or Assisting Suicide,* issued by The Director of Public Prosecutions, February 2010 and available at http://www.cps.gov.uk/publications/prosecution/assisted _suicide_policy.html (accessed on 22/07/10).
11. R *v Lund,* 2007, unreported.
12. White R, Willock I, The Scottish Legal System, Butterworths 1995, for a general overview of how the Scottish legal system works.
13. End of Life Assistance (Scotland) Bill. There is considerable information available on the Scottish Parliament website, including a Briefing Paper http://www.scottish.parliament.uk/business/research/briefings-10/SB10-51.pdf. The videos of evidence, for instance that of the Solicitor General, may be time-limited, but were accessed for this publication at http://www.scottishparliament.tv/popup.asp?stream=http://vr-sp-archive.lbwa.verio.net/archive/280910_ELA.wmv on 1st Oct 2010. For the impact, of any, of European Law on UK decisions, see the speech of Lord Hope in R (on the application of Purdy) (Appellant) v Director of Public Prosecutions (Respondent) [2009] UKHL 45. Available online at http://www.publications.parliament.uk/pa/ld200809/ldjudgmt/jd090730 /rvpurdy.pdf (accessed 1st Oct 2010).
14. The more serious the crime, the more likely it is on the public interest test that a prosecution will follow. Even if, as in the last recorded case, HM Advocate v Brady (October 2006), where the accused killed his brother who was in the final stages of Huntington's disease and was found guilty of culpable homicide and admonished.
15. McCall Smith R, Sheldon D, Scots Criminal Law, Butterworths 1992 for a fuller examination of the different categories of homicide.
16. Ferguson P, Killing "Without Getting Into Trouble"? Assisted Suicide and Scots Criminal Law. ELR 2(3):288-314.

Before you start

How do you plan for a major holiday? What's your style? Do you learn everything you can about the destination? What you need to take? And details such as, how will you cope if you are tired when you arrive and have to remember how to sort out hotels, car hire, transport and any small items you forgot to pack? Some people will immerse themselves in every aspect and then trust to their knowledge and a bit of luck. Others will know it could be a struggle in a strange environment, jet-lagged, the children getting irritable and making demands. And then on top of it all, the airline loses your luggage or a message arrives saying there is a crisis back home.

Everyone has their own way of dealing with a journey into the unknown. The important thing is that you have a way. You are not the sad and lonely backpacker who gets mugged outside the airport because you don't have a clue. You're not the person who assumed everything would go OK because the travel agent said so. You're not the person who gets the wrong bus or jumps into a dodgy taxi at midnight, ending up frightened and alone in a place where no-one speaks your language. And unless you have superpowers, the reason it doesn't happen to you is that, one way or another, you are prepared. Whether you obsessively made and re-made checklists; whether you're a 'frequent flyer;' whether you've got friends at the destination; whether you've talked things over with your family that are with you and the friends and neighbours back home. Whether, in a nutshell, you are supremely confident inside. Not in a foolhardy way: but just knowing that you have the physical, mental and emotional tools to cope. You know the laws of the land, your own capabilities and shortcomings, and what to do in an emergency.

Some people believe death is a journey to another world. Whether you do or not, the process of dying is something that is very real and a journey (towards death) that you only take once. The journey 'of a lifetime' in fact! Death concerns the hereafter, depending on your beliefs perhaps. But the dying process is very real, very much in the here and now. This book focuses on dying; or rather that part of living that you do after all the other parts. It's an important – very important – part of your life. Isn't it worth making sure you do it as well as you can?

Let's try making some checklists. You will no doubt make your own – one that applies to the very specific details of your own unique life and situation. But here's one to start with . . .

o   **Methods** Be intimately familiar with at least two to three self-deliverance techniques. Knowing that you can 'pull the plug' may give you confidence and courage to go on longer.

o   **Wait, and check your prognosis.** Don't rush into anything. Find out the facts and give yourself time to come to terms with them. Don't assume the worst. If you suffer from depression, investigate treatment options (quite often depression can be alleviated completely with modern drugs).

o   **The Law** Be familiar with the current legal provisiojns – just in case. Understand what might happen if you involve others.

o   **Backup plans** Have backup plans for different situations, different stages of physical and mental health. Circumstances can change sometimes without warning.

o   **Last words** Write a letter explaining that taking your life is your decision alone. That it is not due to depression and not due to anything anyone else might say or do. (You might not use it, but it's good practice!) Some people might like to make a voice recording or a video statement.

o **Letters to loved ones** Write letters to each of your nearest and dearest. Remembering the moments you have shared, and that are engraved in their heart, as in yours. Thank them for things that have previously been left unsaid. Some small words of kindness, compliments, things you appreciated about them, or things they did, will mean the world. Remember that if they anticipate your action, it will still involve a certain amount of shock. If they didn't, more words of comfort and explanation may be appropriate. Perhaps make a videotape diary, or audio recordings of your fondest memories and thoughts, maybe a favourite poem or some passages that sum up your values, even a joke or anything else you've shared or would like to share with those close to you.

o **Documents** Prepare, or be able to prepare at short notice, all the documentation that a person will need to attend to matters after your death. Your *last will and testament*. Your bank details. Insurance documents. Any ongoing commitments and contact details for the relevant companies. Life assurance policies will generally pay out as long as you are not, financially speaking, pulling a fast one on the company. If you have taken out a policy shortly before ending your own life, it is unlikely to be paid. If it is a long-standing policy, then the company has little to gain by refusing what would have been due had you died naturally only a short time later. They are generally fair, and will only refuse to pay in 'unreasonable' cases where you've paid them very little and expect them to pay out a lot! Other documents that can usefully be laid out (they may be needed by the registry office before the funeral can take place) include your birth certificate, marriage or civil partnership certificate, NHS medical card, and pension and benefits books.

o **GP contact details** Name, address, and phone number of your doctor and any specialists looking after you. A note attached to your body should explain that it is a voluntary, deliberate act, and that only the doctor should be phoned to sign the death certificate, not the emergency services.

o **FAO** A list of people to be informed, and their contact details.

o **Solicitor** Contact details for your lawyer if you have one.

o **Living Will** Make a Living Will ('Advance directive'). This helps to cover you against treatment you wouldn't want, in the event you cannot speak for yourself.

o **Palliative care** If you have a known condition, learn as much as you can and want to know about it. Also the available treatment options. These may change, so keep yourself up to date and open minded. These can include both modern technology and simple comfort measures. If you suffer with certain groups of diseases (especially cancer), investigate the expert knowledge that a Macmillan nurse can offer (via your GP or primary medical carer.)

o **Pain relief** If you have pain that is not being adequately treated, be prepared to protest loudly until it is – or get someone to do it for you. Better and more effective pain relief is possible than is routinely given (to most people). If you want the best, be prepared to be insistent. Knowing your rights helps you to do this in a polite and assertive way. As with palliative care, getting good pain relief may involve making a fuss. That can include shouting or making a noise. Best of all for getting attention, if you can get a television camera to pick up on your story, you will find the medical services are suddenly falling over themselves to pull out the stops. About 95% or more of pain is relievable. As little as 50% may be routinely relieved. You may need to get insistent. Macmillan nurses are the main UK experts when it comes to cancer pain. They can assist not only with the latest pain relief and medical expertise but with emotional and sometimes financial support. A doctor referral may be necessary, but you can make an enquiry by telephoning freefone 0808 808 00 00.

o **Values History** Consider making a Values History or Values Statement. This is a statement of your wishes, how you want to be treated in your final days, the things that are important to you. It can include small, personal things, such as having your hair done and looking your best, spending quality time with those who you are close to. Things that make life worthwhile, spiritual values, hobbies. Also things that you like to avoid, or things that frighten you.

o **Who will find you & when** Have some thought, if you are likely to be alone in the final hour, how someone will find you. A recorded letter? An arrangement for someone to call if they haven't heard from you? (Finding a body after it has been decomposing for a week or so is not a nice way to find anyone.) One of our Exit workshop participants who lived in a remote area, planned to post a recorded delivery letter to himself and place a note on the door to the postman asking him to call the police. (This is obviously not good idea if you live somewhere where the note might be seen prematurely.)

o **Hotels** What if you die in a hotel? Would it be better if the manager (rather than a chambermaid or young person) is the one to find you? One person left a note on the bathroom door, instructing the person who found it not to enter but to call the manager or the police. A 'Do Not Disturb' notice on the outer door will keep people away until you have outstayed your booking. If you pay for your room in cash and in advance it will avoid problems for the hotel (Accounts are frozen at the point of death).

o **Talk to people** (wherever you can). If those close to you are fiercely opposed to self-deliverance, you may need to use some discretion, for their sake and yours. If your loved ones are more open to such ideas, judge how far you can discuss matters (in a general way) without jeopardising your own plans or freedom to act. One way might be to introduce the subject by means of a Values History (see above). It isn't a matter to raise lightly. Rather (for instance) say to them, "There's something I'd like to discuss with you after dinner." That prepares them, allows them to anticipate spending some time rather than making excuses or brushing it off. Perhaps ask them for their views first (this creates a polite duty to listen to yours!) Instead of diving in, maybe discuss less upsetting subjects first. Things such as life assurance, views about the hereafter, what they think about growing old and how will it affect them. Gradually sense how much detail you and they can comfortably discuss. But if you are unsure whether they already have strong fixed views, sound them out casually by referring to a news story.

o **Make it accessible** You have all the documents, letters, statements. When the time comes, ensure that everything that needs to be found is on a table nearby.

o **Make peace with yourself** Review your life. Ask if you are satisfied with the life you have lead. It was a remarkable journey. There's a saying, "Forgive yourself before you die. Then forgive others." Be generous in how you judge yourself – and others.

o **Talk before the end** Terminal illness and dying can be an isolating and stressful experience both for you and your loved ones. But it needn't be. Conversation and understanding serve several important functions at once. They reduces the sense of being cut off; they create a special time of sharing. By talking you bring each other into your worlds. Ensure those things you always wanted to say aren't left unsaid. But remember people won't understand what you want unless you talk (and listen) to each other. One of the biggest fears about dying is the associated loss of control. By expressing your wishes, an element of that control is restored.

Allow yourself some privacy Make sure you will not be disturbed for at least eight hours if possible. This includes service people who might become suspicious. To guard against unwanted resuscitation, you can prepare a specific clause in your living will, or pin a note to yourself refusing resuscitation and emphasising that going against your wishes will be illegal. Switch off or unplug telephones, answering machines, doorbells.

o **Funeral arrangements** If you have specific wishes about the type of funeral and any details of the service, and whether you would like cremation burial or green burial, make sure that people have been informed or your wishes will be easy to find. (They are not legally binding but will generally be respected.) More than 80% of people haven't written down any preferences around their own death, and less than a third of people have told anyone about the sort of funeral arrangements they would like to have after they die. This is added stress for those left behind.

o **Medical research, organ donation** Check the small print if you are leaving organs or your whole body to benefit science or other people. There are many exclusions that vary from place to place. Allow for funeral plans if your body cannot be accepted for one reason or another. Donating your body for medical research must be done formally and with specific, witnessed consent (in order to comply with the Human Tissue Act 2004). Bodies may routinely be refused if a post-mortem examination has been performed. Organ donation after suicide is extremely rare as the organs cannot be removed sufficiently quickly at the moment of death.

o **What about throwing a party?** It is a chance to say a lot of things in an upbeat atmosphere rather than with your last dying breath. Whether it's full of party streamers or a black-tie dinner. Do it your way! Do some planning and make those farewells meaningful. Spend some time thinking of the positive qualities about those for whom you care. Jot them down if need be. It's also a chance for them to say those nice things about you instead of waiting until the funeral! But you can do the same. Genuine compliments, given or received, help both persons to feel a sense of self worth, to feel good about themselves, to open doors of communication.

o **Your last meal** Bear in mind that food doesn't tend to stay in the body that long. Especially when all the muscles relax at the point of death. A very light, easy-to-digest meal, is the most you want to be carrying around before self-deliverance. It is best to ease off gradually if you want to purify the body. You may want to reduce caffeine and stimulants, red meat and food that probably won't be excreted easily beforehand.

o **Enjoy the journey** Examine your attitude to death. How do you want to set the scene? If you plan to have favourite music, flowers or incense, photos of those dear to you, maybe some poetry or the words in a special book – all these things can be part of your very personal advance planning.

o There are some resources you may find useful near the end of this book for writing down important people to be contacted, your wishes and so on. Or design your own.

Last Acts

The next chapters detail five principal methods. Please become familiar with at least two or three. Reading alone is not sufficient. 'Dress rehearsals' will make you confident by showing up weak points in your knowledge or practice ahead of time, so that they can be safely corrected. They also, through habituation, overcome the ingrained fear of such an act. In the course of each chapter, the material is approached from different angles so that you will have a thorough knowledge of the method. You may be tempted to skip through and just jot down the 'essentials' but this would be a mistake: you will ultimately save time by going through the material methodically and, when it comes to ensuring that your last act in this life is done properly, you will surely find it makes sense to have as comprehensive an understanding as possible so that you can react appropriately to any unforeseen developments or last minute concerns.

Some chapters have a short story or dramatisation to help you visualise the scenario. Research has shown that considering a 'three-dimensional' scene in this way is far more effective at anticipating and solving problems than merely using a checklist of instructions. Please adapt each story to your own lifestyle or circumstances or make your own story so you can picture each stage in some detail.

1. Helium
2. Compression
3. Drugs
4. Plastic Bags
5. Starvation and other means

Last Acts: Before you start

Dear Leonard. To look life in the face, always, to look life in the face and to know it for what it is. At last to know it, to love it for what it is, and then, to put it away. Leonard, always the years between us, always the years. Always the love. Always the hours.

From the film The Hours, by Stephen Daldry

Last Acts:

Saying 'goodbye' is often another way of saying 'I remember.'
Anon

It is only in full and uncompromising awareness of our own mortality that life can take on any purposeful meaning.
Martin Heidegger

There is but one freedom,
to put oneself right with death.
After that everything is possible.
I cannot force you to believe in God.
Believing in God amounts to coming
to terms with death. When you have
accepted death, the problem of God
will be solved – and not the reverse.

Albert Camus

Helium

Story – what you need – main features – general description
– what is the evidence for helium? – how quickly does it
work? – are there any unpleasant side-effects? – checklist –
references & diagrams

Frank's story – a typical scenario

Frank had made his preparations well ahead of time. In the
garage was a cupboard that was always kept locked. He and
Miriam had always had their own hobbies, part of their lives
they kept separate, and no-one ever asked what it was that he
had behind that door. Miriam knew he believed in 'self-
determination', in the right to end life at a time when it felt
right. One evening he had brought the subject up over dinner.

"I'm going to this Exit workshop next Thursday," he mentioned casually. He had been a member for many years now.
"You have a good day out", she replied. "You might want to
stay over – I'm playing bridge that night anyway."

Frank enjoyed the workshop – it was not only a chance to
find out the details he needed to know but he was able to chat
to like-minded people. The next day, he discussed some of the
ideas he had formed with his wife so that she would not be
shocked if the fateful day ever arrived. He also wrote a 'last
wishes' statement that he could leave in the event of his death,
saying how everything was by his own hand and that it was
what he had wanted. Then he went on the Internet and
ordered what he needed. It was easy to find companies that
supplied party balloons and the disposable helium tanks to fill

them. He ordered two, just to make sure. Then he made a shopping list – plastic tubing, some hose clips, a 'T-junction' connector. He checked in the garage to make sure he had a flat screwdriver. In the kitchen were some strong scissors he would use to cut the tubing. The first hardware store he went to didn't have any poly tubing, but the larger one on the edge of town supplied him with everything he needed. It was all in the 'home-brewing equipment' section.

The following week, it was Miriam's turn to play bridge at her sister's, so Frank set aside the evening to put the equipment together and familiarise himself with it. The tanks of helium were quite light and could be lifted with one hand, but they would still need somewhere to be stored, so he cleared out the large garage cupboard. He unscrewed the valve from each tank then checked the tap on each, releasing just a small spurt of gas so he knew how much strength was needed to open and close it. Then he fitted a length of tubing to each – he had bought more than he needed in case he made a mistake, but it was quite straightforward. He connected the tubes from each tank by means of the T-junction – they were a good tight fit – leaving the third opening for the tube that would go to a plastic bag.

When he had been in the store, Frank hadn't been quite sure if the poly tubing he chose would be a good fit for the outlet on the helium tanks. He had bought the diameter of tubing (and matching T-junction) that seemed the closest, but also purchased half a dozen hose clips to make them extra secure if need be.

Frank had obtained a sturdy transparent plastic bag, the opening of which he had elasticated in the way he had practiced at the workshops, using ordinary elastic and masking tape. He had also fixed the end of a longer piece of tubing to the inside of it using adhesive tape. This tube was long enough to lead comfortably from head height (when he was seated in a nearby chair) to the T-junction.

Before making the final connection, Frank tested the bag again for comfort. It wasn't a tight fit – it didn't need to be, as air would have to escape from the bag as the gas pushed it out. He checked that the last piece of tubing, the one attached to the inside of the bag, was plenty long enough to easily reach the T-connection. He also checked he could reach the helium taps from his seat. Then he removed the bag.

When it came to the final part of his dress rehearsal, Frank knew he must take care. Helium acts very quickly, so he could not open the taps while the bag was over his head and all the tubes connected, but he had gone through all the separate stages. The taps worked fine, the bag was comfortable in use (he particularly liked the clear plastic) and the tubes were all the correct length. He made the final connection, fitting the tube from the bag to the T-junction securely, then carefully pushed the assembled equipment into the garage cupboard and locked it.

Each year or so, Frank would re-read the literature, get the equipment out and remind himself of how he would use it. One year, he found that with advancing age he had less strength in his hands for turning the gas taps. Always keen on gadgets, he and Miriam had a couple of devices for turning taps with ease. The one he liked had a good firm handle with an easy grip. It fitted over any tap (like the small one on the helium tank) and made it easier to turn them. It was easy to get a spare one and keep it the cupboard.

It was some years later when Frank realised the time was getting near. He and Miriam had many times discussed dying and understood each other's wishes. Under English law, even if a person ends their life with their own hand, a loved one cannot be in the room at the same time. On the day, Miriam spent the afternoon walking in the park.

When he was alone, Frank pulled the equipment out and got himself comfortable. It took a bit longer these days as it was less easy to get about than it had been. He had only had a very light breakfast, wanting to leave his departed body in a way that would cause minimum mess. He sat in the chair for a little while, contemplating his decision and with some of his favourite Chopin playing softly in the background. A book of his favourite poetry lay in his lap. He also knew that, although this was the perfect opportunity, he could change his mind if he wanted to. But he didn't. His illness was too far advanced and at his last check-up he had asked enough explicit questions to know that, even if he could be kept comfortable in hospital, it was not possible to prevent further deterioration. He left a last loving note to his wife, and also a note to whoever it might concern explaining his actions, how they were entirely his own and well-considered. A book of poetry rested on his lap. He put the last nocturne on 'repeat.' He positioned the bag over his head so the elasticated part was like a headband and squeezed out most of the air. As the gentle piano music rose, Frank reached across and turned on both helium taps quickly in succession. The bag filled with helium. Frank took a last breath then with a whoosh expelled the air from his lungs and immediately pulled the rim of the helium-filled bag down over his face. Within seconds he experienced a light-headed floating sensation as he started to faint. The last thing his eyes took in were a couple of lines from Walt Whitman . . .

What you need

o   A tank of helium - or preferably two
    (about £45 each from party balloon supply companies)
o   some poly tubing
o   an 'equal-T' connector (if using two tanks)
o   Five hose clips (clamps) – optional
o   A screwdriver if fitting the clamps
o   Some fairly sturdy scissors to cut the poly tubing
o   A sturdy plastic bag
o   Adhesive tape and elastic

Helium – you can find companies on the Internet by searching for 'helium balloons' or in yellow pages under headings such as *Parties* or *Balloons*. (As companies change from time to time, there is little point in giving addresses but they are certainly not difficult to find.) If you order by credit card over the Internet, it also avoids the need to speak to anyone personally but these companies generally are not suspicious of people buying

Large disposable tank of helium as supplied for filling party balloons

kits of helium and balloons. Some companies have two products – disposable tanks which are lightweight and sold; and larger, heavier tanks for bigger parties that are only rented. Buy the disposable ones. They will be sent by courier. When the tanks arrive they have a valve to make it easier to attach balloons while inflating them. On all the tanks I have come across, this valve can simply be unscrewed, but if this isn't the case you need to remove it forcibly. Once the valve is off, the helium can be released from the tank simply by opening and closing the tap.

Poly tubing – this is sold for various purposes including home brewing, aquariums and garden water systems. It comes in various diameters and you need some that will fit fairly snugly over the outlet on the helium tank. The first time I bought some, I 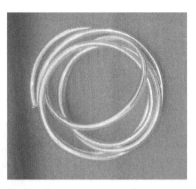 didn't want to walk around the home-and-gardens store carrying helium tanks and hadn't measured it, so I judged it as closely as possible and bought two different diameters and matching T-connectors. When I got back, I found one was a good tight fit (but needed a bit of pressure to fit), whereas the slightly larger one would need hose clips to secure.

An 'equal T' connector – this is simply a hard plastic piping connector with three outlets. It's sold at the same place as the tubing so you can get a T-connector of the right diameter made specifically to fit.

An equal T connector can be used to join two tanks

Five hose clips – if the tubing is a good fit, you won't need these, but if it is even slightly loose they are a good precaution. You place them on the tubing *before* you fit the tubes over the outlet or T-connector then tighten them with a screwdriver. (It may be easier to hold the hose clip stead using a wrench in one hand and the screwdriver in the other.) If you think you might want them, maybe get slightly more than you need in case you damage one – they can be slightly fiddly to tighten. Someone at a workshop suggested using strong adhesive tape or duct tape to secure the tubes once they were fitted. If you do this, do check it from time to time in case the tape has deteriorated and needs to be replaced (the same goes for any tape holding the tubing to the bag).

Plastic bag – the bag you use with helium does *not* have to be very large. It is simply a way of ensuring the helium stays around your mouth and nostrils for a few moments. A sturdy one, such as a large roasting bag, will ensure you don't accidentally damage it on the day. A transparent one is pleasant as you can see out, and looks less morbid to those finding you. It *does* need to be big enough to allow the air to circulate freely. (The bag is very different in size to the one usually used for the *Plastic Bag and Drugs* method.)

Adhesive tape and elastic – tape is needed to prevent the smooth poly tubing from slipping out of the bag. Elastic for securing the bag in this method can be ordinary elastic, about a quarter of an inch wide. The bag does not need to be a tight fit around the neck and the elastic is simply to keep it in place. Any adhesive tape can be used. Micropore tape as sold in chemists is easy and convenient to use.

Main features
Helium provides a totally painless and reliable way to end one's life. Some preparation is needed, as well as basic skills and physical mobility to put the equipment together. Additionally, it requires a safe place to store the assembled kit until

time of need and sufficient privacy to put it into effect. In the unlikely event that the person was disturbed and 'rescued' at a critical moment after losing consciousness, some brain damage could have occurred (as with any other method of asphyxiation, such as drowning). So make sure you *won't* be disturbed!

General description
Helium gas is released into a small bag over the head, displacing the air inside the bag. Breathing continues normally, but the lack of oxygen means the brain is rapidly starved and shuts down, causing death. The presence of helium in the body (for instance in post mortem) is very difficult to detect. Unconsciousness is swift, and there is little discomfort from the carbon dioxide build-up that would normally occur from use of a plastic bag alone.

What is the evidence for helium?
Helium is an odourless, tasteless, colourless, non-toxic gas that is lighter than air and fairly readily available. The 'helium method' was developed by researchers in Canada and the United States and has become an increasingly common method of choice in 'rational suicide' or 'self-deliverance' over recent years. In the UK alone, according to a report by St George's University of London and funded by thee Department of Health, there were 25 helium-related deaths in 2008, an increase from ten in the previous year. It is impossible to survive without oxygen, and helium simply provides a way of displacing oxygen while simultaneously providing a comfortable environment.

How quickly does it work?
Loss of consciousness occurs very rapidly, as with any other method of asphyxiation such as drowning, choking, or

hanging (though without the unpleasantness of those methods). Inert gas is used by vets for putting animals to sleep. In experiments, animals (dogs, cats, rabbits, mink, chickens) showed little or no evidence of distress from inert gas asphyxia, become unconscious after one to two minutes, and die after about three to five minutes. Make sure you will not be disturbed for 30 minutes, just to be sure.

Are there any unpleasant side-effects?
None known.

Checklist

o   Check that assembled equipment is in good order and that you can operate the helium tank taps. You should be familiar with their action, so you can turn them easily, quickly, and to an extent that achieves a steady flow rather than sudden, high-pressure gas.
o   Check that you will not be disturbed.
o   Leave a note for whoever finds you explaining your last act.
o   Exposure to atmospheres containing greatly reduced oxygen (increased helium) can bring about unconsciousness without warning; for the sake of those who may find you, you may want to ensure the room is well ventilated – although the amount of helium, which rises and quickly disperses in the atmosphere is very unlikely to present a danger to others unless you are in a very tiny enclosed space. There have been deaths, for instance, when persons stepped inside a giant helium balloon (the sort used for advertising), but a small canister of helium dispersing into the air is not likely to pose a threat.
o   Variations on the method (instead of using a plastic bag) include use of a gas delivery mask (such as used in hospi-

tals) or a sealed tube tent. If an oxygen mask is used, this is designed to mix the gas with air, so must be modified.

o Nitrogen, or any other inert gas, could be used instead of helium, but is harder to obtain. Rubber tubing could also be used instead of poly tubing. Body bags or mountain survival bags (some with clear view panes) are also adaptable options and can be purchased online.

o Exit suggests following the helium hood method described in this chapter as closely as possible. But not to the point of obsessiveness. As long as the nose and mouth are surrounded by helium long enough for death to occur, the rest is rather like icing on a cake. To underline the simplicity of the method, we'll also describe how a man used helium to end his life in Switzerland with materials obtained the same day and without any preparations. But why not do it as well as you can and with the best possible safeguards? Let us look at the method in detail.

Helium uncovered – everything you need for self-deliverance

Helium has become the number one method of self-deliverance world-wide. It probably vies with all other methods combined. Materials are relatively easy to obtain, no drugs are needed, and it is entirely painless, swift, and certain. This present guide builds on existing knowledge worldwide, shares tips developed from the workshops, as well as the latest ideas analysed and evaluated. But even if it is the most popular, it won't be suitable for everyone. The main reason for this is that a person's circumstances can change unexpectedly, whether due to illness, infirmity or living arrangements. For this reason, it will still be best to familiarise themselves with several methods of self-deliverance.

This section will include:

o   Making a helium hood. How to adapt a bag to make a hood in which to breathe the helium, which will result in death after a few moments.
o   The 'scrunch' method. A particularly effective way of self-deliverance using helium that minimises even slight possibilities of momentary discomfort.
o   Where to buy things - and we review some of the 'gadgets' available worldwide.
o   How to store your equipment discreetly.

Making a helium hood (diagrams 1 – 5)

Making an elasticated bag yourself to use with helium is not a difficult or complicated business. Exit Workshop participants usually make one in the space of a few minutes. A variety of materials can be used to make the elasticated hem. The simplest method, described here, involves some ordinary thin elastic, micropore tape to seal the hem, and an optional toggle to adjust tightness.

Start with a large roasting bag, elastic, and adhesive tape. Use a bag that is about 24" long and wide enough to fit comfortably over the head. These roasting bags or 'oven bags' are strong, see-through bags available from some supermarkets or shops such as Lakeland. It should be large enough to fit comfortably over your head and down your neck. It doesn't need to be larger than this – a large bag could take too long to fill with gas. The open end of the bag is folded inside out for about an inch (like a trouser-leg turn-up). A cut is then made in this hem *(diagram 1)*. Don't cut through the main part of the bag, just the hem. When you have placed or threaded the elastic in the hem, that small cut will enable you to tape the elastic into the hem but still leaving an opening to make a sort of draw-string, or at least pull the ends together and knot them.

Thin elastic (eg approx '4-cord' thickness) is placed in the hem seam, and the seam sealed with tape *(diagrams 2 & 3)*. You will

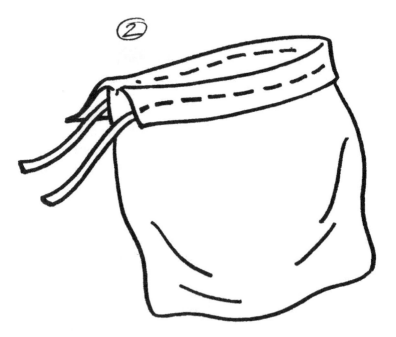

probably find this easiest to accomplish if you lay everything out on a flat smooth surface such as a table. Remember, tape the hem (cuff) shut: don't tape the bag shut! If you have difficulty keeping the elastic in place long enough to tape down the hem, you could do it another way: simply tape down the hem first, and then thread the elastic through it by attaching one end to a large (closed) safety pin while you pass it along the closed seam. (This way is a bit like threading a belt.)

Whichever way you do it, it's not rocket science. Make sure your bag looks similar to the one in diagram 3. You can also strengthen the bag underneath the cut, running the adhesive tape under the opening and under the free ends of the elastic.

You can use any sort of adhesive tape. Some brands may deteriorate in time. Micropore is good – an adhesive paper

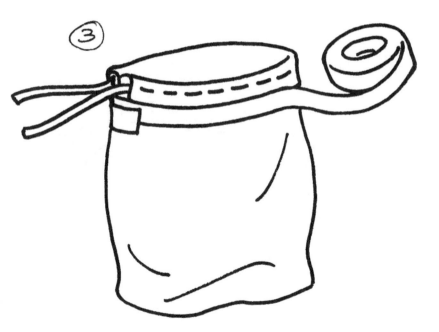

tape sold at chemists for dressing small wounds. Masking tape (as used for decorating) is also a good alternative. But the bag-making process is simple enough: not only will you maybe have two or three attempts in order to get a result that looks tidy, but you should find yourself pretty expert after you've made one. So if you need to make a fresh bag a few years later (if it has been stored for a long time) then you can whip one up in a few moments. (Don't leave it until the last minute though – just in case your fingers are less nimble one day!)

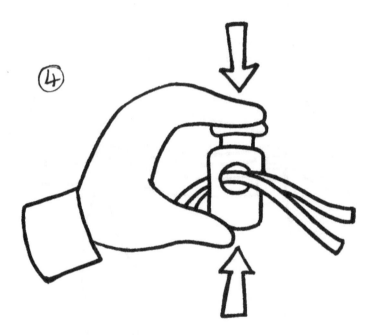

A small toggle may be used to adjust the tension *(diagram 4)*. This is not essential – you can just knot the ends of the elastic after a bit of experimentation to find the correct tightness.

These toggles are available from outdoor adventure suppliers or good habershers such as John Lewis. Or you might even use one from an old anorak. Squeeze the toggle to open it, finger pressure holding it open as you pass both ends of elastic through the opening.

The elastic does not need to be tight. Experiment and knot the free ends of the elastic so the bag closes around the neck but can still be slipped on and off. You may find a toggle makes this easier, as you can adjust the tension. Or you may prefer it without; either is fine.

Once the ends of the elastic are tied (with or without the toggle attached first), a long piece of tubing is fixed inside the bag so the end of the tube is well up inside the bag *(diagram 5)*. The end of the tubing should be near the top of the bag when it is worn, to quickly push any air out of the bag. Attaching adhesive tape to the inside of a bag can be awkward. It tends to stick to whatever part of the bag it touches. To overcome this, turn the bag inside-out for a few moments while you attach the tubing.

This tubing has to fit either the nozzle of the helium tank, or the similar-sized T-junction, so you may want to leave attaching the tubing until later when you have the other pieces of equipment that we will discuss in a moment.

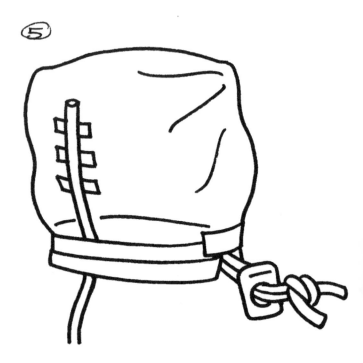

Variations Some people may also prefer to sew a wider strip of elastic to the bag itself, instead of using tape. If you decide to do this, remember to stretch the elastic as you sew, otherwise it will not 'close' the bag. Do this by stretching the bag and elastic over a cereal box.

Another variation is to use a Velcro strap which attaches to itself (available from shops such as the larger hardware stores such as B&Q). The advantage of making a bag beforehand with an elasticated opening avoids the problem of managing bag, rubber bands and tubing, pulling them over the head and making sure everything is in place. Even if an elasticated bag is not used, tubing should be securely attached so it won't slip.

Some people will find this explanation rather wordy. But bear with us. Others people like things explained in a detailed way. Not all of us are equally alert either as our age progresses. So we have tried to avoid the writing style of technical manuals. The aim is to transfer an *understanding* of the mechanics. Small variations are not critical – it's a case of finding what you are comfortable with. Let's go over some details.

The helium 'scrunch' method The most obvious way to use helium for self-deliverance is to arrange all the equipment with the bag over the head and slowly open the gas taps. The 'scrunch' method is a refinement that involves first putting the bag onto the head like a shower cap. The elasticated edge is around the forehead at the front, and nearer the neck at the back. With the bag in position like this, as much air is squeezed out of the bag as possible, using both hands. Then the helium is turned on and the bag quickly fills with gas. When it is full of helium, exhale fully and then quickly pull the bag down completely over the head and face (diagrams 6-10).

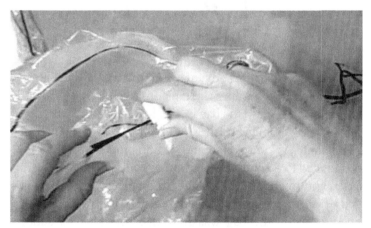

A participant at a workshop in Manchester makes a 'helium hood' out of a roasting bag, elastic, Micropore tape and a small toggle.

There are some distinct advantages to this method. It allows a slight margin for turning the taps on and adjusting them. It means that any air in the bag is greatly reduced from the start, rather than just being pushed out by the helium. The chance of inhaling a mixture of air and carbon dioxide can therefore be reduced to a minimum. Carbon dioxide causes hyperventilation and might account for any momentary distress exhibited by only one or two isolated persons who turned the taps on only when the bag was fully over the head (a sudden feeling of claustrophobia or last minute nerves is also a possible explanation). The evidence for the advantages of the scrunch method are not, on careful examination, overwhelming as other reasons can't been firmly ruled out. Did the person just experience a last minute panic? Were they using a very large bag with a lot of air? Was the gas flow insufficient? But as there are still some unknown factors, it is probably better to be safe than sorry, so the scrunch method seems a very plausible precaution. One should be seated in an armchair (or lying down) so that one cannot fall over, and the tank should be secure — either in its box to stabilise it and/or fastened to the chair with an elasticated bungee cord strap such as used for fastening luggage. Occasionally some small jerking is reported at death or just before, so the possibility of accidentally knocking the cylinder over or dislodging the tubing is to be avoided.

Diagram 6: Place the elasticated hood on the head as if it were a shower cap. The elasticated edge is on the forehead at the front of the head, and at the neck at the back of the head. Any long, loose hair is tied back in case it gets in the way. 'Scrunch up' the bag with both hands, pressing all the air out of it until flat against the head.

Diagram 7: Open the gas flow so there is a steady, gentle, but clearly audible flow of helium. Wait until it has inflated the bag. Note that the bag is not covering the face at this stage.

(Well before you do this, or connect the tubing, experiment *briefly* with the helium tap, just by switching it on and off again very quickly. Both to make sure it is not too stiff but also to accustom yourself to the gas flow. This will be part of your 'dress rehearsal' – not just before you use the helium for self-deliverance.)

(Diagrams 8, 9 & 10): Exhale forcibly, then pull the hood

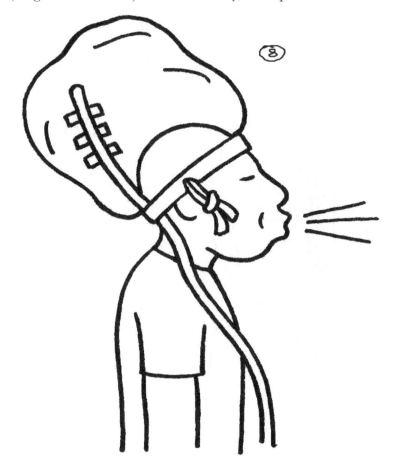

down swiftly. Breathe normally. Death will occur minutes later (consciousness is lost in anything from 20 to 90 seconds).

Fitting the tubing: Attach the longish piece of tubing to the inside of the bag. It needs to be a metre or two long — sufficient to comfortably reach the helium tank at the side of the armchair, or the T-connector. The width of the tubing is about 10 mm. It helps to turn the bag inside out while fixing the tubing in place. In the UK, poly tubing is most easily obtained in person from a home-brew shop (such as Edina Homebrew, 14 Elgin Terrace, Edinburgh EH7 5NW. Their web address is www.edinahomebrewshop.co.uk, although it may not be not ideal for Internet ordering). Addresses of suppliers are both numerous and frequently changing, but as a further example, one member wrote in after a workshop with her 'shopping' successes: "Helium tank (disposable) from Click4 Limited via Internet (£32 for tank); PVC tubing (3/8 inch bore x 1/16 inch width) from Hardware Shed Ltd via Amazon.co.uk (£1 for 3 metres). This size of tubing fits the Click4 Ltd tank exactly. Bag: made from pack of turkey roasting bags bought from Lakeland, Micropore from Boots, and elastic and toggles bought from local haberdashers. The bags may be the most expensive after the helium – one person paid £8 for a pack of 50.

Individual shops may not always have the correct size of tubing in stock, so you may need to shop around or modify the gas nozzle (see *adjusting helium tank nozzle width*, below). Buy your helium tank *first* so you have an idea of the correct width of tubing. If in doubt, buy more than one sort of tubing. You will need between three and five metres if you are using two tanks.

Adjusting helium tank nozzle width

If you buy an expensive ready-made helium hood, say from the GLADD Group, it comes with tubing of the correct size to fit most disposable helium tanks. If you are making your own, you may find it harder to get the exact fit. The larger B&Q superstores, as well as home-brew shops specialising in materials for making beer and wine at home, sell a size often referred to as 12.5mm. This provides a looser fit which needs adjustment. To make the fit tight when there is a discrepancy between the nozzle size and the internal diameter of your poly-tubing, you will need some 'self-fusing silicone tape.' This is available from B&Q stores and plumbers' supply shops. If you can get '10mm' tubing, this is the best. But 12.5mm provides a good fit if you increase the nozzle width with self-fusing silicone tape. This tape is typically used to fix leaky pipes. It is not sticky, but bonds to itself. Cut a few inches of silicone tape from the roll. If it's the wider 25mm-wide tape, cut it in half lengthways first so it is not much more than 10mm wide. Stretching the tape slightly as you use it, wind it around the metal nozzle of the helium tank. Try your 12.5mm tubing and see if it is a good fit. Further secure your tubing with a hose clip or some duct tape.

Quoting precise differences in tube widths might be useful for the technically minded (if all suppliers measured in the same way) but less useful if you do not have a micrometer, or you

If your tubing is not a perfect fit, you can adjust the width of the nozzle to fit the tubing using self-fusing silicon tape, as used by plumbers.

happen to be dealing with a home brew shop that judges tubing by looking at it with the naked eye. Which is why we suggest, buy what looks close until you get a good fit. If you need to make a slight adjustment, silicone tape works a treat. If the tubing is a bit too tight, some (not all) tubing can be softened slightly by running it under hot water first.

Example of a ready-made helium hood kit (Gladd bag)

Other third-party products

Exit members are maybe unlikely to need these items. A bag is easy to make yourself, and flow control, over and above just opening a tap, can be readily adjusted using a tap turner of the type considered presently. But a Gladd Bag (address below) is very serviceable if you don't wish to make your own. The new address replaces that of the old suppliers (who have retired) but the cost is quite considerable for a piece of kit you can easily make yourself. Another talked-about product is the Flow Control Kit, but we would point out to anyone thinking of buying both that the sizes have on occasion not been compatible. You would need to adjust the size of the tail outlet on the Flow Control Kit to make it fit the poly tubing that comes with the Gladd bag. The Flow Control Kit has been engineered to be used with a much narrower tube. You can adjust the outlet size with self-bonding silicone tape. Or buy nebuliser tubing – which does fit the 'kit.' Death by helium inhalation is essentially a simple business, and while the Gladd bag gives an option for someone say, who might have extremely arthritic hands, the Flow Control Kit, in the opinion of this author, is an unnecessary addition. Impressively expensive products will appeal to some, but readers are advised not to be dazzled or intimidated by technology and information overload. (To keep things in perspective, read the *Simplicity Itself* section, below.)

If you want a ready-made helium hood (Gladd bag), these are currently available (at the time of writing) from: GLADD Group, 3755 Avocado Blvd # 166, La Mesa, CA 91941 USA. It is an elasticated bag for use with helium and with tubing attached (ready to connect to two helium tanks). The $60 USD charge includes postage and discreet packaging but does not include helium. The tubing is the correct size to fit directly onto the helium outlet (once the balloon valve has been unscrewed and removed). The Gladd bag complies with this book's recommended size (see below).

The Flow-Control Kit is promoted by an Australian group which also uses the 'Exit' name ('Exit International') and which causes some confusion in view of its occasional high profile activities in the UK. Exit International has also run workshops from time to time in the UK, although the feedback is that they are not as extensive as Exit's full-day and two-day interactive workshops. Many of Exit International's workshops have been cancelled at the last moment due to local complaints and venues withdrawing permission. While this may or may not have certain political value, it does not directly help those who need the information. For this reason, Exit's workshops, in contrast, are low-profile and advertised almost solely via its membership rather than the newspapers. Exit International is not connected to Exit ('Exit' as referred to in this book, based in Edinburgh, Scotland, and pioneers of self-deliverance manuals from 1980 onwards). Exit International have however contributed strongly to keeping the issue of euthanasia in the public spotlight.

Bag sizes for helium When looking at the size of bag used, a few points are worthy of consideration. Some organisations have recommended a largish one of 36" length; whereas the one used in Exit workshops (and also recommended in other manuals as well as indicated in Exit's magazine), is smaller – about 24". The bag size is relevant to the size of the person's head, so it is more scientific just to say one that fits comfortably over one's head rather

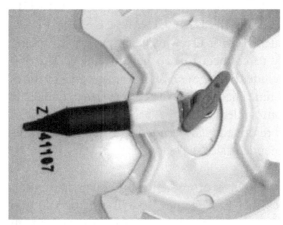

Preparing the helium tank (I).
Unscrew and remove the nozzle attached to the gas outlet

than being overly specific (unless one was to provide a chart of head measurements vs bag measurements - which I think would be a bit silly in the extreme!) The argument in favour of a larger bag is that any remaining carbon dioxide will be diluted faster with the larger amount of helium present. This might be a minimal consideration if using the favoured 'scrunch method' as we call it (collapsing the bag and filling it with helium before pulling it down). But consider how this works in practice. We see a lot of people dress-rehearsing the 'scrunch' in the workshops. They mostly do it quite well – and without a mirror! – but if one were to start with a larger bag, there is also more air to expel. You would see people scrunching most of the air out but unaware that they had just pushed some of it to the side of the bag. The addition of tubing inside the bag makes it harder to 'scrunch' - particularly if it is a longer bag with even more tubing going up to the top. A bag that is 50% longer (36" instead of 24"), holds much more than 50% more air. With the smaller bag, most of the volume is taken up by the person's head! So although the bigger bag is only 50% bigger, it holds maybe several times as much air or gas once it is on.

Preparing the helium tank (II): With the nozzle removed, tubing can be fitted to the bare metal outlet

An advantage of the smaller bag is it fills much quicker and needs less gas to fill it. Gas flow is not a problem if adjusting the gas manually so you can hear the flow. You even have the option of turning it up to fill the bag and then reducing the flow slightly before pulling the bag down. While we recommend the scrunch method as the most favoured option, even if you used a small bag (without the scrunch) and turned the gas flow up swiftly, it would be full of just helium within two or three seconds. Just the same amount of time it would take to fill a couple of balloons at most. The simplest way of adjusting the gas flow, should you want to, is with a prong-type tap-turner.

Adjusting gas flow If you have a bit of arthritis in your hands, you may already be familiar with 'tap-turners.' These are gadgets sold by mobility aids shops to make it easier to turn household taps which are a bit stiff. But dozens of people trying them in Exit Workshops have shown that they are equally useful for everyone when it comes to adjusting the flow on a helium tank. (There are some illustrations of the two types described here as suitable at the end of this chapter.) On most of the disposable helium tanks we have come across, both the 30 and 50 balloon size, a very tiny adjustment of the tap makes a very large adjustment to the flow of helium. A typical helium tank emits a very strong jet of gas if opened fully. Enough to blow up a skirt from the far side of a ballroom! This is far too much for our purposes. Using a tap turner gives easy, precise control over the gas flow, so that you can quickly and easily adjust it to give a strong but steady, gentle flow. Get to know the flow rate by briefly turning the tap on and off once or twice. In choosing a tap turner, not all devices are equally suitable. You need the sort that has a large number of metal or plastic protrusions. They are usually called 'Swedish Tap Turners.' Some suppliers worldwide of suitable 'Swedish Tap-Turners' include: Whistling Tortoise (Tel 0131 225 6365, 42a Hamilton Place, Edinburgh EH3 5AX). It has a handy loop that you can use for attaching it to your wrist if you wish. Email them at info@whistlingtortoise.co.uk (www.whistlingtortoise.co.uk). This 'Swedish tap turner' can also be obtained in the USA by phone or online from: Megamedics - www.megamedics.com (800) 646-2680, or Medical Products Direct.

A slightly different Swedish Tap Turner is available from Help the Aged (Product Code: 105246) £14.94 Tel: 0800 169 1609. This one was a second choice by workshop participants. The handle isn't quite so comfortable to use, but still works fine for the purpose.

Obtaining helium

Helium can be obtained from any party balloon supplier. It is sold as part of a party balloon kit. Helium, being lighter than air, is used to inflate balloons so that they float. Most of the suppliers are mail order, but we have also obtained a

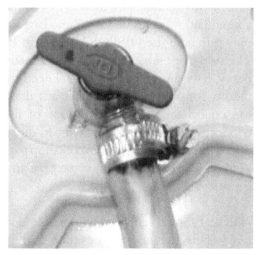

Preparing the helium tank (III). Showing the poly tubing fitted to the outlet. In the diagram, a hose clip has been used for added security. You could also use duct tape wound around the tubing and base of the tap to prevent it slipping off when moving it about.

helium balloon kit from Clintons Cards on the high street.

The tank is very lightweight – it can easily be lifted with one hand. The larger tank is about 18", as is the box it usually arrives in. Here are some suppliers (correct at time of going to press):

1. NotJustBalloons £34.99 + £8 courier (50 balloons size)
01304 812501 www.notjustballoons.co.uk
2. shop.click4warehouse.co.uk £22.57 Delivery (ex. VAT): £6.04
VAT @ 15%: £4.29   Total: £32.90
3. Partyrama www.partyrama.co.uk
E-Mail sales@partyrama.co.uk Tel 0870 0420 165
Gas for 50 x 9" balloons
£27.95 7-day delivery £3.75; 2-day delivery £6.95

When you order helium, there are two main choices. Disposable and non-disposable. Small and large. We recommend you only purchase the DISPOSABLE, and LARGE canister(s). The non-disposable ones are problematic. They tend to be heavy, have a nozzle that you will need strong equipment to modify for use, and the supplier will also ask you when they can collect the empty tank! None of these companies are connected to Exit or any right-to-die interests, so some discretion is advised. As one workshop participant mentioned, "I guess I'll have a party at some time anyway, so I think I'll get two tanks."

Although not essential, many people do decide to get two tanks. This is an added precaution in the unlikely event that one of the jets should get stuck or fail when in use. If you are going to use two tanks, either connect the bag to a T-connector, which you can buy from B&Q, (as in the diagram at the end of this chapter), or tape tubing from both tanks to the inside of your helium hood.

Storing helium discreetly One of the downsides of helium is that it requires a certain amount of equipment that is less than discreet if living with in-laws, for instance. A participant at one of workshop had devised a method of overcoming this, and we include it in case it is useful for other readers. Instead of connecting up the tanks and tubing in advance, nimble-fingered readers might want to consider practice runs in putting it together on the spot. You could keep the helium in

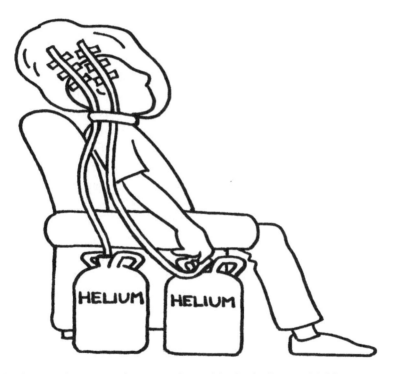

the boxes they arrived in, together with the balloons. Tubing (one length ready to connect to each tank) can be cut to length and kept with a wine-making kit. Roasting bags could be used for the odd Sunday lunch!

Urban myths exposed

Helium balloon kits are mass produced. There is not much variation or much that can go wrong. Helium is an inert gas and doesn't 'go off.' But are you getting pure helium? Apart from any trade description, there is little motive for manufacturers to pollute a successful product. Says campaigner Derek Humphry: "This false rumour about mixing oxygen into helium tanks keeps coming up. I think the opponents to choices in dying start the rumour so as to upset people's plans. The manufacture of helium in disposable tanks is a multi-million dollar international business, so diluting it would be hugely expensive for them, and would also mean it could not be used for industrial purposes. Therefore the helium as sold today is effective for whatever purpose it is needed." Another common, but unfounded, worry is the idea of being 'gassed.' In fact, breathing helium feels the same as breathing air. There is no choking or sensation of gasping for air. Helium is breathed normally. Only the brain notices the difference as the absent oxygen content causes it to cease functioning. Get used to opening and closing the valve (briefly – unless you have a spare tank) so a gentle steady supply can be released. When you hear a light, steady noise, you've got it right. Unconsciousness occurs generally within a minute but can be anything from ten or twenty seconds to ninety seconds or even a couple of minutes. Death follows a few minutes afterwards.

Simplicity itself

The following (true) story is repeated here not as an ideal example to imitate, but as reassurance for anyone that feels that the 'ideal methods' are just getting far too complex! Many things in this books take minutes to demonstrate but longer to explain. Here is how one man used helium as an emergency exit without any advance preparation. This is a back-to-basics painless death. No fancy taps, tubes, special bags. No recipes or technical expertise.

A 64-year-old German man books a hotel room in Switzerland for one night. The following noon, the management forces open the door, which was locked from inside. The man is lying dead on the small single bed. A bag is over his head, held in place by the bag's plastic ribbon drawstring and a rubber band. A safety pin has been used to pull it tight around the neck. A small bottle of helium stands on a table. It wasn't connected to the bag.

He had simply held the bag with the opening downwards while he filled it with helium (which is lighter than air and rises), then carried it away from the source of the gas and put it over his head. It demonstrates that no direct connection between the plastic bag and the gas bottle is essential. And also that a large amount of helium is not really required.

The case was reported in the American Journal of Forensic Medicine and Pathology *(Schon C, Ketterer T)*. It is one of the simplest of helium deaths on record. Whilst it might be very nice to have a large tank or two of helium, proper tubing, perhaps connected with a t-junction, and a nicely customised bag with the elastic fitted into a neat hem, it is hardly essential. All that is needed is enough helium for a few minutes until the breathing ceases. Once the bag is fixed round the neck with an average seal, the gas isn't going to go anywhere. The same gas can repeatedly be breathed in and out. A bag full of helium, exhale fully before putting it on, then swiftly secure it around the neck. I think I'd maybe want to practice a few times with the rubber bands or whatever I was using to hold it in place.

In this case, the man used a garbage bag (17 litre size – not very big). It was the sort that has a couple of plastic ribbons for tying the bag. (These are commonly available from large stores such as some B&Qs – look for packs of 'Clear Storage Bags with Drawstring.') The ribbons can be a bit fiddly to tie shut, so he had just pulled them tight and secured them with a safety pin. The helium tank was rented from a local party balloon shop.

The 'right-to-die' movement sometimes (rightly) accuses the medical profession of 'medicalising death.' Putting a simple, personal business into the hands of the 'experts' who are the 'only ones knowledgeable enough to cope.' But it is also too easy to put the process of self-deliverance into the hands of another group of experts. The right-to-die societies (Exit included!) that teach you the 'best' way.

Admittedly, we can try to help people avoid pitfalls. But this book tries to familiarise you with principles first and foremost. Does it matter whether you are the sort of person that likes a highly technical approach? Or whether you are a down-to-earth personality that just 'gets on with it.?' And remember that the best laid plans can go astray. Perhaps you have your helium kit all ready. Sitting in the cupboard for when the time comes. But you find yourself abroad when things take a sudden and unmistakeable turn for the worse. Hopefully you can still improvise! At the very least, the example of this man in a Swiss hotel room is a reassuring thought to all of us who worry about tiny details, one tank or two, and might panic if we don't have the 'recommended' equipment to hand. If he could do it, so could you.

If people can't follow instructions, or the instructions don't exactly fit circumstances, then it can all be in vain. The style

Exit has found most practical in the UK workshops is to familiarize participants with the principles (by letting them dress-rehearse various approaches); critique the application of the principles; but then empower them by making sure they are practically adept with more than one way (ie both different ways with helium, and different self-deliverance methods). This allows for the fact that their circumstances and capabilities near death may be very different from when they put most of the preparation in. Not to mention different learning approaches that people may have. The various 'do-it-my-way' methods are an excellent foundation and learning tool. This example in Switzerland shows how someone can readily adapt knowledge to circumstances that arise.

Helium autopsies – is helium detectable?

Helium has long been thought undetectable after the event. It is an inert gas and so does not react with any other elements or compounds within the body. Death results from lack of oxygen in the brain, not from the presence of helium. Researchers Ogden and Wooten, for instance, described it as a "potentially undetectable cause of death," and said that, "Helium inhalation can easily be concealed when interested parties remove or alter evidence." Other researchers, Schön and Ketterer worded their paper slightly more cautiously, saying that helium, "leaves only seldom externally visible marks or pathomorphological findings on the body. If the plastic bag and other auxiliary means are removed by another person, the forensic death investigation of cause and manner of death may be very difficult." This is particularly appealing for someone who, for whatever reason, does not want suicide to be generally known as the cause of death, and has a willing helper prepared to (illegally) remove the evidence.

Although these researchers highlighted valuable case studies, their hypotheses are flawed and assume too much. Schön and Ketterer reported the case of a 64-year-old man who achieved suicidal asphyxiation by inhaling helium inside a plastic bag. He probably followed the instructions described in an article about committing suicide written by a medical practitioner from Zürich. Observing cases is one thing. Making generalised assumptions, however reasonable they seem, can be misleading.

There are two main ways that have surfaced for detecting whether a person committed suicide using helium. One is circumstantial. The other is by means of very careful autopsy as special autopsy techniques and devices are required for collection of the gas from the lungs. Authors Grassberger and Krauskopf suggested that, "Because of the diagnostic obstacles involved, it is necessary to rely on good death-scene investigation for situational evidence when the body is discovered." They reported three cases of suicidal asphyxiation with helium gas that were examined at the Department of Forensic Medicine Vienna within three months in 2006. In all three cases, autopsy was unrewarding from the point of view of gross pathology.

A successful toxicological analysis was however reported in Forensic Science International. In this report, initially the autopsy did not show any specific findings nor did the routine toxicological analysis reveal significant information regarding the cause of death.

They describe the procedure: "During autopsy both lungs were subsequently collected in a plastic box filled with water. The box was covered with a lid, leaving as little air as possible in the box. The box was turned upside down, and using a syringe fitted with a T-piece, the residual air was sucked out of the box and discarded. Then long and thick metal needles were pierced into the side of the box to manipulate the lung and press out the gas. The gas volumes escaping from the lung were collected with the syringe from one corner of the box and were pressed into a headspace vial which had been filled with water and crimped closely before."

A volunteer was then used to get an impression of the helium concentrations in the lungs from breathing pure helium. The volunteer simply exhaled deeply and inhaled pure helium once. Part of the exhaled gas was then collected and analysed. Analysing helium presence needs a variation from the usual method where helium is also used as the displacement gas. To analyse the samples of helium, nitrogen was used as a displacement gas. Chromatograms for the gas sample under investigation and the negative control case were taken. Inhalation of helium before death was thus proved. A helium-enriched, oxygen deficient atmosphere could therefore be assumed as the cause of death.

What can be learn from this? Helium death is not easily detectable. It leaves little or no trace. But determined pathologists going to extreme lengths could perhaps ascertain it by the methods described.

Perhaps we can draw this chapter to a close by relating the moving story of Michael Bateman, who described his wife's passing in the *Exit Newsletter:*

"My wife, Margaret had lived in pain and lack of mobility for many years, being bed-bound and totally dependent upon others for the last three. The medical profession has been less than useless and simply made matters worse. As I myself became ill and unable to care for her, she could not bear an indeterminate future in a nursing home. So she decided that the time had finally come to end her own life as the only way out of her suffering.

"We had already decided that helium was the way to go and had obtained all the necessary equipment some time before. With some further adaptations on the tank valves and some help from me she was able actually to turn the taps herself. Margaret filmed her suicide note, telling the world why she was doing it, and actually filmed the start of the process to show that she managed to turn the taps herself. From then on, the whole process was amazingly quick and painless, and I will be eternally grateful for that.

"After the publication of the DPP guidelines as to when they would prosecute or not for assisting a suicide, I did not hide my involvement nor any other aspect of the suicide. This would appear, currently, to mean that it is not in the public interest to prosecute me, although this may still change. Immediately after the event I was arrested and kept in police cells overnight, every member of the family and many friends were questioned both that day and night and over the following weeks. My house was stripped of any possible evidence, filing cabinets, computers, cameras, papers, etc. and my life was brought to a halt. Even now, 2 months on, I have received little back from the police, only pleading with them has obtained just the minimum to keep going, but without insurance, bank information and the like, things are getting left that should be sorted.

"We still don't even have the full autopsy report which I hear has evidence of my wife's illness. The police recognised that we, as a family, were placed in an intolerable position and were suitably sympathetic at a personal level, but their procedures do not cater for this situation and they had to follow what is essentially a murder enquiry.

"I hope that my story will help others to understand the likely persecutions that they will go through, when all they have done is help a loved one to a desired and peaceful end. However, the burden should not be placed upon family and friends, there should be official, medical processes in place, which of course requires a change in the law and a change in attitudes from those who pontificate from the comfort of good health and a cosy life." *Michael Bateman, Exit Newsletter 30(1)*

References

- Auwaerter V, Grosse Perdekampa M, Kempfa J, Schmidta U, Weinmanna W, Pollaka S, Toxicological analysis after asphyxial suicide with helium and a plastic bag. Forensic Science International, Vol 170, Issues 2-3, 6 August 2007, pp139-141).

- Gilson T, Parks B, Porterfield C, Suicide with inert gases: Addendum to Final Exit, Am J Forensic Med Pathol. 2003 Sep;24(3):306-8. (reports on 7 fatalities in Tucson, AZ throughout an 18-month period).

- Glass H, Snyder F, Webster E, The rate of decline in resistance to anoxia of rabbits, dogs, and guinea pigs from the onset of viability to adult life. Am J Physiol 1944, 140:609-615.

- Grassberger and Krauskopf, Suicidal asphyxiation with helium: Report of three cases. Wiener Klinische Wochenschrift, June 2007, 119(9-10):323-325.

- Helium Data and Safety Tips, Western Westwinds Gas Control Technology
  www.westwinds.com

- Herin R, Hall P. Fitch J. Nitrogen inhalation as a method of euthanasia in dogs. Am J Vet Res 1978, 39:989-991.

- Mail Online: Terminally ill doctor survived suicide pact which killed wife because bag used to suffocate himself was too small. http://www.dailymail.co.uk/news/article-1304427/Terminally-ill-doctor-survived-suicide-pact-wife-bag-small.html Accessed 21 Aug 2010.

- Ogden and Wooten, Asphyxial suicide with helium and a plastic bag. Am J Forensic Med Pathol, Sep 2002, 23(3):234-7.

- Schon C, Ketterer T, Asphyxial Suicide by Inhalation of Helium Inside a Plastic Bag, American Journal of Forensic Medicine and Pathology Vol 28, No 4, pp 364-367, Dec 2007.

- Stone G, Suicide and Attempted Suicide: Methods and Consequences, Carroll & Graf 2001.

- St George's University of London, Drug-related deaths in the UK continue to rise, Press Release 24 Aug 2010 http://www.sgul.ac.uk/about-st-georges/divisions/faculty-of-medicine-and-biomedical-sciences/mental-health/icdp/website-pdfs/Drug-related%20deathsfinalPressRelease.pdf, accessed 8 Sep 2010.

- Wanzer S, Glenmullen J, Helium: Newly Used Method to End Suffering. *In:* To Die Well, De Capo Press 2007. Pp115-123.

- Watts R, BC Presence of starch linked to victim and Martens, RCMP chemist testifies. Times Colonist newspaper, Tuesday, October 26, 2004.

Extra information – you may want to read the sections on asphyxia in the *Appendix* to get an even fuller understanding of the physical process.

Swedish tap-turners are an excellent way of adjusting the gas flow carefully

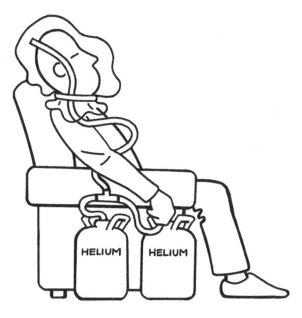

Last Acts:

Let me put this in terms you understand, David. My 'quality of life' – isn't that what you call it? – has dropped below zero. I know there is nothing fatally wrong with me and that I could live on for many years. With a colostomy and some luck, I might even be able to recover a bit of my former lifestyle, for a while. But do we have to do that just because it's possible? Is the meaning of life defined by its duration? Or does life have a purpose so large that it doesn't have to be prolonged at any cost to preserve its meaning?

I've lived a wonderful life, but it has to end sometime and this is the right time for me. My decision is not about whether I'm going to die – we will all die sooner or later. My decision is about when and how. I don't want to spoil the wonder of my life by dragging it out in years of decay. I want to go now, while the good memories are still fresh. Help me find a way.

David Eddy in A piece of my mind – a conversation with my mother, quoted by Geo Stone in Suicide and Attempted Suicide

He searched for his accustomed fear of death and could not find it.

Leo Tolstoy

Strange it's always the living, that fear the idea of the dead. Goodbye.

Roy Harper

Compression

Story (tourniquet method) – ratchet tie-down – other variations (continuous looping; suspension) – finding the carotid arteries – extra safety using a bag – what you need – main features – general description – what is the evidence for compression? – further cases from the medical literature – how quickly does it work? – are there any unpleasant side-effects? – checklist – references

Main features
Compression provides a simple method of ending one's life that is not dependent on having previously-acquired equipment or drugs to hand. Properly done, there is little or no discomfort and it can be performed without arousing too much unwanted attention. The ease with which it can be achieved makes it suitable both as a mainstay method, but particularly for emergencies if one becomes confined to a nursing home or hospital bed.

Concerns over the possible survival of the brain stem (which have occasionally been documented in rare non-suicidal compression cases involving healthy young subjects) have prompted greater emphasis on using a plastic bag in conjunction with this method. A small bag, such as that described for helium (a large roasting bag) is suitable. No other preparation is needed, and such a bag is small enough to be folded discreetly or even used to hold toiletries and so avoid suspicion. The only other implements are material with which to make a tourniquet and some sort of rod with which to tighten it. Such things can be found impromptu or kept with one at all times.

There are a number of variations on the 'compression technique' depending on personal preferences and availability of equipment. Marjorie's story illustrates the Tourniquet Method (which is the most common method in this category). The other major variation is the Ratchet Tie-Down, which is explained in detail afterwards. All the various compression methods involve compression of the carotid arteries without interrupting the breathing.

Marjorie's story

It had happened quite unexpectedly. What had seemed like a routine trip to hospital suddenly developed into something serious. They would do everything they can, but Marjorie was not expected to recover. Her careful plans to make sure the end was at a time of her choosing were not going quite as expected. In hospital, she had no access to pills or helium. She lay awake for a couple of nights making her plans, going over all the possible materials and making her choice. It didn't take too much to ask the nurse to bring her handbag for her so she could get one or two small items. She wanted her mirror and

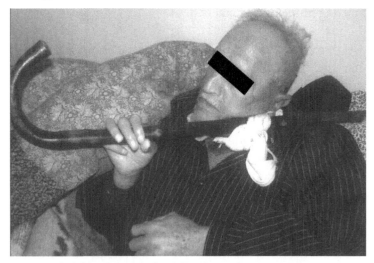

Pathology photograph of a suicide using tourniquet compression

her lipstick, but most importantly she knew that in the inside zipped compartment were a pair of stockings. She had also managed to hide a spoon from dinnertime – a good metal spoon, proper cutlery, not like the stuff you got in some of the places she had been in.

Marjorie made sure her 'implements' were in a place where she could get at them easily, without making any noise that would attract attention, and not somewhere the nurse might find them and wonder what on earth this quiet little lady was going to do with them. She waited until the early hours of the morning when the ward was quietest until she made her move. Under the cover of the bedclothes, she made her preparations. This was where all the dress-rehearsals would now come in handy! If she hadn't practiced many times beforehand when she was fit and healthy, working it all out now may well have been beyond her: but she knew what she was doing. Taking one of the stockings, she knotted it loosely but comfortably around her neck. She wanted to allow about three or four inches when the loop was pulled and the elastic of the stocking was at its full stretch. Too much and the

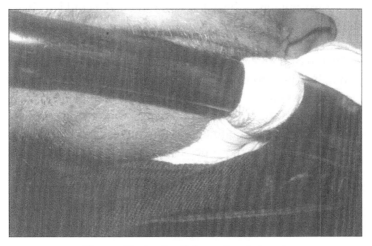

Close up of the tourniquet in the previous photograph

process would be cumbersome. Too little and the stocking would be uncomfortable even before she started. She tied it in a good knot that couldn't slip – a 'reef knot' I believe they called it, she reminded herself.

She remembered the many times she had practiced the technique, using her thigh at first so she could see what she was doing. If you started with the stocking looped around your thigh, one end in each hand, then knotted it – right over left and tuck it under, that was the natural way to do it. The second knot, the one that made it so it wouldn't come undone, started the opposite way: it went, left over right and tuck it under. (If you did two 'rights over lefts', you ended up with a 'granny knot' or slipknot.)

Carefully she positioned the loop around her neck so it was high up, well above where a man's Adam's apple would be. She knew that having it low on the neck would cause discomfort, since pressure lower down would compress the windpipe, and this was not her intention. Marjorie decided to slip part of the pillowcase under the loop as well – not strictly necessary, but when the nylon was tightened it could dig in to the skin a bit so might as well make it comfy with some padding. Next she slipped the spoon between her neck and the nylon of the stocking. Then she tightened the nylon loop as if tightening a tourniquet or turning the hands of a clock. In the practice sessions she had used a variety of implements that came to hand, some were a bit longer, some the length of a spoon. She had experimented turning the spoon in one direction and then the other to see which suited her best. After several turns she could feel it was quite tight – not far to go now. The spoon would not unwind itself – it tended to catch on the jaw or collarbone – but Marjorie would be lying down so there was also the bed there and she could be sure that, once the desired pressure had been achieved, it would remain.

Marjorie spent a few minutes lying quietly and pausing. Once more, she warmly reviewed all the wonderful things she had enjoyed in her life. She thought of her loved ones, and the sealed letter she had placed in her bag addressed to them, making sure they knew she was ending her life in the way she wanted, and that it was her decision alone, her wish.

As a final double safety measure, she unfolded the large roasting bag she had kept in her purse. She loosened the tourniquet slightly, just enough to be able to tuck in the edges of the bag. Slipping the bag over her head she knew this was her fond farewell to the world. She tucked it in securely all around the tourniquet.

Then she tightened the tourniquet some more until the woozy feeling started to come over her. One more turn. The pressure was compressing the carotid arteries. Marjorie lay on her side, inclined downwards, breathing calmly as she fainted. No fresh blood reached her brain. Five minutes later, Marjorie was dead.

Note: most recorded examples of suicidal compression follow the pattern just described but without the addition of a plastic bag. The bag is simply an extra safeguard – anoxia is caused by the tightening of the tourniquet. Unconsciousness and death follows. In very rare cases, it might be possible for the

Reef knot (correct)   Granny knot (wrong)

Diagrams showing the correct and incorrect way of tying a knot that doesn't slip brain stem (not the brain) to survive with the tourniquet alone, so the bag is recommended as an extra safeguard. A senior neurologist has suggested that, "death from carotid occlusion alone usually results from brain swelling and herniation that destroys the brainstem. It is not clear whether the pathophysiology of strangulation is simply one of asphyxia that would cause damage to both brain and brainstem or of carotid occlusion that might affect only supratentorial structures." Using a bag ensures that there is no possibility of survival in any sense.

Ratchet Tie-Down
The ratchet tie-down is a main variation on this method. What Marjorie achieved with a handmade tourniquet is here achieved with an easy-to-obtain, inexpensive piece of equipment. Some people find the ratchet off-putting. You can skip this section if you wish.

You might want to purchase one and familiarise yourself with it before deciding if it is to be one of your methods of choice. You will find them at various retail stores such as those that stock materials for home improvements or car accessories. The usual purpose is for such things as securing luggage on a car roof rack or holding items securely on garage walls; the load stays secure because the webbing tightens and stays locked in place with every pull, until you release it by pushing the thumb lever.

Some people find working the ratchet tie-down comes quite naturally and also like the aesthetic appeal (it looks nice and neat once in place) – others find it quite the opposite and even distasteful. In the workshops, persons who have already used them for ordinary purposes, were naturally inclined to physical work involving ratchets, and more men than women, preferred them. Those who had difficulty working them initially also seemed less inclined to favour them. Although it comes with full instructions, some may find it awkward to use or worry about operating the release mechanism once the tie-down is in place.

An example of a suitable 'hookless' ratchet tie-down

There are two main types of ratchet tie-down – ones with a hook and ones without. The only type that you are interested in is the one without (see illustration). It is possible to place the loop from the ratchet tie-down around the upper part of the neck, tightening with the ratchet until the carotid arteries are compressed sufficiently for the blood supply to the brain to be interrupted (without interrupting the breathing). This results in loss of consciousness followed by death.

It is very important to familiarise yourself with the way the ratchet tie-down works before placing it around your neck. **The thumb release mechanism generally needs a bit of practice. Read the instructions on the box and experiment with strapping down luggage or using it on your thigh (where you can see what you are doing and remove it easily).**

Only practice with the ratchet on your neck if you are extremely confident that you can operate the mechanism easily and release it when required. If possible, do your dress rehearsal with a trusted friend, and keep a pair of scissors handy just in case it gets stuck or you can't operate the release mechanism once the ratchet is in place.

Some people will find that, once fitted, the ratchet tie-down is more aesthetically pleasing than many other methods. The webbing material is also comfortable against the neck and generally will not necessitate additional padding.

Using ratchet tie-downs

The ratchet tie-down is simply a mechanical refinement of the tourniquet method that appeals to a small number of people. Trim off excess strapping – only about a metre is needed. Then thread the strapping: it is a bit like threading the film in an old-fashioned camera. Practice on your thigh for dress rehearsals, and especially practice undoing the ratchet, which is much harder than loosening it.

Step by step:
o   Work the handles until the slot is exposed on the centre spindle.
o   With the handles in a 'V'-shape, feed a few inches of the free end of the strap through the centre of the spindle (A). This part is like threading a bobbin or

camera sprocket. Insert the strap from the top of the 'V' shape.
o Crank the handle to secure the strap (two or more layers of strap must be wound around ratchet reel for a secure hold.) See diagram (B).
o Tighten as needed by cranking the handles a few turns.

To release the ratchet:
o Compress the spring release bars and open the handle 180° until it clicks. (You can still release the strapping if it won't open to 180° but it may require more effort.)
o Firmly pull apart each side of the secured strap (C).
o Compress the spring release bar again and return to the start position.

Other variations on the compression method:
Successful suicides have been recorded in the medical literature with two other methods – continuous looping and suspension.

a) Continuous looping means simply passing a cord around the neck quickly with many turns, using a material that doesn't slip. Nylon coated cords, for instance, tend to slip, whereas many cords (such as traditional string) create a certain amount of friction. Simple knots with some of the turns may help. Once the cord has been wrapped tightly around the upper part of the neck it tends not to slip and, if there is sufficient pressure to occlude the arteries, death results. This variation is only recommended in an emergency (for instance if no other materials were available). You need to be agile enough to wrap the cord quite quickly for a lot of turns. For comfort, some padding is desirable, especially if using thin cord or string. A number of deaths have been recorded where a person has simply had time to wrap stockings around the neck and tie them at the nape of the neck.

b) Suspension is a gentle method that has been recorded frequently in the medical literature. It does not require suspension of the whole body (as in hanging) but simply uses the weight of the upper body to apply pressure via a large loop or strap to the carotid arteries. For instance, *Bhardwaj and Rautji* cite a case of a male, ". . . suspended . . . with his feet touching the ground." The loop can be attached to any fixed object such as a door handle, hook, ceiling fan, stair rail or kitchen bar. The loop is placed around the neck in such a way that, by slumping forward (facing the floor), pressure is placed on the carotid arteries. The carotid arteries are compressed with as little as seven pounds of pressure (the jugular veins with even less – about four and a half pounds). This varies greatly between individuals, but is quite small, which is why a sitting or semi-reclining position is sufficient. A massive 33 pounds of pressure, in contrast, is needed to compress the airway. Suspension does not require much knowledge and can be accomplished even by invalids.

How to find the carotid arteries
This is usually quite easy (but don't worry if you can't find them!) The instructions from St John's Ambulance suggest: "With the head tilted back, feel for the Adam's apple with two fingers. Slide your fingers back towards you into the gap between the Adam's apple and the strap muscle [the easily identifiable muscle running up the side of the neck from the shoulder blade to the hinge of the jaw] and feel for the carotid pulse." You are feeling under the jaw bone at the front/side of the neck. Use the pads of the fingers rather than fingertips or thumbs. Some people have a stronger (or more apparent) pulse here than others. In workshops, most, but not all,

participants were able to identify the carotid artery success-fully. Knowing where it is will make it easier to understand what you are going to accomplish when you compress it with the ligature, but don't worry if you can't feel the pulse.

Making extra sure – using a bag for safety

Some people will use compression as a last resort when no other method is available to them. The tourniquet alone stops oxygen reaching the brain, resulting in permanent uncon-sciousness. A resultant swelling in the brain usually also destroys the brain stem (located at the base of the brain, controlling automatic functions even into permanent vegeta-tive state). Yet in exceptional cases the brain stem could survive. There are reported cases of strangulation in healthy people where the brain stem has survived and the person remained permanently unconscious in PVS. So a sensible additional precaution might be to place a small to medium bag over the head and slipped under the tourniquet or tie-down. This will ensure breathing stops and even the brain stem cannot survive. The roasting bags used in the helium chapter for making helium hoods are quite sufficient. Further research is needed to understand why documented cases of suicidal compression without any bag have clearly resulted in death rather than PVS. But meanwhile the additional safeguard seems both sensible and very little trouble.

Experiments by many people and on several occasions in the workshops have demonstrated that there is plenty of time to apply the tourniquet after placing the bag over one's head. (Note these were done in the safety of company!) No feelings of stuffiness or discomfort were experienced. Practice apply-ing the tourniquet swiftly and safely before experimenting using a small bag. The whole dress rehearsal should be done very quickly at this stage. It is highly unlikely that a person would get 'stuck' or pass out accidentally, but we very strongly recommend that you do such a dress rehearsal in the company of a trusted friend or partner for safety's sake. Place the knotted loop over the head. Some people, especially if they have a very wide head and a very narrow neck, may find it easier to tie the loop once it is around the neck instead of beforehand. Learn how to make a secure knot blindfold when tying the ends of your strip of material together to form your loop. Even without the bag, you probably need to do this at some point as the angle means you can't judge the distance and appropriate place for the knot without a mirror. Have a pair of scissors to hand for safety – the loop is quite loose, but might not be loose enough to pull over your head again. Once the loop is tied loosely around your neck, practice inserting the stick and tightening it quickly like the hands of a clock – to the point where it catches on your jaw or shoulder, not to the point where it makes you dizzy. Then take the stick out and place it nearby. Put the roasting bag over the head and tuck it in all the way around under the tourniquet. Insert your stick and turn it swiftly till it can catch. The whole procedure takes less than half a minute.

When it comes to do the procedure for real, the only difference is an extra turn or two to ensure you go dizzy and pass out. This will occur before you run out of oxygen if you are using a plastic bag as well.

The compression method is particularly suited for unforeseen circumstances, such as hospitalisation. When in such a desperate 'emergency' situation, detailed fine tuning may seem superfluous. Additional use of a plastic bag may even be so difficult that the benefits seem to outweigh the burdens. In an emergency situation where you have very few choices left, choose the least worst option.

What you need
For the tourniquet method:

o   Only household equipment is needed although any of the following may come in useful:
o   Stockings, bowtie, rope, flex, window sash-cord or webbing. The type of material used in a ratchet tie-down is quite adaptable and can be purchased easily (you can use almost anything from which you can make a tourniquet loop – be inventive!) Note that some neckties tend to be 'stretchy' and are less than suitable; stockings, on the other hand, will only stretch so far. For the workshops, we used many materials, but especially rufflette. This can be purchased from John Lewis' or haberdashers (it's used for trimming curtains). You need a width of about 25mm. A very narrow width can be uncomfortable and a very wide strip will be difficult to twist effectively when you insert the stick.
o   Padding. If you want to obtain one, a foam cervical collar or a section cut from one (buy on the Internet from medical suppliers) is excellent, but almost any padding will do.
o   A plastic bag if desired. Large roasting bags (the very large size) are a good choice.
o   Mixing spoon, large pen, sturdy artist's brush, or similar (anything which you can use as a rod, your 'stick' to turn the tourniquet).

Although favourite materials can be obtained in advance (and especially for practice purposes), suitable implements can be found in most situations and environments with a minimum of fuss or trouble. You might even want to make an occasional habit of looking round a new room or environment and thinking, "What would I use?"

Choosing a bag

Most people will use the largest size of roasting bag available. Try it on for size when you get home just to make sure. It needs to be long enough so you will be able to tucks the edges under the tourniquet of your choice. Apart from that, it is not really critical.

For the ratchet tie-down method:

o   A ratchet tie down, the sort without hooks
o   A bag for extra safety, as above.

General description of what happens

Pressure is applied by one of a number of means such that the arteries and veins in the neck that supply blood to and from the brain are compressed though without enough pressure to compress the windpipe (In the classic judo 'choke' for instance, which uses the same principle, pressure is often achieved by pulling cross-wise on the lapels). Without a fresh supply of oxygenated blood, the brain then dies within a few minutes. (Allow 20 minutes however to ensure you will not be disturbed.) As with other methods of starving the brain of oxygen, interruption early on could lead to brain damage.

What is the evidence for compression?

The evidence for compression comes from three main sources. Firstly, in the medical literature, many cases have been reported although it is far less common than other methods of asphyxia. For instance, one study found that suicides by means of ligature compression in Berlin occurred about once a year. Nineteen cases over a period of 20 years were reported by *Maxeiner & Bockholdt (2003)*. Similarly in a study of asphyxial deaths in Turkey, ligature deaths accounted for less than three per cent *(Azmak, 2006).*

Secondly, in the academic literature concerning sexual deviance, many cases of auto-erotic asphyxiation are known. This seems strange at first, but they are relevant inasmuch as the same technique is employed, compressing arteries to stop oxygen to the brain, although with entirely different intentions. One partner applies pressure to the other's neck to obtain a 'high' by partial stopping of oxygen to the brain, or self-induced compressions for the same purpose. Fatalities occur when the pressure is continued for too long. The quantity of documented cases enables greater study of the physical process by which anoxia is achieved painlessly.

Thirdly, the technique used by martial arts experts (and for some time the police) of applying pressure to an opponent is well understood. The 'lateral vascular neck restraint' (or 'sleeper hold') was once a widely taught choke in law enforcement, performed from behind by putting an arm around the neck with the crook of the elbow over the midline of the neck. By pinching the arm together while assisting with the free hand, the carotid arteries and jugular veins would be compressed on both sides of the neck. Correctly applied, this caused unconsciousness without putting any pressure on the airway. In 1981, a class action suit was brought against the City of Los Angeles over fatalities connected with carotid artery control holds. Whereas judo practitioners are expert at not continuing the choke long enough to cause death, police were generally less skilled.

Inexpert application of a choke hold is also believed to have caused cardiac arrest, particularly in someone with underlying heart disease (there is some evidence showing that a reflex action alone from pressure to the vagus nerve can cause death in this manner). *Prahlow,* for instance, makes mention of the 'carotid body,' a specialised group of cells within the wall of the carotid artery that, when stimulated, can result in significant changes in heart rhythm and rate, as well as blood pressure.

A 'blood choke,' or carotid restraint, specifically refers to a chokehold that compresses one or both carotid arteries and/or the jugular veins without compressing the airway, causing a hypoxic condition in the brain. Regardless of who the opponent is, a well applied blood choke leads to unconsciousness in 4-10 seconds, and if released, the subject usually regains consciousness in double the time the choke was applied after he had blacked out (e.g. a choke applied for fifteen seconds after the person passed out results in the person regaining consciousness 30 seconds later). Applied for longer, they are lethal. In ordinary language, a person passes out when the brain doesn't receive oxygen. If the deprivation is continued, death results. Compressing the arteries requires a fraction of the pressure to compress the airway in the throat. This is also seen in the difference between traditional manual strangulation and properly applied blood chokes. The latter require little physical strength, and can be applied successfully by a comparatively weak person. There are many cinematic depictions if you want to visualise the difference. Old James Bond movies will have the secret agent or the villain simply applying fingertip pressure to points on the neck until the victim faints and slides to the floor. Similarly the Japanese film *In the Realm of the Senses* depicts erotic asphyxiation between lovers – the pressure applied to the neck generally stopping short of unpleasant. It is not more pressure that is needed to cause death – simply a longer time period. (For those considering these films, the Japanese movie is a tasteful, critically acclaimed and award winning film – but it is also very sexually explicit.)

Finally there are well-documented cases of 'choking game' deaths. These involve youths seeking a brief euphoric state caused by cerebral hypoxia (see, for instance, *Toblin et al, 2008,* who recorded 82 deaths of this kind in the USA).

It was first brought to the author's attention by judo practitioners writing in saying how it was 'the simplest form of suicide' and explaining the technique of judo holds that can be readily adapted for self-inflicted, painless asphyxiation. But it was only during work for his Masters degree at Glasgow University that a pathologist alerted him to the high incidence in the pathology literature, conveniently disguised. As one police surgeon writes (Henry, 1966), "The confusion and embarrassment felt by a person discovering a body who has died through sexual asphyxia is likely to be considerable. Attempts may be made to disguise the nature of the death to medical attendants and to investigating police officers." A review of published studies soon confirmed both the prevalence and method used. The number of reported and well-documented cases is now huge.

Some further cases from the medical literature

1. A woman aged 73 was lying full length on the floor of a bedroom, which she shared with another patient in a nursing home. The bed clothing had been thrown back in a manner consistent with getting out of bed. There were no signs of any struggle. She was dressed in a nightgown and a brown stocking was round her neck; the fellow of a pair was seen suspended over the head of the bed. The stocking was applied with a half-

knot at the nape on the first turn and with another half-knot at the front of the neck. The first turn was tight, but the second, although close to the first, was easily released. There were no other signs of violence, but a little bleeding, which produced a small stain 1 in. in its diameter, had occurred from the nose; the stain was directly below her nose. Her face and neck, above the ligature, were congested and of purple colour. Bleeding had occurred beneath the conjunctivae [eyelids], but petechial haemorrhages [pinpoint haemorrhages often found in asphyxia] were not seen in the skin of the forehead and face. The tongue protruded, but was not bitten; she had dentures, but these were on her bedside table.

2. In one case, however, a 53-year-old man succeeded .. .. He wrapped twine around his neck 35 times, tied a knot and tightened it. He then bent forward on his knees with his head down, which increased his neck circumference, and thus, pressure from the twine; this is the posture in which he was found. Since this is an unusual position, the police were initially suspicious. However, there was no internal damage to the fairly delicate anatomical structures in the neck, a fact consistent with suicide, but not murder.

3. A 70-year-old-man was found dead in his room, a piece of belt-like cloth wrapped around the neck, knotted, and tightened by a walking stick. He was found lying on the bed, with his feet touching the floor. His hand was still on the walking stick which was seemingly used by him for a tourniquet effect. This case study included photographs of the diseased with the tourniquet still in place, reported in the

American Journal of Forensic Medical Pathology *(Atilgan, 2010)*.

There are many more case histories, often with ingenious variations. Additionally, the case histories in autoerotic asphyxiation show examples of unintentional death. Most involved males, although one study *(Byard et al 1993)* looked at differences where women were involved, particularly noting how neck padding had been used to avoid chafing. There is no need to go into too much graphic detail (the sample of literature quoted at the end of the chapter will provide the necessary documentation for the serious researcher). All the cases involve a degree of neck compression, a few with the addition of a plastic bag. One particular amusing case (amusing of course except for the deceased and those who knew him) is perhaps worthy of mention to give the gentle reader an idea. The man in question had rigged a complex system of pulleys to apply pressure to the neck, compressing the arteries and producing a 'high' whilst indulging in solitary sexual activity. To tighten the ligature, but not to a deadly degree, he had attached the pulley to a garden lawnmower. A stake in the lawn prevented the power lawnmower from going too far. Except it rained, and the stake came loose . . .

How quickly does it work?
Like helium, compression works by starving the brain of oxygen and takes no more than a few minutes. Occasionally fatal cardiac arrest can be triggered at the same time. This is due to 'reflex vagal inhibition' – a mechanism that may sometimes leap into action as the vagus nerve in the neck is depressed, particularly in the elderly or if there is some underlying heart disease. Studies using an apparatus causing rapid carotid occlusion and quoted by *Oehmichen et al* demonstrated loss of consciousness in seven seconds.

Are there any unpleasant side effects?

There may be slight discomfort from the pressure on the neck, though this is not enough to interfere with breathing. As the blood supply to the brain is interrupted, there is a sense of dizziness or fainting, followed by unconsciousness and death. Judo practitioners have described their experience of losing consciousness from compression-technique judo holds as 'quite pleasant', like controlled fainting. This tallies with the reports of brief euphoric state caused by cerebral hypoxia in studies of youths playing the 'choking game.' Photographs of persons who have ended their life by compression, such as those reproduced in this chapter and in other studies (such as Di Nunno, Constantinides et al, *Self-Strangulation – An Uncommon but Not Unprecedented Suicide Method*) show the deceased peacefully at rest with the ligature in place. The difference in length between the tightened ligature and the uncompressed neck is quite small – for instance a tightened ligature of 30cm on a neck of 35cm.

Checklist:

o   You need two or three items: something you can make a strong loop with, and something you can use to tighten the tourniquet. Make a list of suitable household items. Even get into the habit of looking around or imagining yourself in other situations such as hotels, nursing homes, or on holiday – what would you be able to use in an emergency? You will find there are types of material that are more comfortable, but stockings are fairly easy to obtain at any hour of the day or night (for instance, from 24-hour petrol stations). People have used belts, suspenders, shoelaces, scarves, handkerchiefs, neckties, shirtsleeves, pantlegs, and undershirts, among many other things. Shop around for a suitable roasting bag or similar.

o If using an elasticized material (such as stockings or tights), make the loop the size you want when the material is at its maximum stretch.

o A fraction of the pressure that would compress the windpipe is needed to compress the carotid arteries (these supply oxygenated blood to the brain). Avoid placing pressure on the windpipe though by keeping the loop higher around the neck rather than lower down. Padding may be used for extra comfort – find out by experimenting with different loops and see which ones are comfortable without padding (don't cut into the skin) or which ones need padding.

o Practice making the tourniquet on your thigh first, rather than your neck. This allows you to see what you are doing. Make sure you can do the knot easily.

o When you come to practice the tourniquet around your neck, maybe have a pair of scissors handy to cut the practice stocking (or cord) should you need to.

o A wooden kitchen spoon is excellent for practice. Try turning it until you can feel the pressure (but not causing you to feel dizzy or faint). See how it catches on the collar bone or jaw. Decide if turning it in one direction or the other feels to work better for you.

o The tourniquet 'lever' can be placed at any point, but at the side and towards the front of the neck is perhaps easiest and most comfortable – and also positioned well to catch on chin or collar bone. (Do experiment – it is the quickest way to understand it!)

o The pressure needed for self-deliverance is the same pressure that is needed to cause you to become dizzy and faint, so exercise due caution during your dress rehearsals.

o Remember, keep the tourniquet high up on the neck to minimize uncomfortable pressure on the windpipe and maximise pressure on the carotids.

o   Make sure the knot is secure and does not slip.

o   Ensure the fitted loop is sufficiently distant from the neck (about two or three inches) to allow the 'stick' (pen, spoon, etc) to be inserted and turned. You need to be able to turn the stick like the hands of a clock to tighten the tourniquet.

o   Ensure the loop isn't *too* big. Otherwise you will end up turning it for a long time to make it tight enough. By the time you feel the pressure on your neck, the twists in the loop will have become very unwieldy.

o   Practice until you can do it comfortably, effectively and safely. Practice very carefully at first, especially if practicing on one's own. You can go almost to the 'dizzy point' and no further.

o   You do not have to tighten the tourniquet to a dangerous degree in dress rehearsals. The loop will acquire a natural tension so you can experience the stick catching against the jaw or shoulder-blade.

o   Everyone's physical dimensions are individual, so experiment. For some people turning it clockwise will be best, for others anti-clockwise. If you have a very pronounced jaw, it will catch differently. But it works for everyone and there is nothing very complicated about it. This whole chapter is describing a process that can be demonstrated in a matter of seconds.

o   If you want to experience the 'dizzy point' when you are practicing alone, simply apply pressure at the pulse points, as explained (in the event of fainting, your hands fall away so you are not in danger). This is *not* recommended as a regular practice though. If you are in poor health, exceptional care is needed so as not to trigger the vagal reflex and you should *not* go as far as making yourself dizzy in a dress rehearsal.

o It is not necessary to be able to find a pulse for the technique to work. Some people's pulse is more pronounced than in others.

References:

- Atilgan M, A Case of Suicidal Ligature Strangulation by Using a Tourniquet Method, American Journal of Forensic Medicine & Pathology: March 2010, Vol.31, Issue 1, pp 85-86.

- Atanasijević T, Jovanović AA, Nikolić S, Popović V, Jasović-Gasić M, Accidental death due to complete autoerotic asphyxia associated with transvestic fetishism and anal self-stimulation - case report, Psychiatr Danub. 2009 Jun;21(2):246-51.

- Azmak D, Asphyxial deaths: a retrospective study and review of the literature, Am J Forensic Med Pathol. 2006 Jun;27(2):134-44.

- Becker R, Sure U, Petermeyer M, Bertalanffy H, Continuous intrathecal baclofen infusion alleviates autonomic dysfunction in patients with severe supraspinal spasticity, J Neurol Neurosurg Psychiatry (letters to the editor) 1999;66:114.

- Bhardwaj DN, Rautji R, Sharma RK, Dogra TD, Suicide by a transvestite or sexual asphyxia? A case report, Med Sci Law. 2004 Apr;44(2):173-5.

- Behrendt N, Buhl N, Seidl S, The lethal paraphiliac syndrome: accidental autoerotic deaths in four women and a review of the literature, Int J Legal Med. 2002 Jun;116(3):148-52.

- Blanchard R, Hucker SJ, Age, transvestism, bondage, and concurrent paraphilic activities in 117 fatal cases of autoerotic asphyxia, Br J Psychiatry. 1991 Sep;159:371-7.

- Byard RW, Hucker SJ, Hazelwood RR, A comparison of typical death scene features in cases of fatal male and autoerotic asphyxia with a review of the literature, Forensic Sci Int. 1990 Dec;48(2):113-21.

- Byard RW, Hucker SJ, Hazelwood RR, Fatal and near-fatal autoerotic asphyxial episodes in women. Characteristic features based on a review of nine cases, Am J Forensic Med Pathol. 1993 Mar;14(1):70-3.

- Clark M , The autoerotic asphyxiation syndrome in adolescent and young adult males January, 1996 Referenced at http://www.tcfcanada.net/articles/aea/youngmales.htm

- Di Nunno N, Costantinides F, Conticchio G, Mangiatordi S, Vimercati L, Di Nunno C, Self-Strangulation: An Uncommon but Not Unprecedented Suicide Method, American Journal of Forensic Medicine & Pathology September 2002, 23(3): 260-263.

- Doychinov ID, Markova IM, Staneva YA, Autoerotic asphyxia (a case report), Folia Med (Plovdiv). 2001;43(4):51-3.

- Egge MK, Berkowitz CD, Toms C, Sathyavagiswaran L, The choking game: a cause of unintentional strangulation, Pediatr Emerg Care. 2010 Mar;26(3):206-8.

- Ernoehazy W, Hanging Injuries and Strangulation, eMedicine Specialties > Emergency Medicine > Trauma & Orthopedics, http://emedicine.medscape.com/article/826704-overview, accessed 1st Oct 2010.

- Hall C, Butler B, National Study On Neck Restraint In Policing, http://dsp-psd.pwgsc.gc.ca/collection_2007/ps-sp/PS63-2-2007-1E.pdf 2007, accessed 2 Sep 2010.

- Henry RI, Suicide by proxy: a case report of juvenile autoerotic sexual asphyxia disguised as suicide. A common occurrence? J Clin Forensic Med. 1996 Mar;3(1):55-6.

- Hawley D, McClane G, Strack G, Violence: Recognition, Management, and Prevention, A Review of 300 Attempted Strangulation Cases - Part III: Injuries In Fatal Cases, Journal of Emergency Medicine 21(3), pp. 317–322, 2001.

- Information on 'finding the carotid artery' from St John's Ambulance manuals.

- Jenkins A, When Self-Pleasuring Becomes Self-Destruction: Autoerotic Asphyxiation Paraphilia, American Alliance for Health, PE, Recreation and Dance National Conference and Exposition on March 25, 2000 in Orlando Florida, and also published in the International Electronic Journal of Health Education.

- Kano J, Kodokan Judo: The Essential Guide to Judo by Its Founder Jigoro Kano, 1986 Kodansha.

- Koiwai E, Deaths Allegedly Caused by the Use of Choke Holds (Shime-Waza) http://www.judoinfo.com/chokes5.htm

- Koops E, Janssen W, Anders S, Püschel K, Unusual phenomenology of autoerotic fatalities, Forensic Sci Int. 2005 Jan 17;147 Suppl:S65-7.

- Macnab A, Deevska M, Gagnon F, Cannon W, Andrew T, Asphyxial games or "the choking game": a potentially fatal risk behaviour, Injury Prevention, 2009;15:45-49.
- Maxeiner H, Bockholdt B, Homicidal and suicidal ligature strangulation—a comparison of the post-mortem findings, Forensic Science International, Vol.137, Issue 1, 60-66 (14 Oct 2003).
- McClave J, Russell P, Lyren A, O'Riordan M,Bass N, The Choking Game: Physician Perspectives, Pediatrics 2010;125;82-87.
- Mifune K, White F, The Canon of Judo: Classic Teachings on Principles and Techniques (this book, as well as Kano, infra, also details the 'Kappo' safety technique of resuscitation when respiration has ceased due to use of choking techniques).
- Mohr W, Petti T, Mohr B, Adverse Effects Associated With Physical Restraint. Can J Psychiatry, Vol 48, No 5, June 2003.
- Money J, The Breathless Orgasm: A Lovemap Biography of Asphyxiophilia, Prometheus Books 1991.
- Multi-Society Task Force on PVS, Medical Aspects of the Persistent Vegetative State, NEJM 1994, 330(21):1503.
- Oehmichen M, Auer R, König H, Forensic Types of Ischemia and Asphyxia, in: Forensic Neuropathology and Associated Neurology, Springer 2005, Part III, Chapter 14, pp293-317.
- Ohlenkamp N, The Judo Choke, Judo Trends Magazine January 1966.
- Pomfrett C, private correspondence, 2010.
- Prahlow J, Asphyxial Deaths, in: Forensic Pathology for Police, Death Investigators, Attorneys, and Forensic Scientists, Humana Press 2010, Part 3, pp388-418.
- Posner J, private correspondence 2010.
- Sauvageau A, Racette S, Autoerotic deaths in the literature from 1954 to 2004: a review, J Forensic Sci. 2006 Jan;51(1):140-6.
- Sauvageau A, Geberth VJ, Elderly victim: an unusual autoerotic fatality involving an 87-year-old male, Forensic Sci Med Pathol. 2009;5(3):233-5. Epub 2009 Jun 9.
- Sheleg S, Ehrlich E, Autoerotic Asphyxiation: Forensic, Medical, and Social Aspects, Wheatmark 2006. This work contains a very extensive list of further references and source materials.
- Stemberga V, Bralić M, Bosnar A, Coklo M, Propane-associated autoerotic asphyxiation: accident or suicide? Coll Antropol. 2007 Jun;31(2):625-7.

- Stone G, Suicide and Attempted Suicide: Methods and Consequences, Carroll & Graf 2001.

- Toblin RL, Paulozzi LJ, Gilchrist J, Russell PJ, Unintentional strangulation deaths from the 'choking game' among youths aged 6-19 years - United States, 1995-2007, J Safety Res. 2008;39(4):445-8. Epub 2008 Jul 9.

- Wijdicks E, Varelas P, Gronseth G, Greer D, Evidence-based guideline update: Determining brain death in adults, Neurology 74, June 8, 2010:1911-1918.

- Zecević D, Suicidal strangulation with a double-knotted noose, Journal of Forensic Sciences Vol 27 Oct 1982.

A friend, reflecting on the time her cancer had been diagnosed as terminal, said, "Being terminal just meant that at last I acknowledged that death was real. It did not mean that I would die in six months or even die before the doctor who had just given me the prognosis. It simply meant that I acknowledged that I would die at all."

From Who Dies by Stephen Levine

We have gazed too long at the stars together to be afraid of
the night.

On the tomb of a Christian astronomer, written by his partner

I am too tired
To move on, or to mind the paths travelled.
Where I find moonlight and gentle breezes,
I shall unload, lay down, and rest in peace.

Helen Chen

Drugs

Introduction – main features – using chloroquine – general description – myths about chloroquine – what is the evidence for chloroquine? – how quickly does it work? – are there any unpleasant side-effects? – obtaining chloroquine – anti-nausea drugs – obtaining sleeping tablets – shelf-life of drugs and buying drugs abroad – Mexico – buying drugs on the Internet – the best way to take tablets – what you need – preparation and method – barbiturates and other drugs – checklist – references

Introduction
Often when people think about drugs for suicide their attention turns to one of two main groups. Attempted suicides are common with the highly available but highly unsuitable drug paracetamol (known in the US as acetaminophen). Paracetamol is likely to cause very painful yet non-fatal internal organ damage. More educated persons, and members of right-to-die organisations, sometimes go on a (often fruitless) quest for what they believe is a perfect drug. They spend much time and energy writing letters to find out if barbiturates are available in Mexico or through the Internet, oblivious both to the dangers of such a quest and to the reality – which is that suitable drugs can usually be obtained fairly easily at home.

If, because of your medical condition, you happen to have a good supply of barbiturates, these can be ideal on their own (see later this chapter). Otherwise there is one drug on which there is more accumulated evidence for its use in suicide than any other, but it is a drug which must only be used with great care and in combination with a specific range of other drugs. That drug is chloroquine.

Main features

In the US a prescription is needed, but in most other countries chloroquine is available without prescription (see later in this chapter for ways of obtaining chloroquine). This makes it attractive as a 'drugs only' method as long as you also have (or can obtain) enough suitable sleeping tablets to ensure a deep sleep. Chloroquine is not a gentle drug however. A person using chloroquine needs to be confident of completing the procedure effectively and not vomiting the large amount of drugs ingested.

Using chloroquine

Although chloroquine ingested in sufficient doses is undoubtedly fatal, a proportion of people (about one in five) experience side-effects, therefore a suitable sedative is needed in conjunction with the chloroquine. A further concern is that a large group of sedatives – benzodiazepines – interact with chloroquine and are even used as a standard hospital treatment for chloroquine overdose, so the choice of sedative is important.

Benzodiazepines – the drugs generally to *avoid* in combination with chloroquine if possible– include temazepam (although this is one of the drugs of choice for use with plastic bags – see next chapter). Most benzodiazepines end in '-azepam' and so are readily identifiable. These include nitrazepam (Mogadon), diazepam (Valium), flurazepam (Dalmane), loprazolam, lormetazepam, and temazepam (Restoril, Normison). In the preceding list, I have given some of the *brand* names in brackets. These change from time to time and vary from country to country. If in doubt, examine the packaging or literature enclosed with the drug to find out the *generic* ingredient. This is the chemical name of the drug and does not vary. Some of these drugs are also prescribed for anxiety.

So what sedative is suitable for use with chloroquine? The most obvious drug of choice is zolpidem (known in the US as Ambien). If you obtain zolpidem in the UK, it may be packaged as zolpidem or have the brand name *Stilnoct* added. A very important point is that zolpidem tablets are tiny, making them easy to swallow (and they doesn't interfere with chloroquine). It is a prescription drug for sleep disorders, but widely prescribed and so relatively easy to obtain. Certain other sleeping drugs are also fine in combination with chloroquine *though preferably not benzodiazepines such as temazepam.* However, if you only have benzodiazepines, the statistics do indicate that if you have managed to ingest sufficient chloro-

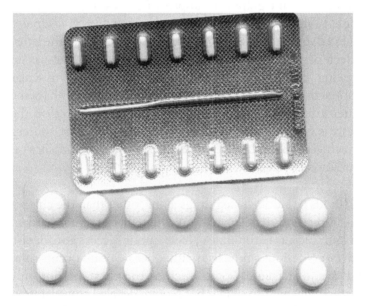

Comparative size of zolpidem (top) and temazepam (bottom)

quine, no amount of benzodiazepine will interfere with a fatal outcome.

A similar sounding drug but one that should emphatically not be used with chloroquine is zopiclone. Great confusion, with tragic consequences, resulted when one translator of *Departing Drugs* added their own recommendation without the permission of the authors – to use zopiclone with chloroquine. This didn't come to light for a long time as Exit failed to monitor closely the translated copies of its book being sold in the Netherlands. The illegal copies have since been withdrawn. A group of authors calling themselves the Wozz Foundation (in: *Humane Self-Chosen Death, 2006* – see: *Guide to Suicide Guides,* this volume), correctly claimed that chloroquine and zopiclone is a combination to be avoided. They incorrectly claimed (alongside some graphic examples of distressing deaths) that the authors of *Departing Drugs* ever recommended it. *Wozz* also claimed that benzodiazepines are not an antidote to the lethal effect of chloroquine on the heart and that their use in treating chloroquine poisoning is to suppress muscular contractions and epileptic seizures. While they clearly have the latter effect, suggesting they do not alter the effect on the heart is contrary to both mainstream and specialist sources which very specifically note the effect of benzodiazepines on cardiotoxicity in chloroquine poisoning.

Methods of suicide using drugs alone, other than the chloroquine method, tend to rely on drugs that are very hard to obtain (such as barbiturates), have a poor success rate, or else have very serious side effects either before death occurs or in the event of failure. Some (such as tricyclics) are not only increasingly hard to obtain but require detailed consideration as to whether they are suitable for a particular individual. As these drugs collectively form a tiny area of suitably dignified means of death, they will be considered towards the end of this chapter.

General description – chloroquine & sedatives
An anti-nausea drug is taken some time before the main drugs. A large dose of chloroquine is taken (about 50 pills) followed by enough of the appropriate sleeping tablets to ensure deep sleep. (If drugs other than chloroquine are used, an anti-nausea drug is still required.)

Myths about chloroquine
There are a number of myths about chloroquine frequently banded about, so it is necessary to address them directly.

Myths about chloroquine (1): a failed attempt can result in blindness
This is a common objection, often suggested by doctors who have a passing, inadequate knowledge of chloroquine. They have learnt that chloroquine can cause blindness in toxic doses. This is true, but leaves out the essential factors: chloroquine is only known to cause permanent blindness when there is long-term overdose, not a single overdose. Any visual disturbances are considered reversible with an acute (one-off) overdose. This is known from a large number of reputable studies, such as those published by the World Health Organisation and the Toxicology Management Review (see appendix). What is worth stressing however, is that chloroquine is a very dangerous drug and not suitable for the faint-hearted. Recovery from a failed attempt (compared to a failed attempt with a plastic bag) could potentially be very distressing.

Myths about chloroquine (2): are any sleeping pills suitable?

This is also untrue and widely recognised now following the revelations in the book *Departing Drugs* and publication of *The Chloroquine Controversy* (which is reprinted in the appendix). Before that, some organisations, even with medical advisors, had suggested using chloroquine with benzodiazepine -type sleeping drugs. True, if you ingest enough chloroquine there is very little that can be done to prevent death, even with medical treatment; but it makes little sense to take the standard antidote (benzodiazepine) with the drug chloroquine itself. Following publication of *The Chloroquine Controversy,* organisations that had previously recommended the use of benzodiazepines with chloroquine withdrew their publications, in some cases replacing them with *Departing Drugs.* But concern over chloroquine (and lack of understanding) has in many cases not persuaded many right-to-die societies to re-introduce chloroquine among their recommended methods (with appropriate cautionary advice about benzodiazepines). This is regrettable, but with the increasing popularity of helium as a method is less important than in the past.

The original recommendation for chloroquine (without the precautions over benzodiazepines) came from doctors. Similarly, the concerns over chloroquine and blindness have also come from doctors. In both cases doctors have spoken from inadequate knowledge and their advice was accepted simply because they were doctors. One should remember that doctors are expert in the use of drugs to heal, not in their use for suicide. Similarly, doctors that practice euthanasia are expert in the specific drugs they use, but often less accurate elsewhere unless they have done their research. Doctors do, however, tend to be quick to acknowledge flaws in their beliefs, as they have done when we have presented them with peer-examined, scientific data and published proof. Many authors on self-deliverance, like the proverbial doctor, encourage an almost religious acceptance that what they say is gospel. This book takes no such attitude and encourages readers to sceptically examine *every* recommendation, particularly in any absence of supporting data. *Five Last Acts,* whether in the main body or the Appendix, includes many references so you can verify and have scientific confidence in our written assertions.

Remember that drugs like benzodiazepines can remain in the system for a while – for several days after taking them. If you have been taking them for any other reasons, it may be advisable to allow time for them to completely leave the body.

What is the evidence for chloroquine?
Chloroquine has a long history and has been routinely provided to armed forces stationed abroad. Given that suicides among this group of the population are noted rapidly, there is a remarkable amount of data in the medical literature on suicide by means of chloroquine – more so than with any other drug studied. See the *appendix* for some of the many medical sources on death by chloroquine.

How quickly does it work?
The time varies, but several uninterrupted hours should be set aside. As it is normally taken with sleeping tablets, unconsciousness ensues quickly (in cases where sleeping tablets are not taken, unconsciousness often occurs within half an hour, but sleeping tablets are very strongly recommended in case it does not!)

Are there any unpleasant side-effects?
Very possibly – at least if appropriate sleeping tablets are not taken. Of the various side-effects, the most serious is extreme hyperactivity and convulsions, which affects one in five people taking a chloroquine overdose without sleeping tablets. Therefore, although it is a reliable method of suicide, it should really only be considered in combination with suitable sleeping tablets. In the case of a failed attempt, there may be some persistent side-effects, including disturbances to vision, but not permanent ones.

Obtaining chloroquine
Chloroquine is commonly dispensed as an anti-malarial. This means it is available from any chemist (for instance in the UK) without prescription but at the discretion of the pharmacist. The chemist may ask where you are going. Anti-malarials are used for travel to most parts of Africa, the hot parts of South America, Central America, and South-East Asia. The chemist will probably also enquire as to how long you are going for. Working out the exact number of tablets needed against malaria uses a formula that includes a period before and after travel as well as weekly dose while you are away, so the chemist will expect you to state a time period rather than a number of tablets. Some people will ask for sufficient for their whole family travelling together. People who are stockpiling the drug for use in self-deliverance will often visit several chemists to ensure a sufficient supply. If you really are planning on getting drugs to prevent malaria, you may want to look into it more carefully for that purpose (mosquitoes have developed resistance to chloroquine as many areas). Sometimes a chemist will suggest more modern or area-specific drugs, but I usually say I prefer chloroquine as it doesn't upset my system. The main brand names of chloroquine are Nivaquine and Avloclor. Sometimes they come in foil packs and

sometimes loose. The most common size is 200 or 250mg. Fifty of this strength of pill is recommended. Less will probably do, but this is a dosage that no-one has survived, out of many hundreds of suicides.

Anti-nausea drugs
If you are taking a large number of tablets, the stomach's immediate reaction will be to try to vomit them up, therefore you need an anti-nausea drug (sometimes called an anti-emetic or anti-sickness or travel-sickness drug) to control and prevent any nausea and vomiting. There are many adequate ones available over the counter, or you can use a prescription drug such as metaclopramide or prochlorperazine. If you buy them over the Internet, take some reasonable precautions (such as testing the prescribed dosage when you are feeling nauseous). Although the usual precautions apply (see *Buying drugs on the Internet*, below), as most of these drugs are quite cheap there is not the same motivation to sell counterfeits.

One thing to be aware of with anti-nausea drugs is that some of them cause drowsiness. This is particularly true with some of the antihistamine preparations. Unless you are specifically using the drug to cause sleepiness, check the details carefully. There are too many to list, but antihistamines fall into two categories, those that also cause severe drowsiness and those that do not (or cause less drowsiness). Ask the pharmacist (and also check the notes on the packet when you buy them) or your doctor. Try the normal dosage recommended for travel-sickness or other genuine medicinal reason and see if you feel drowsy. Hyocine is an anti-nausea drug that is also available as a patch applied to the skin rather than as a tablet. It may cause some drowsiness though. Not all anti-nausea drugs are used for travel-sickness. Metoclopramide, for instance, is ineffective for tummy upsets caused by travel so won't be offered for that purpose. (Metoclopramide is the anti-nausea drug of choice in Dutch euthanasia.)

It has been pointed out that some anti-emetics focus on upset stomach whereas some, for travel sickness, act on the brain's balance receptors. Therefore a favoured recommendation and easily available is an over-the-counter drug called Motilium (generic name: domperidone).

The exact choice and number of anti-nausea drugs is far less crucial than using common sense. Ideally you would take an initial dose a couple of hours before the self-deliverance drugs and a further dose about twenty minutes before taking lethal drugs. You would increase the normal dose slightly, but not excessively.

Anti-nausea drugs are also routinely prescribed for certain conditions, as part of advanced palliative care, and commonly in patients with advanced cancer.

Obtaining sleeping tablets such as zolpidem (Ambien)
When will a doctor prescribe these sleeping tablets? Not just because you fancy some, that's for sure! Your doctor is responsible for your 'whole being' health so this means that if he or she is convinced that your *sleeping problems are interfering with a normal life* then a prescription can be justified. For instance, if your lack of normal sleep means you cannot perform your job properly or it is interfering with a normal social life. Sleeping tablets are usually prescribed on a short term basis (they can't be taken on a daily basis for a long period as their effect wears off or they become addictive). Sometimes if your doctor trusts you to use drugs sensibly and not too often, a more regular small amount may be pre-

scribed. Prescribing will normally follow the 'least medication needed' option, which goes something along these lines –

1. Serious sleep problem.

2. Doctor suggests lifestyle changes or occasional use of over-the-counter medication.

3. Patient tries this *for a month or so* and reports back that sleeplessness is still a serious problem. (Each stage requires a certain amount of time to give it a proper chance of working, so can rarely be skipped.)

4. Doctor prescribes a mild sleeping tablet such as zopiclone for occasional use. (Note the similar spelling: zopiclone is a markedly different drug to zolpidem.)

5. After maybe a couple of months, the patient reports back that it has some effect but does not really work that well at providing reliable sleep, and/or there are unpleasant side-effects such as upsetting the system in some way. zopiclone, for instance, can sometimes cause mood changes or daytime clumsiness or daytime restlessness.

6. Doctor prescribes zolpidem or the (benzodiazepine drug) temazepam (also called Restoril), possibly in the lowest dose. Although temazepam tablets tend to be a bit bigger than zolpidem tablets, they are quite suitable for the plastic bag method.

7. Repeat of stage (5), at which point doctor prescribes different drug (zolpidem or temazepam) or a different dosage.

Another reason sleeping tablets are prescribed is for long-haul travel. If I am flying a considerable distance and have to give a lecture shortly afterwards, it is important I get a good sleep on the plane. I generally ask my doctor for a small number of sleeping tablets and indicate any that, from experience, I find ineffective or unpleasant!

Zolpidem usually comes in tablets of 5mg or 10mg. Temazepam tablets and capsules vary. In the UK, Temazepam is available in 10mg and 20mg doses (which are very roughly equivalent to the 5mg and 10mg zolpidem strengths). It costs the NHS roughly twice as much as temazepam, but is still an inexpensive drug.

Zolpidem is an excellent drug of choice in combination with the plastic bag. It can also be used with chloroquine. Temazepam is not strongly recommended with chloroquine but is an adequate drug for use with the plastic bag method.

Buying chloroquine – a reader's experience
An Exit member who attended a workshop bought some chloroquine afterwards and then wrote in to the Exit Newsletter recounting her experience:

"I bought 120 tablets of chloroquine (Avloclor) with no difficulty. First, I consulted the reputable travel health website www.fitfortravel.scot.nhs.uk (run by NHS Scotland) and looked at the malaria map for a number of countries and what anti-malaria drugs would routinely be prescribed for them. I discovered that northern and southern (not central) India and Central Asia fit the bill because chloroquine is the drug of choice for these areas. (If you choose India, you are recommended to take chloroquine and proguanil, so more complicated.) Central Asia is subject to malaria from May to October only.

"I simply went to three chemists and said I was going on a tour of Central Asia for two weeks in late September. I went to a couple of Boots and neither asked any further questions, although one did ask me to complete a form to say I had been advised to take chloroquine. I also went to a small independent chemist who asked which countries I was going to in Central Asia. I listed Armenia, Azerbaijan and Kyrgyzstan. This chemist obligingly showed me his crib sheet of malaria countries and recommended drugs, and all countries in Central Asia – apart from Kazakhstan – are deemed to require chloroquine from May to October (even though most tourist sites are in cities, which are all malaria-free!) If I had been asked for any more detail, I would have said I was going to visit Mount Ararat in Armenia, which is a tourist highlight and which is definitely in a malaria area.

"The rules for chloroquine are that you take two tablets a week for one week before the visit, during the visit, and for four weeks afterwards. So I said I was going to Central Asia with my husband for two weeks. This meant I would need more than one pack for the two of us (ie. fourteen pills each; packs of twenty tablets) and would be given two packs by each chemist. Tablets cost £2.50 per pack at the local chemist and £4.30 per pack at Boots!)"

Note: Boots is a leading UK chemist shop and has sometimes been known to ask people to sign a disclaimer form for you to acknowledge they have given you advice for this product.

Buying drugs abroad and shelf-life of drugs

Some people get stuck on the idea that they can find the perfect chemist somewhere abroad, maybe Mexico, and get their dream prescription. The logic of spending much time, effort and money on such a quest seems dubious. Firstly, it is usually relatively easy to get the usable drugs in your home country where you know they are genuine and in good condition and where you are not breaking any laws. We do not recommend you go abroad especially to look for prescription drugs. But if you do buy drugs abroad, some common sense observations will help you determine their worth.

You need to know that they are genuine and secondly that they have been stored in suitable conditions. Many pharmacies in hot climates will keep main drug supplies in a specially air-conditioned room – some will not. Drugs sold in foil packs are less likely to have deteriorated than those that are not, and tablets/pills are more resistant to deterioration than capsules. Tablets are hard, compacted, whereas capsules are soft and more easily affected by external conditions. Generic drugs may be just as good as branded ones or they may (in poorly controlled countries) be weaker. I've seen accompanying small print that said where the actual drug was not available a suitable 'substitute' would have been used in manufacture. Even if it appears branded this is not a cast-iron guarantee of authenticity: there is a large black market in counterfeit drugs, even down to the packaging.

When it comes to sleeping pills, if you believe you have a genuine product, you can test them in the normal way – to see if a normal dose will give you a good night's sleep, and also (as a precaution) find out how many you need to get eight hours sleep in daylight hours. Obviously most drugs other than sleeping tablets cannot be tested in this way. (One doctor,

Philip Nitschke of Exit International, an organisation unconnected to Exit, also sells a kit for testing barbiturates purchased in this way. http://www.exitinternational.net/).

Another common but largely unfounded worry about whether
drugs have been affected by storage after the shelf-life or 'use
by' date.

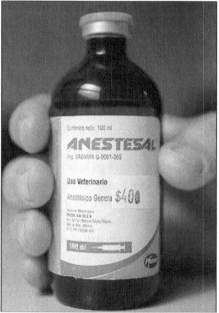

Example of Mexican Veterinary Nembutal

Here is a quotation
from the Wall Street
Journal:

"The expiration date,
required in several
countries, specifies
the date the manu-
facturer guarantees
the full potency and
safety of a drug.
Most medications are
potent and safe after
the expiration date. A
study conducted by
the U.S. Food and
Drug Administration
covered over 100
drugs, prescription
and over-the-counter. The results showed that about 90% of
them were safe and effective as far as 15 years past their
expiration date. Joel Davis, a former FDA expiration-date
compliance chief, said that with a handful of exceptions -
notably nitroglycerin, insulin and some liquid antibiotics -
most expired drugs are probably effective." *(Cohen, 2000)*

Testing drugs is a very expensive business. Most people who obtain drugs for medicinal reasons will renew them or use them within a relatively short space of time, so there is no need for drug companies to test them for many, many years. This does not mean they suddenly become useless, merely that they have not been tested. In the case of tablets, if they have been kept in dry conditions at a reasonable temperature, it is unlikely that they will deteriorate for a very long time. For chloroquine, just get new ones every few years or so (or if you live in the US, whenever you travel outside). For sleeping tablets, if you have kept them for a long time, test them with the 'estimating dosages' experiment. If you get a good eight hours sleep in the day time with, say, two, then just multiply that number by ten for use with a plastic bag or chloroquine.

There are reliable stories of persons travelling to Mexico and buying barbiturates over the counter by asking for the veterinary brand names and saying it is for 'putting down their pets', then bringing them home and using them without getting caught on the way. Previously it was reported that you might easily walk into a doctor's office, pay a consultation fee of around $50, and then complain of serious insomnia and ask for a prescription of Nembutal or Seconal, saying it was the only sleep-aid that would work while you are travelling in a hot country. It is clear that such opportunities change frequently and that might be much harder to do now. Barbiturates are highly controlled substances and possession of them without a legal prescription is a serious offence. I am aware of people who obtained veterinary barbiturate just a few months ago in Mexico: but by the time you read this book, will that option have become more difficult as well? The barbiturate commonly used both in animal euthanasia and in the Netherlands for voluntary euthanasia is Nembutal (the generic name for which is pentobarbital, a short-acting barbiturate). The usual dose of Nembutal prescribed for assisted suicide in Oregon is 9gms, whereas Dignitas in Switzerland prescribes 12 gms. If you are caught at customs, the likelihood is that the drugs will be confiscated and you will face a very serious charge. Think twice before breaking the law. Apart from anything else, if you are caught you may face a situation where it is almost impossible to put any plans for self-deliverance into action. For those who feel undeterred by these considerations, the following should be considered. Once again, I am not advocating breaking the law at all. But knowing the facts may help dissuade you, or at least put you in a position to decide one way or the other.

o Two bottles of (liquid) veterinary Nembutal would be needed.

o A single bottle contains 6gms in 100ml of elixir. (A size that fits easily in your hand.)

o They are not expensive – probably no more than £20-£30.

o American dollars can usually be used in Mexican border towns.

o Many people make short excursions to do tourist shopping across the border in Mexico from the U.S.

o The language in Mexico is Spanish, but some very basic English may often be understood in border towns.

o Do you really think you are good at avoiding suspicion? In the 'Vetinaria' chemists? And when going through Customs?

o Trade names on the bottle include Anestesal, Sedal-Vet, Pentobarbital Injectable, Sedalphorte, Barbital, Sedalpharma.

o It is illegal to take it out of the country.

o   It is illegal to take it through the U.S. when completing your flight home and U.S. Border Controls may be especially hard.
o   It is highly illegal to bring narcotics into the U.K.
o   Posting Nembutal home probably incurs an even greater risk of detection at Customs.
o   Possible sentences could include a jail term of several years or a heavy four-figure fine.
o   If you are very ill, consider whether you will be able to drink two bottles unaided.
o   Without knocking them over?
o   When Nembutal in liquid form is drunk, an antiemetic (anti-sickness) drug should also be swallowed approximately 30 minutes before the lethal overdose. This is done because large concentrated doses of pentobarbital may cause vomiting.
o   What is your back up plan if no nembutal is obtained?
o   Chemists selling the drug frequently cease to do so. It may even take an extra day or two in Mexico to look for other suppliers..

Buying drugs on the Internet
Similar concerns apply as buying from abroad. Regulations (such as which drugs can be mailed from which countries to which countries) change from time to time, as do web addresses. There are many reputable firms online and also many involved with counterfeit drugs or simple fraud. While you may find some useful drugs online but we do not recommend it as a primary route. You will not be able to buy prohibited drugs such as barbiturates legally on the Internet. There are many cases of people online charging anything from ten to a hundred times the cost of veterinary Nembutal from Mexico. And many cases of people being defrauded with non-

genuine materials. Even if you do manage to buy controlled drugs such as barbiturates over the Internet or by mail, you are still committing a very serious and punishable offence. A recent article in *The Economist* magazine noted that crooks are growing ever more technologically sophisticated. Some can even counterfeit the holograms on packets that are meant to reassure customers that pills are genuine.

Gulp or grind? – the best way to take tablets

How do you usually take tablets? Some people gulp them down with barely a sip of water. Some people like a slug of whisky, and some almost half a pint of water. Some people can take several at once, and some will struggle over one. Your ability to swallow tablets may also vary according to how you feel or other factors. No-one has yet invented a simple and reliably painless 'one-tablet solution' for self-deliverance. Most tablets are quite bitter tasting. The degree of difficulty swallowing sufficient of the drugs concerned can be factor determining how suitable this method is for you. Remember it may change once you are very ill.

To overcome the worry about swallowing tablets, many people will grind them up and then mix them with something like apple sauce or chocolate pudding. These are two of the more popular foodstuffs to hide the taste, but bear in mind they are unlikely to mask it entirely. Grinding tablets up also has the advantage that they will be absorbed slightly quicker once in the stomach. If you plan to grind them up, a small mortar and pestle from a kitchen accessories shop will make the job easier. Or a 'pill crusher' which can be found in some healthfood stores and chemists. A sensible amount of sauce or pudding is enough to mix the tablets but not too much. If it is more than a few spoonfuls you may start to feel sleepy before you have finished swallowing the tablets.

An alcoholic drink to wash them down is quite acceptable. Alcohol increases the effect of many sleeping drugs but can also irritate the stomach. The general rule is to drink alcohol if you feel inclined to do so, but not vastly more than you would usually. Stick to your usual tipple or increase it slightly. Don't go to great excess, especially with a form that you generally avoid. Whisky, for instance, disagrees with my digestion whereas I can enjoy wine without an upset stomach. Let your body be your guide, as it varies greatly from person to person. Understand also that antacids can slow the rate of absorption of chloroquine and so should be avoided.

What you need
For a drugs-only self-deliverance:

o A lethal quantity of drugs.
o A handful of anti-nausea tablets.
o A mortar and pestle for grinding up drugs (helpful, not essential). A coffee grinder could conceivably be used.
o Apple sauce or something to mix the drugs with (helpful, not essential). Partly melted ice-cream or sorbet (about half a cupful) is an option, possibly sweetened with honey. Milk products are generally avoided as they slow absorption, but a *little* milk may help to line the stomach just enough to decrease irritation. A little food should be just as effective – something light, such as toast. Generally you do not want to have too much in your stomach.
o Undisturbed time – at least several hours.

For using drugs with a plastic bag for self-deliverance, please see the *plastic bags* chapter)

Preparation and method
Firstly you might want to estimate how high on your preference list this method is, and your next most preferred method. After stockpiling sufficient drugs, get an idea of how easy or difficult it will be for you to swallow them. Sleeping tablets can work quite quickly – will you have the time and ability to swallow all that you need? If you want to know exactly *how* bitter-tasting the drug is, try just one tablet with the apple sauce and taste it as part of a dress rehearsal. If and when the time comes, you will need to act decisively and quickly, so estimate your own ability to swallow all the drugs effectively.

Next, go over in your mind the exact scenario, several times. Plan your timetable. The order in which the drugs should be taken is anti-nausea drugs, followed by a gap to let them work, then the chloroquine, then the sleeping drugs immediately afterwards or at least within a few minutes.

Make sure everything is arranged, notes written, the place warm and comfortable, *before* you start. You will probably unplug the phone and disconnect the doorbell. If in a hotel, you have left the *Do Not Disturb* sign up.

When taking sleeping tablets, especial care must be taken to ensure the full amount intended is consumed swiftly. There have been cases of failed suicides where the person fell asleep before finishing swallowing the drugs.

Other drugs – barbiturates
If you have access to barbiturates then these are normally sufficient to induce sleep and death quite safely on their own. Anti-nausea medication is still required, as mentioned above, and you need to pay particular attention to making sure you swallow sufficient of the drugs swiftly so that you do not pass

out before finishing them. Sleep is normally followed by respiratory depression and death. Beyond that, there are a few considerations as follows:

Although death will normally occur within a few hours, in rare cases it may take longer. Cases of persons being alive (in a coma) up to four days before dying have been recorded. Certainly the precautions against being disturbed should allow for this. The use of a plastic bag in addition can securely avoid this drawn out possibility.

There are three broad categories of barbiturate according to their duration of action in therapeutic doses. Long-acting barbiturates include barbital and phenobarbital (Veronal, Luminal, Gardenal). Medium-acting barbiturates include butobarbital/secbutobarbital, mephobarbital, amylobarbital (Soneryl, Butisol, Meberal, Amytal). Short-acting barbiturates include pentobarbital, quinalbarbital/secobarbital (Nembutal, Seconal). Tuinal is a mixture of amylobarbital and secobarbital. While this classification is helpful for therapeutic purposes, shortness of action is not equated with lack of toxicity. Long-acting barbiturates have caused the most fatal poisonings, but some authorities believe the short-acting ones lead to a deeper coma. If given a choice, the short-acting ones or a combination of both seem overall preferable. Pentobarbitone (pentobarbital) is used for euthanasia in the Netherlands. In practice, their availability is so scarce that it is a case of using what you have or, if you are not sure if you have sufficient, using them to cause deep sleep in combination with a plastic bag or chloroquine. Much more can be written on this, but with barbiturates being so hard to obtain it would seem to be overloading the reader with unusable information.

A minimum recommended lethal dose is 60 capsules of 100mg Seconal or Nembutal. The usual three or four anti-nausea pills are taken half an hour to twenty minutes beforehand. It is also best, if possible, to take a beta blocker with the anti-nausea pills, such as three tablets of 80mg Inderal (propranolol hydrochloride). This reduces the blood pressure and makes the system immune to adrenalin. Although the 6 grams recommended above may be optimal, more may be desirable if your stomach can stand them, and death has frequently been recorded with as little a 3 grams of butabarbital. In the Netherlands, 10 grams (100 x 100mg) of pentobarbital is used, and even then a secondary drug (delivered by injection) is the norm.

In Britain, all barbiturates are classified as Controlled Drugs. Preparations containing secobarbital (quinalbarbitone) are in schedule 2 of the Misuse of Drugs regulations along with cocaine. Receipt and supply must be recorded in the Controlled Drugs Register. Barbiturates are also controlled as Class B drugs under the *Misuse of Drugs Act*. Doctors can still prescribe them and patients take them, but unauthorised possession or supply is an offence. Maximum penalty is five years imprisonment and a fine for possession, and fourteen years imprisonment and a fine for supply. If prepared for injection, barbiturates are regarded as Class A drugs with even more severe penalties.

If a suicide attempt with barbiturates fails, there may be some lingering disorientation but no seriously disturbing long-term effects.

Alcohol greatly increases the effect of barbiturates. A reasonably large amount is a good idea – as long as you don't take so much that it makes you vomit. This varies from person to person, so know your usual alcohol intake (or the amount you can drink without vomiting).

Other drugs – Orphenadrine, Propoxyphene, Tricyclics
These have been listed in *Departing Drugs* or *Beyond Final Exit* and are sometimes acceptable drugs. Compared to the main methods described in this book, they are no longer drugs of choice. They will be considered briefly.

Orphenadrine
Orphenadrine is prescribed for a variety of conditions including Parkinsonism and as a muscle relaxant. Three grams (30 times 100mg tablets) is considered reliably lethal. Side-effects are potentially very serious though, including hallucinations and possible seizures. It is best avoided unless you feel you do not have other options. If you do use it, be sure to use plain tablets, ground up, *not* orphenadrine compounds.

Propoxyphene (and Dextropropoxyphene)
This painkiller drug is less widely available now. Many forms available were combinations with drugs such as paracetamol or aspirin, which have very serious side-effects in failed overdose. It was considered a suitable drug for use in combination with the plastic bag (or with other sedatives) but is being withdrawn in most countries. Seizures are also a possible side-effect.

Tricyclics
Tricyclics are a class of anti-depressants. They are sometimes prescribed less than before, as the newer SSRIs (anti-depressants like Prozac) are considered to have a lower side-effects profile – in other words, side-effects don't include possible death. Prozac (fluoxetine) is considered by some studies to increase the lethal effect of the tricyclics if taken in

combination. Alcohol or barbiturates increase the toxicity. Some studies have suggested diazepam increases the toxicity of amitriptyline. Of all the tricyclics, amitriptyline is generally the most useful in self-deliverance.

But tricyclics are a complex area for use in self-deliverance. Some are highly sedating and some less so. Those with *sedative properties* include amitriptyline, clomipramine, dosulepin (dothiepin), mianserin, trazodone amd trimipramine.

The *less sedating* ones include imipramine, lofepramine and nortriptyline.

If you have sedative tricyclics (ones from the first list), especially if you have amitriptyline, they may be considered a suitable sedative if you take precautions. Firstly, if you have been taking them for a therapeutic reason, you need to stay off them for a few weeks to ensure you have not become acclimatised to them. Then, a few weeks before using them for self-deliverance, you need to do the *Estimating Dosages* experiment to see if a small dose knocks you out for several hours of daytime sleep. With this amount as a base increase your planned self-deliverance dose by a factor of ten if you are using them with the plastic bag. Individual reaction to tricyclics varies.

Although there are numerous cases of suicide with tricyclics alone, there are so many variables that they cannot be confidently recommended as a stand-alone self-deliverance drug.

Other drugs not mentioned so far
There are many drugs that can kill you, but very few that can do so reliably and painlessly. There are also drugs on which

there is insufficient information to make a recommendation one way or the other.

Checklist

o If you are using chloroquine, do you have suitable (preferably non-benzodiazepine) sleeping tablets to take with it?

o Do you understand the dangers associated with various drug-orientated methods of self-deliverance?

o Have you taken into account your ability to swallow the required amounts of drugs, either in tablet form or crushed up? Do you have an alternative method should you one day be in a condition that eating and swallowing is slow and difficult?

o Have you made suitable arrangements not to be disturbed?

o If in doubt about any of the aspects of your drugs-only plan, have you considered using a plastic bag as an additional safeguard?

References

• Cohen L, Many Medicines Prove Potent for Years Past Their Expiration Dates, Wall Street Journal, 28 March 2000, 235 (62): A1).

• Crouch B, Toxicological Issues with Drugs Used to End Life. *In:* Battin M, Lipman A (eds). Drug Use and Assisted Suicide Haworth Press 1966:211-222.

• Docker C, Smith C, et al, Beyond Final Exit, Right to Die Society of Canada 1995. This volume includes authoritative articles and further references for barbiturates and tricyclics.

• Fake Drugs – Poison Pills, The Economist Sep 4 2010, p73.

• Hawton K, Simkin S, Deeks J, C-proxamol and suicide: a study of national mortality statistics and local non-fatal self poisonings, BMJ 2003;326:1006-1008 (10 May).

• Humpry D, Final Exit, 3rd edition, Dell 2002.

- Jamison, S. When Drugs Fail: Assisted Deaths and Not-So-Lethal Drugs. *In:* Battin M, Lipman A (eds). Drug Use and Assisted Suicide Haworth Press 1966:223-243.
- Koichiro Kumagaim, Yoshio Yamanouchi, Kunihirom Atsuom, Noritamti Ashirmo, Antiarrhythmic and Proarrhythmic Properties of Diazepam Demonstrated by Electrophysiological Study in Humans, Clin. Cardiol. Vol. 14, May 1991.
- Linden C, Rippe J, Irwin R, Manual of Overdoses and Poisonings, Lippincott Williams & Wilkins 2006.
- Nitschke P, Stewart F, The Peaceful Pill Handbook, Exit International US Ltd 2006. (nb Exit International US is an international Australian-based organisation. It is not connected with Exit, an international organisation based in Edinburgh, Scotland).
- Olson K, Poisoning and Drug Overdose, McGraw Hill, 2007.
- Riou B, Rimailho A, Galliot M, Bourdon R, Huet Y, Protective cardiovascular effects of diazepam in experimental acute chloroquine poisoning, Intensive Care Medicine 1998, Vol.14, No.6.
- Shannon M, Borron S, Burns M, Haddad and Winchester's Clinical Management of Poisoning and Drug Overdose, Saunders; 4 edition (May 24, 2007).
- Tadaylhjkirio Kmi. D.. Kikuoa Rakawam.. D.

For an authoritative list of further references to articles on chloroquine from the medical press, see the chloroquine section in the appendix of this book.

Last Acts: Drugs

The benefits of living long are now being balanced, often towards imbalance, of living too long. The theme that repeatedly emerges from doing the numbers game in ageing and dying is that timing is everything. Outlive your money, your friends and family, or your health, and institutionalised dying will be your future. One option for many has been to cancel that future by taking their own lives

From A Social history of Dying by Allan Kellehear

Forgive yourself before you die. Then forgive others.
Morrie Schwartz, American educator and writer (1916 - 1995)

Against you I will fling myself unvanquished and unyielding, O Death!

Epitaph of Virginia Woolf

Plastic bags

Story – what you need – main features – general description – what is the evidence for plastic bags? – how quickly does it work? – are there any unpleasant side-effects? – checklist – references & diagrams

Jennie's story

Jennie drew her life to a close using one of the most traditional of methods – sedatives and a plastic bag. The sedatives weren't the cause of her death, but they were sufficient to ensure she was deeply unconscious when the oxygen in the bag was exhausted. Everything was planned carefully and she had practiced the 'dry-run' on many occasions – she would place a couple of rubber bands around her neck then slip the bag over the top of her head and tuck the ends in underneath the bands. It was a large bag to give the drugs time to be fully effective. She had experimented with several variations – two bags inside each other, a large garden garbage bag, one of those 'compression' bags used for storing clothes (she had cut the seal off to make it easier to tuck under the rubber bands) – in fact whenever she was out shopping she was always on the look-out for suitable bags. She used two rubber bands in case one broke. They were the right size, fitting quite snug around her neck without being in the slightest uncomfortable.

The bag she had settled on was see-through plastic. This was nice. It let the light through as well as looking less unpleasant to whoever would eventually find her. Everything was arranged. She had her anti-sickness pills ready to be taken twenty minutes or so beforehand, then the sedatives that she would take immediately before arranging the bag (putting the bag on quickly before they started to make her feel drowsy). She also had a book of Keats, her favourite poetry, to hand, and a CD of Beethoven's 2nd symphony which she would listen to while making the preparations and leave playing as she 'went under.'

Jennie's 'kit' that she had put together over the years also included a wide-brimmed hat and a painter's mask. Some of the literature suggested them to keep the plastic of the bag from being sucked against the face; but she found with the bag she had chosen it was not necessary – the plastic material was quite heavy and, when she shook the bag to get lots of air inside prior to putting it over her head, it didn't seem to fall against her face even after several minutes. Practicing with the bag but without the sedatives was quite safe – you never became drowsy and could take the bag off long before the air got hot and difficult to breathe (that would take up to half an hour at least).

Jennie lived with her son. Under English law, no-one could be in the house at the same time that she made her 'exit' so she was careful to make sure he was going to be out for a good few hours. Her son was sympathetic to his Mum's beliefs and understood her tact and why she wanted to make it clear to everyone that this would be her act, without anyone's help or assistance. When he had left, she also unplugged the phone, removed the batteries from the doorbell, and did a last mental check to make sure no visitors were expected.

The amounts of drugs were carefully laid out. She had used the 'estimating dosages' routine (see *Frequently Asked Questions)* and avoided taking any of the drugs for medicinal purposes for some months so her body was not accustomed to them at all (in other words, she didn't have an acquired tolerance that sometimes occurs with frequent dosaging).

Jennie knew she could relax until the last minute and that then she had to act swiftly. Once she started taking the sleeping tablets, all the preparations had to be completed quickly before they started taking effect. As an extra precaution, she had taken some anti-nausea pills a couple of hours ago. She ground up her sleeping tablets ready to be mixed with some chocolate pudding. She left her farewell note where it would be easily found. She hadn't eaten all day, wanting to keep her stomach fairly empty. Now she treated herself to a small meal – some toast and croissants – and took another dose of anti-nausea tablets, just over twice the therapeutic amount. They were the sort that did not make you overly drowsy, but she could still feel the effect. Fortunately she was well rehearsed.

With an eye on the clock, Jennie waited about twenty five minutes for the anti-nausea pills to be absorbed. She switched her music on. Then she mixed the ground-up tablets with the pudding. She placed the rubber bands around her neck before downing the mixture in a few spoonfuls, washing it down with a glass of champagne she had placed nearby. Without pausing (the sleeping tablets could start to work within half a minute!) she slipped the bag over her head and tucked it securely under the rubber bands, checking all the way round so she knew it was a good seal. She sat back in her comfortable armchair and had time to pick up her Keats. It was a large print volume and she could see the lines clearly through the plastic bag.

> But this is human life: the war, the deeds,
> The disappointment, the anxiety,
> Imagination's struggles, far and nigh,
> All human; bearing in themselves this good,
> That they are still the air, the subtle food,
> To make us feel existence, and to shew
> How quiet death is.

How does it work?
Very soon after taking the sleeping tablets and quickly donning a plastic bag, the person falls into a progressively deeper sleep. The air in the bag is gradually 'used up' – the lungs remove oxygen from the air with each inward breath. That oxygen is transferred to the blood which in turn keeps the brain alive. The outward breath contains a higher proportion of carbon dioxide and eventually the air in the bag contains insufficient oxygen to oxygenate the blood and keep the brain alive (anoxia). The process is hastened by the build up of carbon dioxide, which is toxic in higher concentrations. When the entire brain ceases to function, all the automatic processes of the body also stop: death occurs.

Drugs to use with plastic bags
Any sleeping drug of your choice that is effective. This can be from over-the-counter drugs, if they work for you, to the stronger ones obtainable on prescription or sometimes via the Internet. Test them with the *Estimating Dosages* routine. For a fuller description of various options and approaches to obtain them, please review the *Drugs* chapter.

What you need
o   A suitable bag. The preferred size is shown in the diagrams, but you may select a smaller one as long as you are aware of the difference this presents.
o   A couple of elastic bands.
o   Sufficient sleeping tablets to put you in a deep sleep.
o   Some anti-nausea tablets.
o   Lots of practice putting the bag on!
o   Other options include a wide brimmed hat or painter's mask to keep the bag away from your face. Many people

will find these unnecessary, but you will be able to tell during your dress-rehearsals if your bag has a tendency to fall against the face.

Main features
The plastic-bag-plus-drugs method is historically the most established method of self-deliverance that is still used today. It is a 'safe' method in the sense that if a person doesn't get it quite right, the worst that is likely to happen (unless they are disturbed) is that they wake up with one hell of a hangover. It requires relatively little in the way of equipment or know-how. Some people find the plastic bag method unaesthetic.

General description
It is important to understand the mechanics of the 'plastic bag method' to avoid errors. It is a good method, but many failures have also been reported. Failures can usually be explained by the wrong size of bag being used, or occasionally the wrong type of plastic.

The use of sedatives is not just to cause sleep, but a sufficiently deep sleep for you to be immobilised. Otherwise it is quite possible that you will tear the bag off in your sleep. You know how most people toss and turn occasionally in bed at night? If something (such as the bed quilt) falls over the face and makes it too hot to breathe comfortably, you will probably move or push it off without waking up – it is an automatic reaction to carbon dioxide.

As the air in the bag is used up (similar to when you get 'hot and stuffy' under the bed covers), what happens is that the percentage of carbon dioxide in the air is increased as a result of exhalation. One of the side-effects of breathing a higher concentration of carbon dioxide is hyperventilation – an increase in the depth and rate of breathing – and you easily become more physical as a result.

Without putting too fine a point on it, it is easy enough to calculate the given amount of air in a bag and roughly how long it will last. Although they vary slightly from one individual to another, we also know the amount of time that sleeping drugs take, firstly to put you to sleep (which is very quick) but also, more importantly, how long it takes before you are immobilised and not going to thrash about a lot.

Early self-deliverance manuals recommended a medium to small sized plastic bag. Although there are many successes with such a bag, we know from the calculations just described that the volume of air in a medium sized bag is insufficient to allow time for the drugs to immobilise you. Which is why there are many cases of people 'waking up' and wondering how the bag got torn off.

Off course, if this happens to you, you will probably not have anything more serious to deal with physically as a result of the failed attempt than a bad hangover, but psychologically the experience can be traumatic and frustrating. To avoid this, find a larger bag – no need to measure it, but the picture is a good guide. When you are sitting with the bag on, then if it comes down to your knees (in sitting position) then that is a good size. Give it a good shake before you put it on (to fill it with air) and you will have about an hour of comfortable breathing before the oxygen runs out – which is plenty of time for the drugs to work fully.

When the oxygen runs quite low, insufficient oxygen will go into the blood, which means not enough oxygen gets to the brain. Deprived of oxygen for a few minutes, the brain shuts down and then death occurs.

Using a *larger* bag represents the safest course, but some people will choose a medium sized one because it is more comfortable or easier to use or they just prefer it in some way. If it is quite sturdy there should be no problem, but armed with the full facts you can now make your own choice.

We'll look at the details of obtaining and using the best sized bag later in this chapter. The ideal bag size can be determined roughly like this. With you seated in an armchair and the bag over your head and secured around the neck: does the other end of the bag reach down more or less to your lap? If it does, that is an ideal size when we are talking about a 'large bag.' This rough approximation is based on a rectangular bag. Some bags, such as those sometimes used for storing clothing, may be square-shaped, so you can allow for the difference. When in use, the bag should be full of air, but size is not rocket-science and you shouldn't worry unduly over an inch or two.

In some cases where people have been suffering intensely, a *small* bag has successfully been used. This is not the pleasantest way to go, but there is a trade off between how desperate the circumstances are and any further discomfort that can be tolerated. Using a small bag is straightforward death by suffocation. Some tranquillisers might be taken to ease the unpleasant sensations in such a case. Persons using a small bag (rather than bag + drugs) can potentially reduce the time and discomfort very considerably by combining it with a compression tourniquet (see the chapter on compression).

Try out as many different bags as you can in a dress rehearsal. Not when you are sick, but when you are well, so you can make your mind up which one to use well in advance should the need ever arise. Bags with very thick plastic require a bit more manual dexterity to position. If the bag is quite thin, you might want to use two bags, one inside the other. You could even make or obtain a customised bag with a velcro strip for fastening it around the neck. You want to know how to get it on with ease (when you are adding rubber bands to keep it in place, a bit of practice comes in handy.) Remember the sleeping tablets may work very quickly, so there is no time for fumbling.

To summarise:

o A small bag is ok for emergency but will cause feelings of discomfort if the drugs have not taken effect (combine with compression instead).
o A medium bag is popular, but there is a chance you might thrash about in your sleep, possibly even tearing the bag.
o A larger bag (see diagram) may be harder to manipulate (if it is thicker plastic) but ensures you are in a deep sleep as oxygen runs out, so when done properly is more foolproof than using a medium sized bag.

Note: the above considerations apply for the drugs+bag method. The helium method, in contrast, uses a small bag.

If you are unable to get anything else, over-the-counter sleeping drugs (available in most countries) can be used, but a safer option is modern prescription-only sleeping tablets such as zolpidem (Also called Stilnoct. In the US they are called Ambien). Over-the-counter sleeping medications often contain the antihistamine diphenhydramine – their effectiveness is lower than prescription drugs and may also vary over time.

Zolpidem is fast-acting and also has the advantage of usually being supplied in a very small tablet, which makes it easier if you are swallowing quite a quantity. (n.b.: zolpidem is rarely lethal in itself: it is taken as a drug to put you in a deep sleep so that you will not experience any gasping for breath when the oxygen in the bag is used up.)

It has sometimes been possible to buy zolpidem on the Internet without a prescription. If you do so, beware that there is a burgeoning market in counterfeit or substandard drugs on the Web and you should be careful about sources; and also test a small quantity properly before relying on them for self-deliverance. Does one or two put you to sleep properly in the daytime (in other words, when you wouldn't normally just drift off)?

Most people will obtain zolpidem from their doctor and simply stockpile it. For more advice on obtaining zolpidem, see the 'obtaining sleeping tablets' section in the previous chapter on Drugs.

What is the evidence for plastic bags?
Use of plastic bags for suicide is long-established and attested to by police reports, newspaper reports, medical journal reports, eye-witness accounts and so on. The science involved is fairly straightforward.

What is the evidence against plastic bags?
The reason for failures with plastic bags are now fairly well established. The evidence comes largely from reports of right-to-die societies by people who have failed. Exit received a number of such reports and the Dutch right-to-die society told the authors of *Departing Drugs* of many failed attempts. This led to further research. Scientific calculations (as well as descrip-

tions of failures) showed that some failures were due to too small a bag. In these cases, a person's oxygen supply ran low while they were asleep but before the drug had put them in a sufficiently deep sleep. A small number of failures could not be attributed to this cause. Collaboration with the physics department of a major university brought to light that some plastics are oxygen-porous. These plastics are not generally employed in the type of bags used in suicide, but are hard for the user to identify.

How quickly does it work?

With the type of bag in the illustrations, up to a little over one hour. A smaller bag will mean less time, but increases the (small but harmless) risk of failure. Once the oxygen supply has been fully depleted, the brain shuts down in a matter of minutes and death occurs.

Are there any unpleasant side-effects?

Not really. A good-sized bag will overcome any worries about hotness, or stuffiness.

Myths about plastic bags (1): the plastic bag method is foolproof

Actually there are many failures with plastic bags. I once spoke to a man who had failed six times before getting our literature and understanding how to do it in a way that minimizes failure. Exit similarly has many reports of failures from other countries. The slightly reassuring factor is that failure with the plastic bag does not generally lead to any serious complications (other than the trauma of having failed after such a momentous decision). You can try again. But it is helpful to understand how things can go wrong and so minimize the chance of failure.

Myths about plastic bags (2): any reasonable plastic bag will do

The most common culprit of failure is too small a bag – a 'medium' sized bag. This can result in lack of oxygen and hyperventilation (a reflex action involving an increase in the depth, rate, and duration of breathing which, in this case, is triggered by carbon dioxide build-up). This can happen even when the person is asleep. If it happens too early, and the person is not so deeply asleep as to be incapable of reflex action such as struggling, they will often tear the bag off in their sleep, eventually waking up hours later and wondering how on earth it happened. This is not to say there have not been many successful suicides with a medium sized bag; but if you want to avoid this particular danger a larger bag means the carbon dioxide poisoning (which causes the hyperventilation) does not occur until later on. By this time the sleeping tablets have put the person in a *deep* sleep so no movement is possible.

Finding a suitably large bag can present difficulties, especially if you want a large one made of clear or semi-opaque plastic. A brand that particularly caught our attention was a range called Poly-Lina clear storage bags (1500mm x 900mm in packs of ten.) These are available from some B&Q stores and can be easily adapted. If your local store doesn't seem to have them, try phoning round. You can identify them by the barcode which is 5 010234 773903. The barcode remains the same even if you find them through another supplier (such as Amazon). These bags are quite thin and easy to handle. Some other bags, even though they are an ideal size, are often made of thick plastic. This can prove unwieldy if you are trying to tuck the edges under rubber bands positioned around your neck. To get round this, adjust the size of the opening. You can do this by sealing off part of the width using masking tape or similar. If you shorten the section of bag that you are sealing off, this will leave a narrower 'neck' that can fit over your the head and be tucked into the rubber bands.

Of the thicker semi-clear bag, one of the early favourites at workshops were bags sold as large compression sacks at Lakeland. These are storage bags made for putting seasonal clothes or bed-linen in, or for travel. After filling the bag, pressure is applied to squeeze the air out through a seal at the neck of the bag, resulting in a smaller overall size for storage. If you use one of these compression sacks, check the size is large enough, then cut off the seal and adapt it in the way described above.

Fill the bag with air!
This rather obvious point is too easily overlooked. The idea of having a big bag is that it holds sufficient air to sustain you until the drugs place you in a very deep sleep. But a flat bag contains no air. A flat bag that you just put over your head contains a bit of air. Give the bag a shake before putting it on so as to fill it up with air.

Plastic bags are not 100% (but 98 or 99% is close)
Plastic bags and drugs, correctly used, are a reliable way of achieving self-deliverance. In the tiny number of cases that go wrong after correct preparations, the drugs are such that one will simply wake up feeling rather hung-over. But why should even a tiny percentage fail if the correct bag size has been used with the correct drugs? The most likely culprit, though rare, is 'the wrong type of plastic'. Some plastics are oxygen-permeable, which means that, over a period of time, oxygen particles can seep through the bag, and possibly in sufficient quantities to maintain life. This accounts for those cases where a person wakes up hours later, head still inside the bag, and the

bag intact and in place. To a non-physicist, this sounds so surreal that it was a long time before cross-disciplinary investigations revealed this fact about certain plastics. Permeability can now be understood by anyone with access to books on physics such as those listed in the appendix (see the end of the references list in the section *Finding the Truth about Plastic Bags*). The number of bags affected is small. With this method, unlike some methods, one can simply live to fight another day. But although plastic is supposed to have an identifying mark, in practice such marks are often not present. So it is almost impossible to guard against – but fortunately rare enough not to worry about.

Checklist
o   Have you practiced thoroughly?
o   Have you got everything in place so that you have the minimum to do once the sleeping tablets have been consumed?
o   Have you made sure you won't be disturbed?

Diagrams show two alternative relaxed and comfortable postures for using the plastic bag. In the first one, the person is in an ideal armchair, leaning back, and the chair is such that falling out of it is unlikely. The size of the bag in the diagram is a good indication of the ideal size when using a 'larger' bag.

A lying down position is the next best option.

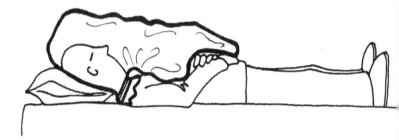

References:

- Hunt AC, Camps FE, Plastic-bag Suicide, Br Med J. 1962 February 10; 1(5275): 378.
- Johnstone JM, Hunt AC, Milford Ward E, Plastic-bag Asphyxia in Adults, Br Med J. 1960 December 10; 2(5214): 1714–1715.
- Please see also the articles in the *Appendix* for a list of references.

She did say towards the end: 'Dying's hard work, you know, you have to do it on your own. Dad can't help, mother and father are no use either.' She died during the night while her son, who was keeping vigil, was making a cup of coffee.

From a case study in *A hastened death by self-denial of food and drink*, by Boudewijn Chabot

I am ready to meet my Maker. Whether my Maker is prepared for the great ordeal of meeting me is another matter.

Sir Winston Churchill

There is a dignity in dying that doctors should not dare to deny.

Anon

Starvation and other means

Overview of methods so far – starvation – main requirements – best approach – detox practices – how long does it take – are there any unpleasant side-effects? – main features – other means - firearms – jumping/drowning – charcoal tents, carbon monoxide and exhausts – hypothermia – methods not recommended – checklist – references

In the last four chapters we've explored the main methods of self-deliverance. For enduring peace of mind, I recommend that you are thoroughly familiar with at least two or three of them. There are many other methods, but most rely on drugs that are difficult to obtain, or are unreliable, or carry a high danger of increased suffering in the event of a failed attempt. Importantly, you can rarely predict with certainty your situation near the end of life, so you may have to make your choices according to circumstances.

Under Helium, we looked at a method that is entirely free of discomfort and suitable in most situations where you have the freedom to put the equipment together in advance, store it securely, and have access to it when the time comes.

Under Compression, we looked at a set of simple methods that have minor discomfort at the most and can be used in a wide variety of situations, including hospitals and nursing homes, when you maybe don't have the freedom to get hold of drugs or equipment.

Under Drugs, we dispelled myths about chloroquine and sleeping tablets, as well as looking at the main other drugs of interest, as stand-alone drugs or for use with a plastic bag.

Under Plastic Bags, we cast an intense spotlight on the variations, showing the different reliability and comfort factors.

In this chapter we will look at methods – especially starvation – that are significant enough to be of interest to a proportion of readers and that, correctly used, can also result in a good death. They give you another string to your bow in addition to the methods of the preceding chapters. As with all methods, our aim is to separate fact from fiction, and remove the myths that can obscure a proper, safe understanding of how to go about things. For a fuller examination of very unsuitable methods (which is beyond the scope of this book), I respectfully refer readers to Geo Stone's excellent study, *Suicide and Assisted Suicide (1999)*, which examines lesser known methods quite clinically.

Starvation

By starvation I mean cessation of eating and drinking, voluntary refusal of food and liquid, fasting and dehydration, or a number of other descriptions. We are talking about food *and* water, and ensuring that it is a voluntary choice throughout by the person concerned. But for the sake of brevity, we'll call it starvation, in recognition of the physical process in which the body is starved of sustenance in the form of food, nutrients and liquids.

Of all last acts, there is probably no better example of how individual the choice of method is than starvation. It is not just about wanting to do it and having access to some pills or equipment. It will be possible for some individuals and not others. It may be physically unsuitable for you. It may be unsuitable on account of your situation in relation to those close to you and how that will develop. It might be unsuitable based on the degree of perfectly lawful cooperation your doctor is willing to provide. It may be unsuitable if you have no-one to provide comfort care. Starvation looks simple. It is not. Yet performed successfully it has much to recommend it.

In studies conducted in Oregon and the Netherlands, nurses reported little or no suffering and pain. But these results are of patients in carefully monitored situations. Attempting it unaided, and in a country less sympathetic to aid-in-dying, can bring all sorts of problems. Recent UK newspaper told of two distressing deaths by starvation after being 'advised' – rather irresponsibly in this author's opinion, to use it as a method by a right-to-die society. Extensive preparation and fine tuning are required. Undertaking it without due preparation and resources can be very distressing. (Case studies reported by *Chabot, 2008,* have expanded many of the comfort care provisions which were examined at shorter length in the earlier edition of this book.)

Do you recall the early suggestion when you started reading this volume? Imagine your death as perfectly as possible – and then imagine possible complications and how you would handle them. In the case of starvation, the 'complications' are highly likely and must be planned for responsibly and ahead of time. Let's go through the method and the complications so you can see what is involved. It is not the easiest way to end one's life, but it is very possible if done properly.

The road to a peaceful death by this method is not only narrow, but after a certain period there is no turning back.

Unlike the other methods, death is not achieved in a matter of minutes or hours. So the emotional strain placed on carers is great, as is the strain on the dying person to manage what they are going through.

The time taken can be approximately two weeks. You will stop food first of all, cleanse the system, then reduce liquids to zero. Someone will need to be on hand to look after you as you get too weak to look after yourself. Starvation has the attraction of seeming more 'natural' to some persons. A passive process, rather than actively using drugs or mechanical means to end one's life. One expires gently. And although the presence of relatives during the process may be a strain, it might also be an attraction, especially to UK residents for whom the ambiguous assisted suicide law (on whether being with someone may involve an illegal act) does not apply with starvation (unless the relatives were denying food and drink to the person dying, in which case different, more stringent laws would apply).

The complications to be handled fall into three categories:

o *Nursing needs.* These involve care of the mouth so that it doesn't dry out completely. Although not 'medical,' there is more to it than there sounds. Advance planning, acquiring and testing various forms of mouth hydration are strongly recommended unless one has a specialist nurse on hand who is familiar with all the options. If blisters and scabs are allowed to develop, they may get to the stage where they are difficult or even impossible to treat.
o *Medical needs.* Conditions commonly medicated include sleeplessness, anxiety, occasionally breathlessness, and pain. Some of these can be self-medicated if one has a suitable supply of the necessary drugs, but GP or hospice support is strongly recommended.

o *Emotional needs.* These are perhaps the most challenging, even with all-round prior agreement, and the main reason when people change their mind. You are not 'here today, gone tomorrow.' So your loved ones may have the sensation of watching you wither away. If it becomes too difficult for them, the urge will be to stop putting them through such trauma. This is probably best addressed by open discussions.

Let's look at each of these in some detail.

Nursing needs – Mouthcare and mouth hydration

The mucous membranes of the lips and mouth are quite sensitive. They become easily damaged as liquid intake ceases and must be cared for properly. Much of the research and preparation can be done by the person themselves. Providing the comfort during the period of self-deliverance then becomes simple care that could be arranged by relatives, but expert help may be needed in some cases. Good mouth care should be commenced beforehand. A soft toothbrush should be available for care as the self-deliverance progresses (children's toothpaste is less abrasive than the usual sort.). The sort of aids that are also helpful include a nebuliser, which is a device usually used to administer medication in the form of a mist inhaled into the lungs, and of which there are many different kinds. A hand-held atomiser performs a similar function. They can be used to moisten the mouth without supplying the body with liquids (as

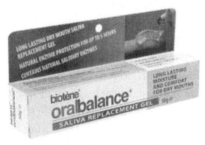

Example of saliva-replacement gel

a drink would). There are mouth sprays and saliva substitutes, and the person planning a self-deliverance through this method can have a dress rehearsal by desisting from liquids for a few days and finding out which saliva replacement products work best in their particular case, both for comfort and for avoiding the sensation of thirst brought on by a dry mouth.

Saliva-gel can be placed on a piece of gauze and rubbed on the gums and roof of the mouth. Some people like a sugar-free gum. Eye-gel and nasal sprays are good to have on hand in case one feels a need for them, and Vaseline can be used on the lips. A humidifier might be placed near the bed to counter-act any dryness in the atmosphere. To prevent fungal infections in the mouth, a gauze soaked in alcohol-free chlorhexidine solution can be used on the gums and tongue.

A glass of water should always be available by the bedside in case the patient decides to break his or her cessation of liquid intake. Simply stopping food without stopping liquids will mean the process takes much longer, but some people may prefer that, perhaps slowly reducing the amount of liquid to about half a glass or 50cc of water before the end of the first week. But another use of liquid is control of lucidity. Drowsiness will set in after a few days of ceasing liquids. This can be controlled to an extent – for instance, if one wants to be more lucid for periods spent talking with loved ones. A small amount of water intake – say half a cup or less – will likely cause some of the urea (which is causing the drowsiness) to be excreted. Although it prolongs the dying process, it may be desirable for some last quality moments with relatives, for instance. A Macmillan nurse will be able to advise should oral care become very problematic.

Medical needs – alleviating any pain and symptoms

In some cases of self-deliverance through starvation, little medication has been needed, or else it has been possible to obtain beforehand the medications most likely to be needed. Most of the well documented successful cases however have been in countries where one would not expect such formal opposition to the idea of ending one's own life. For example, paracetamol to control pain and discomfort, temazepam for anxiety and to help with sleeplessness. But there have also been cases where more elaborate procedures were called for – carefully increased high-dose morphine and subcutaneous Midazolam and other specialised medications that the patient is less likely to have been able to obtain routinely on prescription.

Emotional needs – continuous sharing

The largest reported reason for persons abandoning their attempted self-deliverance, both in Dutch and American studies, is not wanting to cause distress to loved ones (who cannot bear to watch the process). In some Asian communities or traditions, a person planning to die will leave their family and go elsewhere – almost as if going to meet death halfway – and in some cases receive appropriate care. This would be almost unthinkable in the West. Maybe for an afternoon – but not for a period of weeks (or even the ten to fourteen day average). For this reason, it is essential that the persons closest to you, if you seek to go along this road, are as fully aware of the process and its ups and downs as you are. This is not a case of a quick 'reassuring chat' – they need to know details of the complications that may occur. Just as doctors and specialist nursing should be available if needed, even more so is the need for those closest to you to understand what is happening, how it will happen, and how they will handle their feelings. If it comes to a battle of wills where you try to exert your wish to die over them, you may find it is a battle for which you lose the taste. Whereas the other four methods discussed have you in complete control, here there is more of an alternation. For instance, succumbing to the dying process but then exerting a controlled will to delay it a little longer to have quality time (as discussed above regarding water intake and lucidity). A good relationship with the doctor is required so that there is understanding and a sense of working together – not simply fulfilling legal require-ments to give you pain relief.

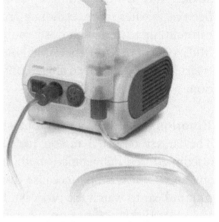

You might also wish to give some thought to carrying on normal needs. For instance, it is possible to wash your hair in bed. *Batiste* make a shampoo that you can spray on your hair, leave for a few minutes, and brush out.

A nebuliser can provide a fine mist

Small details like looking one's best, even if one is as haggard as Gandhi, can be important in one's dying days.

Main requirements

A careful review of the literature (see *Appendix*) indicates that the main requirements are threefold:

o   A physical check-up by a qualified medical practitioner to make sure you do not have either a body type or existing prognosis that is likely to lead to complications; together with careful preparations on your part, researching mouth care products and maybe even finding (or hiring) a special mattress.

o   Nursing and possibly medical care, both for providing comfort care and to initiate emergency action if unbearable complications occur; ideally one should have not just a supply of suitable medications that might be required, but a cooperative doctor or palliative care nurse who can tailor them to your condition or provide other ones as your situation progresses. The most common are medications to control sleeplessness, anxiety, pain, confusion or extreme discomfort, although some or all may not be required in any particular case.

o   A considerable amount of will-power. Both yours and in the people who will be close to you in your final days, so you can work together to achieve dignified death.

What is the best way to approach self-deliverance through starvation and dehydration?
First of all, get a good idea of what is involved, especially the dangers. You can do this by careful reading of the appendix on starvation in this book. Next you might consider the variety of circumstances that could trigger such a decision. In some terminal illnesses (including many cancers), the body will naturally start to shut down and the desire for food and water will become less. Drastic reduction of food and water in such circumstances may speed up an inevitable process. A medical examination may also reveal if underlying illnesses or conditions may precipitate other problems.

Next, ask yourself how strong is your will-power. When you first stop eating, your desire for food will probably be very strong. After three days it will probably be very small. Following a 'detox' practice (see below) will give you a better understanding of how your body reacts to foods and liquids. It will enable you to better plan a healthy diet beforehand, and a sensible reduction that maintains essential nutrients and avoids strong foods (such as red meat) that place a greater strain on the body. You can also discover for yourself if carbohydrates increase 'food withdrawal' and a sense of hunger if stopped (which might encourage you to avoid them as you approach the point where you embark on your self-deliverance.)

Before starting your fast in earnest you might also want to take a mild laxative to help cleanse the colon – any food left lying inside can cause problems later on.

You might want to go to further lengths. An anti decubitus mattress is a mattress often used in combination with your normal mattress. Its special structure is designed to spread your weight evenly and so prevent bed-sores. A bed-pan or incontinence pads may be useful options. Unless those close to you have some familiarity with the dying process, you might want to discuss ways of sharing some understanding on such points. We tend to shield ourselves from dying. Except for nurses and others who know about such things first hand, reality can come as a shock. Regarding equipment, the British Red Cross may be a useful source of help – you can look up your local branch in the phone directory.

A 'detox' practice

You might like to experiment with this by doing a controlled health-fast – the sort of thing yoga practitioners recommend – and the sort of 'detox' that is also encouraged at many health retreats. Many people will approach a detox fast by consuming only fruit and vegetable foods, while eliminating caffeine, tobacco, alcohol and sugar. Work up to a full day when you drink only fruit juice. The hunger pangs are strongest at first, especially if you are used to a diet of three meals a day with lots of red meat. After 36 hours (a full day plus the night-time each side) you may feel more in control of your hunger. The full details of controlled fasting-for-health are beyond the scope of this book and you may wish to look into it further before attempting more than a one-day fast. There is no direct correlation between 'detox' fasts and fasts-to-the-death, but it will give you an idea of some of the territory.

Fasting to death – how long does it take?
On the basis of reports by nurses, patients in hospice care who voluntarily choose to refuse food and fluids usually die a 'good' death within two weeks after stopping food and fluids. A Jain woman reported in the media after fasting to death in India also fasted for two weeks.

Are there any unpleasant side-effects?
Yes – but not in all cases. The precautions listed under *Main Requirements* (above) are to minimise the risk of unpleasant side effects – either by alerting the person to their likelihood in his or her particular case or having the facilities on hand to cope. Weakness, blindness and internal organ failure are among extreme possibilities. Many people may consider the first two bearable, especially with a carer on hand, but internal organ failure can be extremely painful. Again, a carer with at least basic medical knowledge can, in such circumstances, arrange emergency medical treatment if required. In cases where there is no internal organ failure, a carer can play a major part in reducing serious discomfort. Ice chips to moisten the lips, being moved to avoid bed sores (when too weak to move oneself), and other comfort-care measures are necessary for any Westerner contemplating death through refusing food and water.

Main features

Fasting to death has a certain lifestyle attraction. It is perhaps the only 'passive' method of intentionally ending one's life and has an appeal, whether aesthetic or to accord with a person's beliefs, over the more active methods. In certain instances it has not been regarded as 'suicide' and avoids the stigma that some people attach to that word. Legally, it probably allows both a person to be present (in jurisdictions such as England, presence at a suicide could normally be construed as criminally aiding and abetting) or palliative care to be administered during the process. An advantage is that it cannot be done impulsively and is seen not to be done impulsively. It requires a great deal of will-power and is not suitable for all personalities or body types.

Some other equivocal methods of self-deliverance:

Use of firearms

Most right-to-die activists and researchers, largely because of the inherent violence and the disagreeable nature of others later finding a body with gunshot wounds to the head, have shunned the idea of using firearms for suicide. Suicide by means of a firearm is not without other problems, but as it is a not uncommon method it should perhaps be considered in passing, especially as it has a high success rate.

Suicide by using a gun is more prevalent in countries where guns are easily available or else where the person has ready access to a gun because of profession (as is the case, for instance, with farmers or military personnel). Across the US, firearms are used in approximately 60% of all suicide deaths. Failure (which is not uncommon) results in devastating injury. Many intended suicides by gunshot leave the person alive but brain-damaged. Placing it to the temple risks the skull changing the bullet's trajectory. The gun must be powerful enough for the attempt to succeed. Placing the barrel in the mouth pointing upwards towards the brain is the most reliable. This results in penetrating the telencephalon (cerebrum). Care must be taken not to lean forward – failures have been attributed to leaning forward at the last minute or to jerking the gun as it fires – and so altering the path of the bullet. If you buy a gun for the purpose, be sure to practice with it first. The one time the present author used a gun (on a firing range), he was surprised by the amount of recoil, even though he was expecting it.

A main consideration in using a firearm successfully would be having some knowledge, experience or training with firearms. Other considerations include minimising the upset to others by appropriate choice of location (cleaning body tissue off walls and ceilings is a particularly gruesome task.) It is incorrect to assume someone is always immediately incapacitated, or unable to inflict more than one gunshot upon themselves. In one documented case in Australia, a man committed suicide after repeated attempts. He first shot himself in the chest with a pump action shotgun. The load passed through the chest without hitting a rib, and went out the other side. He then walked fifteen meters, reloaded, leaned the shotgun against his throat, and shot his throat and part of his jaw. Breathing through this gunshot-inflicted tracheotomy, he reloaded, walked 136 meters to a hill slope, lay down on the slope, held the gun against his chest with his hands and operated the trigger with his toes for a final shot that managed to kill him.

Jumping and/or drowning

The Hong Kong JC Centre for Suicide Research and Prevention reported jumping from heights to be the most common method of suicide in that city *(1998-2008)*. The question of consideration to others mentioned previously applies doubly. Cleaning up the mess will be an unpleasant task. Persons witnessing the death may be traumatised. If jumping from a building, there is the danger that someone might be killed when you fall on them. People also underestimate the height of buildings needed for a successful suicide. There are cases of people surviving (although totally paralysed) after jumping from as many as six stories. Jumping from ten stories or more is 100% successful. High cliffs stand a better chance of success if there is no chance of the fall being broken on the way. Jumping in front of trains is not only traumatic for the driver, but has a high failure rate (about 50 per cent), with people being pushed underneath and sustaining terrible injuries. One study *(Moore & Robertson, 1999)* identified 51 survivors of jumping and firearms suicide attempts. Of those that jumped (31 out of 51), the estimated average height from which the subjects jumped (and lived with terrible injuries to tell the tale) was 25 feet. There is also a suggestion that people jump from high buildings 'as it is more convenient.' Madelyn Gould, a clinical psychologist, told ABC News *(Friedman, Inside the Mind of a Suicide Jumper)* that "In New York City, jumping is certainly more common than in other places because we have high buildings . . . Usually the method is chosen because it's accessible."

Of those jumping from a height into water from bridges, the strength of the water flow and the height both make a difference. Most suicides from the Golden Gate Bridge in California (250 feet above water) are successful: only about one per cent are not. The average speed upon hitting the water is estimated at 75 miles per hour. In one study of survivors *(Rosen 1975)*, most blacked out before hitting the water, and all reported the experience as pleasant (although two sustained fairly serious injuries). The height of the Golden Gate and similar bridges (and perhaps the location which some see as romantic) form a different scenario to many attempted suicides by jumping and drowning.

Persons jumping from much lesser heights into water may have a very different experience. In the Thames of London some are washed ashore to survive, sometimes after suffering irreversible brain damage. On average over 50 people lose their lives in the Thames each year and about 80% of these are by suicide according to police reports. The impact with the water following a jump from even a low bridge may expel air from the lungs. Clothing may provide some buoyancy initially due to air being trapped inside it but gradually this will be lost. The impact on entry from even a moderate height into water may expel most of the trapped air unless the clothing is waterproof with good neck and wrist seals. Police reports regularly speak of unconscious or semi-conscious casualties floating in the water within five minutes of entry. The movement of water around a bridge often produces eddies that can pin a victim to the legs of the bridge (above or below the waterline) or suck her or him in under it. Fresh water is faster than sea water due to absorption via the alveolar membranes.

Drowning is not a strongly recommended method and may be quite unpleasant. But some people are attracted to it. Most Golden Gate Bridge suicides are unconscious before they hit the water. Spasms are typical when drowning and strong alcohol intake beforehand are likely to reduce unpleasantness of side effects. Alcohol may affect the cardiovascular response to submersion. Drowning in an older person may trigger a heart attack. Ice-cold water will trigger different bodily reactions to warm water, but these don't as yet provide hard or fast evidence of the preferability of one over the other.

Charcoal tents, carbon monoxide and exhausts

Before catalytic converters (which reduce the emission of carbon monoxide) were fitted to cars, this was a popular form of suicide. A hosepipe was run from the exhaust into a semi-closed window and the car kept running, usually in a locked garage. Carbon monoxide (not to be confused with carbon dioxide – a gas which we exhale when breathing) is tasteless and odourless. Its toxicity stems from the fact that it drives oxygen out of the red cells of the blood and thus deprives the body and brain of its normal supply of oxygen. A concentration of even one per cent in the air can lead to death. The greater the concentration, the faster death occurs (it can be anything from a minute to two hours). Failed attempts result in varying degrees of brain damage. One woman I spoke to still

charcoal burner

has recurrent memory loss a result of a failed attempt many years ago. One study suggests that a person's lifespan can also be reduced due to damage to the heart muscle.

If you have the mechanical knowledge to remove the catalytic converter from your car, and you have a reliable enough engine that won't cut out, it is still a possible method. Just be aware of the serious dangers if it goes wrong (the motor cutting out or you being discovered and 'rescued'). Bear in mind you are probably breaking the law by removing the converter. In the UK, if your car was registered after 1st August 1992 you must have the converter present and working for the MoT. Previously registered cars can have the converter permanently removed.

Another method gained popularity in Japan after 1998. Charcoal briquettes (the sort used in barbeque grills or stoves) burnt within an enclosed area, such as a small sealed room, tent, or car, produce large amounts of carbon monoxide. In a typical scenario, the windows of a rented van are sealed with vinyl tape from the inside, and four charcoal stoves placed on the floor. Charcoal burner heaters can be purchased online or from garden and patio accessory shops. The combustion produces carbon monoxide which rapidly decreases the ability of blood to deliver oxygen to the body, eventually resulting in death. Although painless, it can endanger persons entering the closed space, and if the self-deliverer is interrupted they may recover but with permanent brain damage. In November 1998, a middle-aged woman in Hong Kong committed suicide using this method inside her small, sealed bedroom. She is thought to have invented it using her chemical engineering background. After details of her suicide were widely publicised in the media, many others attempted and succeeded in committing suicide in this way. Within two months, charcoal-burning had become the third major method of suicide in Hong Kong. Charcoal-burning suicide accounted for 1.7% of Hong Kong suicides in 1998 and 10.1% in 1999. By 2001, it had surpassed hanging as the second most-common method of suicide in Hong Kong (second only to jumping), and accounted for about 25% of all suicide deaths. Interestingly, the method is not strongly associated either with right-to-die adherents or the mentally ill, and a lack of parallel decreases in suicides rates using older methods with the rise of charcoal burning suicides suggests people are not using it 'in preference' to another method. Charcoal-burning suicides have since spread to mainland China, Taiwan and Japan but are rare in the West.

Hypothermia

Death from exposure to cold has only a moderate success rate. It requires *reliably* cold temperatures over a sufficient period for death to occur. Failure can produce severe and lasting injury. Some drugs, such as barbiturates, chlorpromazine and even paracetamol (acetaminophen/Tylenol) accentuate symptoms of hypothermia. Immersion in cold water causes loss of body heat at a much faster rate than air at the same temperature. Hypothermia is relatively painless but has potentially dire consequences if interrupted (for instance if someone spots and rescues you). In can be as quick as half an hour in freezing cold water or a couple of hours on land. Wearing little clothing helps, and fat people will take longer to die than thin people. Some sedatives are desirable. The amount of time needed varies considerably but several hours are needed. Uncomfortable if not painful, the main danger is rescue or a warming of weather conditions.

Methods not recommended

Slitting one's wrists is not as reliable method as it is sometimes portrayed in the movies. A *Guardian* newspaper interview with the paramedics who attended the alleged suicide of David Kelly says, "Over the years they have raced to the scenes of dozens of attempted suicides in which somebody has cut their wrists. In only one case has the victim been successful." Finding a suitable artery requires greater knowledge of anatomy than most people possess. Usual attempts tend to sever the surface veins. These veins are neither particularly large nor carry as much pressure as the arteries, and so such cuts are often not life-threatening. They can clot before a fatal quantity of blood is lost. If you were intent on trying this method, one of the easier arteries to sever is the radial artery, which is fairly near the surface and where the wrist and thumb come together (feel for the pulse there). Failure may result in simply severing the flexor tendons. Doing it in a bath of warm water can help prevent clotting, as might four to eight aspirin an hour beforehand. A local anaesthetic spray could be used to make it easier (It will probably be rather painful). It might be an idea to cut both the wrists and ankles. But cutting has a very low success rate.

Poisonous plants – although there are a number of plants that are reliably poisonous, they are not reliably lethal or free of very unpleasant side-effects. Various sorts of hemlock are undoubtedly poisonous, but the side-effects differ markedly from the tale of the supposedly peaceful death enjoyed by Plato. See the separate chapter for details.

Checklist

o   The methods in this chapter all carry a certain risk. Have you fully understood the risks and how to cope with them?

o   Have you acquainted yourself thoroughly with several of the main methods from previous chapters?

o   If you are reasonably healthy at the moment, have you looked ahead and considered the various situations which you may find yourself in?

o   Have you prioritised your methods yet also know enough methods to be adaptable to changing or unexpected circumstances?

References n.b.: For extensive references about starvation please see Appendix.

- Adamson E, The Complete Idiot's Guide to Fasting, Alpha Books 2002. (An excellent starter on 'detox' fasting.)

- Albury N and Wienrich S, Practical Care at Home, In: The New Natural Death Handbook, Rider 2000.

- American Heart Association, Guidelines for Cardiopulmonary Resuscitation and Emergency Cardiovascular Care, Part 10.3: Drowning, Circulation. 2005;112:IV-133 – IV-135.

- Arehart-Treichel, J, Terminally Ill Choose Fasting Over M.D.-Assisted Suicide, Psychiatric News January 16, 2004, Volume 39 Number 2.

- Blumenthal I, Carbon monoxide poisoning, Journal of the Royal Society of Medicine 2001, 94:270-272.

- Bungardt N, Dettmeyer R, Madea B, Suicidal shot in the mouth with an unmodified blank cartridge pistol, Archiv für Kriminologie 2005 Jul-Aug;216(1-2):1-6.

- Braun W, Sallekhana: the ethicality and legality of religious suicide by starvation in the Jain religious community (unpublished).

- The Bridge – a thought-provoking film about suicides, Exit Newsletter 2007 27(1):10-12.

- Chabot B, A hastened death by self-denial of food and drink, Amsterdam 2008.

- Chung W, Leung C, Carbon Monoxide Poisoning as a New Method of Suicide in Hong Kong, Psychiatric Services June 2001, 52(6):836-837.

- Finkel A, Carbon Monoxide, in: Hamilton & Hardy's Industrial Toxicology 1983 (4th ed) 157-170.

- Forgey W, Hypothermia: Death by Exposure 1985 ICS Books.

- Ganzini L, Goy E, Miller L, Harvath T, Jackson.A., Delorit M, Nurses' Experiences with Hospice Patients Who Refuse Food and Fluids to Hasten Death, New England Journal of Medicine, Vol 349:359-365 July 24, 2003 Number 4.

- Haw C, Sutton L, Simkin S, Gunnell D, Kapur N, Nowers M, Hawton K, Suicide by gunshot in the United Kingdom: a review of the literature, Med Sci Law. 2004 Oct;44(4):295-310.

- Herdson P, Shotgun suicide with a difference, MJA 2000; 173: 604-605.

- Henry C et al, Myocardial Injury and Long-term Mortality Following Moderate to Severe Carbon Monoxide Poisoning, JAMA. 2006;295:398-402.

- Idris A, Berg R, Bierens J, Bossaert D, Branche C, Gabrielli A, Graves S, Handley A et al, Recommended Guidelines for Uniform Reporting of Data From Drowning, Circulation 2003;108;2565-2574.

- Friedman E, Inside the Mind of a Suicide Jumper, ABC News, http://abcnews.go.com/Health/MindMoodNews/story?id=529 4404 2 July 2008, accessed 13 Sep 2010.

- Kahn M, Lazarus C, Owens D, Allowing Patients to Die: Practical, Ethical, and Religious Concerns, Journal of Clinical Oncology, Vol 21, No 15 (August 1), 2003: pp 3000-3002.

- Knight B, Immersion and drowning, in: Legal Aspects of Medical Practice, Churchill Livingstone 1997 (Chapter 18).

- Lambert M, Silva P, An update on the impact of gun control legislation on suicide, Psychiatr Q. 1998 Summer;69(2):127-34.

- Liu K, Beautrais A, Caine E, Chan K, Chao A, Conwell Y, Law C, Lee D, Li P, Yip P, Charcoal burning suicides in Hong Kong and urban Taiwan: an illustration of the impact of a novel suicide method on overall regional rates, Journal of Epidemiology and Community Health 2007; 61:248-253.

- Loewy E, Terminal Sedation, Self-Starvation and Orchestrating the End of Life. Archives of Internal Medicine 161:329-332, Feb 12, 2001.

- McCann R, Hall W, Groth-Juncker A, Comfort Care for Terminally III Patients - The Appropriate Use of Nutrition and Hydration, JAMA. 1994;272:1263-1266.

- Moore G, Robertson A, Suicide Attempts by Firearms and by Leaping From Heights, Am J Psychiatry 1999; 156:1425–1431.

- Oehmichen M, Auer R, König H, Drowning, in: Forensic Neuropathology and Associated Neurology, Springer 2005, Part III, Chapter 14 - Forensic Types of Ischemia and Asphyxia, pp295-296.

- Orlowski J, Drowning, Near-Drowning, and Ice-Water Drowning, JAMA July 15, 1988 (Editorial), Vol 260(3)390-391.

- Peterson L et al, Self-Inflicted Gunshot Wounds: Lethality of Method Versus Intent, Am J Psychiatry 1985, 142:228-231.

- Piper T, Tracy M, Bucciarelli A, Tardiff K, Galea S, Firearm suicide in New York City in the 1990s, Injury prevention : Journal of the International Society for Child and Adolescent Injury Prevention, 2006 Feb;12(1):41-5.

- Preston T, Mero R, Observations Concerning Terminally Ill Patients Who Choose Suicide, in: Battin M, Lipman A (eds) Drug Use in Assisted Suicide and Euthanasia 1996 Halworth Press: 183-192.

- Rosen D, Suicide Survivors: A Follow-up Study of Persons Who Survived Jumping from the Golden Gate and San Francisco-Oakland Bay Bridges, J Med 122:289-294, Apr 1975.

- Ryles J (Macmillan Head and Neck Clinical Nurse Specialist), Evidence based mouth care policy, Doncaster and Bassetlaw Hospitals NHS Foundation Trust, REF: PAT/PA 17 v.1, 2007.

- Seabourne A, Seabourne G, Suicide or accident - self-killing in medieval England, The British Journal of Psychiatry (2001) 178: 42-47.

- Steel E (director), The Bridge, 94 minutes (film), 2006.

- Stone G, Suicide and Attempted Suicide, Carroll & Graff 1999.

- Stuttaford T, Fumes that can kill, The Times (newspaper) Sep 22 1994.

- Stark C, Gibbs D, Hopkins P, Belbin A, Hay A, Selvaraj S, Suicide in farmers in Scotland, Rural Remote Health. 2006 Jan-Mar;6(1):509.

- Thom S, Keim L, Carbon Monoxide Poisoning: A review – epidemiology, pathophysiology, clinical findings and treatment options including hyperbaric oxygen therapy, Clinical Toxicology 1989 27(3):141-156.

- Tsunenari S, Yonemitsu K, Kanda M, Yoshida S, Suicidal carbon monoxide inhalation of exhaust fumes Investigation of cases, American Journal of Forensic Medicine & Pathology. 6(3):233-239, September 1985.

- Vayvada H, Menderes A, Yilmaz M, Mola F, Kzlkaya A, Atabey A, Management of close-range, high-energy shotgun and rifle wounds to the face, The Journal of craniofacial surgery 2005 Sep;16(5):794-804.

- Wanzer S, Glenmullen J, Voluntary Refusal of Hydration, Accompanied by Physician- Administered Sedation as Needed. *In:* To Die Well,De Capo Press 2007. pp97-103.

Appendixes

My aim in the body of this book has been to make the text readable enough to convey the necessary knowledge to anyone. Some of the research behind the conclusions however, is more technical, and needs to be included for reference, or to cast aside worries about whether the information is reliable. We would urge every reader to investigate methods for themselves. Do not believe something just because a doctor or campaigner said it was so or a famous speaker on euthanasia proclaimed it successful. The methods in *Five Last Acts* and our conclusions about them are well-researched but, on the above advice, it makes good sense to verify that for yourself!

These appendixes present ideas from a slightly different angle. You can take the references and follow them up in any good medical library, such as the ones attached to larger universities. You can search toxicology manuals, such as Martindale's, to find out more about specific drugs. Bear in mind, at this point, that drug companies test drugs for their *therapeutic* purposes only. If the manufacturers (or toxicology* manuals, or doctors – who are also trained in therapeutic use of drugs but rarely in their use in suicide) say such-and-such a dose can be fatal, that is exactly what they mean – not that it necessarily *will* be fatal! The information they provide may offer clues but their aim is at odds somewhat with ours. A further (and in many ways better) approach is to look at statistics on successful and unsuccessful suicides. If you investigate chloroquine, for instance, you will find a wealth of data available. (Anecdotal evidence also has a place, but mostly suggestive – especially when it contains reports of failures: several drugs and certain ways of using plastic bags have been discovered to be flawed by following up the leads from failed attempts.) Eventually there comes a reasonable cut-off point where, with a given method or drug, no-one survives. Anyone can research this – you do not need a medical degree, but you need the patience to understand the terminology so you clearly follow what is being said. If you are doing serious research, after you follow your conclusions to a logical result, it is worth having them reviewed by an expert in that field who is qualified to assess the hypotheses in case you have missed something.

Information on new methods has been published in the *Exit Newsletter* (formerly *Voluntary Euthanasia Society of Scotland Newsletter*) or in *Beyond Final Exit*, the companion book to our 1993 manual *Departing Drugs*. Ordering back copies is not only time-consuming and expensive but for ease of reference the articles need to be gathered together in one place. In addition to background material based on the workshops, these appendixes therefore also includes reprints of key articles, updated where appropriate.

I was sometimes asked why I have not just updated *Departing Drugs*. If you are interested, I recommend you obtain the original. There is no need for an update: some of the drug names have changed (but that can easily be ascertained by looking at the box and referring to the generic, or chemical, name of a drug); more importantly, knowledge of viable methods has grown and, rather than overload the reader with an encyclopaedic account of every possibility, I have distilled the essential methods in this volume to take this into account.

*A guide to what is meant by 'Lethal Dose' in toxicology literature is given is Crouch B, Toxicological Issues with Drugs Used to End Life. In: Battin M & Lipman A, (eds) Drug Use in Assisted Suicide and Euthanasia, Pharmaceutical Products Press 1966, 21-214:
"The majority of lethality data come from toxicity studies performed in laboratory animals that are conducted during preclinical trials or from case

reports. The Lethal Dose$_{50}$ (LD$_{50}$) is an experimentally derived dose that causes death in 50% of a sample of animals which receive the agent. . . . Extrapolation of LD$_{50}$ data from animal research to estimate the lethal dose in humans is problematic. Humans may have marked differences from animals in the absorption, distribution, metabolism and excretion of the substances.

What is asphyxia?

Understanding asphyxia helps us understand several of the five 'Last Acts'.

It maybe helps to consider asphyxia in some of the following terms.

Asphyxia is a process (rather than an event) that involves cutting off oxygen from brain by:

o   Interference with breathing (e.g. suffocation with a pillow, drowning, hanging, or pressure on the chest or larynx)
o   Removal of oxygen from the air (e.g. by inert gas such as helium or the 'plastic bag + drugs method')
o   Preventing oxygenated blood from reaching the brain (e.g. pressure on the carotid arteries – compression method)
    and/or
o   Preventing oxygenated blood from entering the brain (e.g. pressure on jugular veins which prevents exit of used (de-oxygenated) blood – compression method)

It explains how, in different ways, the plastic bag, compression and helium all cause death. Many other methods of death can be attributed to asphyxia – such as drowning or car exhausts, but the ones listed in the main part of the book are the ones with least risk and with little or no discomfort.

A more detailed explanation of asphyxia is given by *Prahlow:*

"The term *asphyxia* literally means *without a pulse,* but the more common and accepted definition means *without oxygen.* More precisely, it refers to a lack of tissue oxygenation (delivery of oxygen to the body's cells). Clinically, the term *hypoxia* refers to the lack of oxygen. Anything that results in lack of tissue oxygenation could be considered an asphyxial process. If this definition is taken to the extreme, then all sorts of other mechanisms of death actually incorporate an asphyxial component. For example, if a traumatic injury results in extensive bleeding, the lack of blood, which functions to deliver oxygen to tissues, leads to the lack of tissue oxygenation with eventual death."

Prahlow goes on, however, to limit his discussion to the types of cases that 'are traditionally considered asphyxial in nature,' these being suffocation, where there is a failure of oxygen to reach the blood, strangulation or compression of the neck, and thirdly chemical asphyxia, where poisoning prevents tissues from using the available oxygen (which happens, for instance, with carbon monoxide). Cyanide, in a variety of chemical forms, is also a deadly poison that acts as a cellular asphyxiant, though a very unpleasant one. (When cyanide has been ingested, a frequent autopsy finding is haemorrhage of the lining of the stomach.)

The term 'environmental suffocation' is sometimes used when oxygen is lacking or has been physically displaced from the environment, as occurs in altitude mountaineering or the use of helium in self deliverance. Oxygen is normally present in the air at about 21 per cent. When it drops to around twelve to fifteen per cent, dizziness is apparent. When the oxygen content drops to about six to eight per cent, unconsciousness occurs, although rapid treatment can still prevent death. At less than six per cent, death occurs in six to eight minutes. At a mere two to three per cent, *Oemichen et al* (quoting earlier research) suggest that death occurs in 45 seconds. With the helium method, the oxygen content of the air breathed is reduced almost to zero within a few seconds.

References

- Oehmichen M, Auer R, König H, Forensic Types of Ischemia and Asphyxia, in: Forensic Neuropathology and Associated Neurology, Springer 2005, Part III, Chapter 14, pp293-317.

- Prahlow J, Asphyxial Deaths, in: Forensic Pathology for Police, Death Investigators, Attorneys, and Forensic Scientists, Humana Press 2010, Part 3, pp388-418.

Please see individual chapters for more references

Asphyxia and the 'right-to-die'

Helium, carbon monoxide generators, 'de-breathers', the 'COgen' self-deliverance device and self-asphyxiation in various forms have all hit the news repeatedly in recent years. This chapter examines some of the methods hitting the headlines and asks are they trends, or simply 'trendy' and media-grabbing?

In 1995 *Exit* Research Associate Cheryl Smith published a groundbreaking article, Carbon Monoxide for Self-Deliverance, in *Beyond Final Exit*[1]. The volume also included a chapter on nitrogen and other inert gases and mentioned helium. Since then, hardly a year has gone by without proclamations about new 'suicide machines', most of which rely on some device to ensure that the person committing suicide dies (within minutes) of asphyxiation[2] by inhaling increased volumes of carbon monoxide or helium. When one of the most popular books on self-deliverance, *Final Exit*[3] by Derek Humphry, went into a third edition, a noticeable addition was a chapter on helium.

Carbon monoxide

Carbon monoxide[4,5] is a highly poisonous gas and has long been used for causing death. In Greek and Roman times it was used for executions. In high concentrations it causes death within minutes. Before natural gas, it was the component that allowed people to die by putting their head in an unlit gas oven. Until catalytic converters arrived, it was the component of car exhaust that enabled suicide by car fumes. More recently, Dr Kevorkian used cylinders of carbon monoxide attached to a gas mask (available at military surplus or medical supply stores) and a hose. A gas mask is not essential – any relatively enclosed space will do (such as a tent, or a tube tent as sold quite cheaply at outdoor adventure shops for emergency use). Even cylinders are not essential – quite fortunately as they are not that easy to buy. A popular method in the East is the use of hibachi or charcoal burners (or any other carbon based fuel). Which brings us to some of the drawbacks: If you fill an area with carbon monoxide, that may also be poisonous to anyone finding you. If you leave something burning, it might end up causing damage by fire – even damaging the means of deliverance if you use a tube tent. The main danger of this (and all) asphyxia methods however is the possibility of brain damage if the process is interrupted due to intervention, running out of gas, or tearing or removing the gas mask, plastic bag or tent while unconscious. This can be minimised by using a high concentration of the gas, which causes most rapid loss of consciousness but, as with any method of self-deliverance, the dangers are to be taken seriously – injuries include dementia, psychosis, paralysis, cortical blindness, memory deficits and parkinsonism; the latter two are the most common.

Carbon monoxide has limited uses in medicine and in metallurgy and I found six UK suppliers on the Internet (using a 'Google' search), but given the concerns about carbon monoxide poisoning it is likely that any would-be purchaser would need to convince the supplier that they had a bona fide trade use in mind.

Notwithstanding these problems, there is plenty of room for experimentation. A standard laboratory method for producing carbon monoxide for instance is by using concentrated sulphuric acid to dehydrate formic acid.[6] Philip Nitschke is an Australian campaigner who, like *Exit* here in the UK, has run self-deliverance workshops. He has put much time into trying to develop a carbon monoxide generator or 'COgen' as he terms it. Nitschke's prototype device replaced the rather unaesthetic gas mask with nasal prongs such as are often used to deliver oxygen in hospitals and which, unfortunately, also mix the inhaled gas with air).

Helium

Helium is a colourless odourless gas which is not combustible. As helium is less dense than nitrogen, breathing of a mixture of 80 per cent helium and 20 per cent oxygen requires less effort than breathing air. Such mixtures have been used in patients with acute obstructions of the respiratory tract. Mixtures of helium and oxygen are used by divers or other workers working under high pressure to prevent the development of caisson disease (decompression sickness, or 'the bends'). Breathing helium speeds up the vocal pattern and increases vocal pitch. Death by breathing helium is caused by displacing the oxygen that the brain needs to stay alive. Unlike carbon dioxide, it does not cause hyperventilation (rapid breathing) and the associated discomfort.

One of the great advantages of helium over carbon monoxide as a means of self-deliverance is that it is easily available. Party balloon kits, available by mail order, include canisters of helium.[7] An ever increasing number of successful suicides are being reported using this method. The helium tank is connected to a hose, the other end of which is firmly attached by tape to the inside of a medium sized plastic bag. Tranquillisers or sleeping tablets (and anti-emetics) may be taken beforehand for added comfort, as described in detail earlier.

As with other forms of asphyxia, interruption may result in permanent brain damage so, although the method is relatively straightforward, care would obviously be needed.

Footnotes

1.Beyond Final Exit is no longer in print, but key articles have been re-published in Exit Newsletters.

2.Asphyxiation is commonly associated with suffocation or choking - but it simply means a loss of oxygen to the brain and so covers a wide range of methods, not all of them necessarily uncomfortable.

3.See subsection on helium. The helium bag technique is also explained in a chapter of Final Exit 3rd edition, by Derek Humphry, which is obtainable through any good bookstore.

4.See also separate section in the chapter on starvation and other means, this volume.

5.Not to be confused with carbon dioxide, which is the gas we exhale and which has very different properties.

6. $HCOOH > CO + H_2O$.

7. At the time of writing, UK suppliers of helium balloon kits that can be found on the Internet include: Imagination Creative Balloons, 3, Dunkerly Street, Oldham, OL4 2AX, England (Tel/Fax: +44 (0)161 626 8734 Internet: www.flowermill.co.uk/balloons Email: balloons@flowermill.co.uk) who offer a helium tank ("Each helium tank will fill approximately 40-50 9" latex balloons") for £42 plus £9.95 for postage and packing; or Icarus Limited, Broadgate House, Church Street, Deeping St. James, Peterborough, PE6 8HD England,
tel: +44 [0]1778 347609 or www.connected.org.uk/icarus/index.html or email them at enquiries@icarusballoons.co.uk They offer three different sizes of helium canister.

Finding the truth about plastic bags

Numerous press reports, both before and after the first 'self-deliverance' manuals appeared in 1980[1], have ensured that plastic bags have long been known as a method sometimes used in suicide. The exact practicalities have been debated at greater length in various books since[2], but there remains concern over some details, especially in the light of reported failures with the method.

The aim of this article is to assemble some of the pertinent issues and scientific theory and act as a focus for developing thought on this method of self-deliverance. Feedback is encouraged.[3]

Popularity
Plastic bags, combined with drugs, are often seen as the method of choice,[4] yet the pitfalls are considerable. On the other hand, some people view bags as unaesthetic or undignified – these factors come down to personal preference or other methods being ruled out for one reason or another. Large plastic bags are seen as a device for suicide when accompanied by ingestion of drugs. (Small bags have been used for suicide when combined with various gases, mostly helium,[5] and involve altogether different considerations.) Not *always* reliably, they have been used as a suicide device with non-lethal drugs.

> On paper it seems easy: a terminally ill person secures a plastic bag over her head, nods off with the help of an appropriate dosage of prescription barbiturates, and dies in her sleep from asphyxiation due to lack of oxygen. To a desperately suffering individual, this will

often seem like a comfort and a realistic option. In fact it is much more complicated.[6]

General methodology and reactions in use

The recommended method with step-by-step instructions is detailed in *Departing Drugs,*[7] as well as this book, but an overview of the process follows for our current purpose. To live, we need oxygen. When we lose the availability of oxygen we asphyxiate ('suffocate'). Common methods of asphyxia include drowning, strangulation and obstructed airways. Asphyxia can also be caused by the absence of oxygen in an environment where we are free to breathe, such as inside a plastic bag (while technically suffocation, this does not necessarily mean that there will be the reactions commonly associated with suffocation, such as struggling – the large amount of nitrogen remaining in the plastic bag allows breathing to continue). We produce carbon dioxide (CO_2) as a waste product. It is a colourless and odourless gas, acidic in taste in concentrations above ten per cent. The body is very sensitive to high levels of CO_2 and when they are present involuntary reactions will normally include an increased rate of breathing and may include panic. You can try this with an ordinary plastic bag over your head. In a minute or two you will become very conscious that you need to breathe fresh air. Even though you have yet to experience oxygen deprivation, your body has become aware of high levels of CO_2 and is automatically alerting you to seek fresher air. As the effect increases, you will hyperventilate (breathe more quickly with increasing depth and duration).

The most important physiological effect of carbon dioxide is to stimulate the respiratory centre.[8] The stimulation is pronounced at levels of five per cent and above.[9] As much as 30 per cent may be tolerated for some time provided the oxygen supply is adequate.[10] Oxygen deprivation begins when oxygen levels have fallen to twelve per cent, and the symptoms of headache and rapid breathing become severe when it falls to eight per cent. Unconsciousness and death do not occur until the oxygen is down to five per cent, "unless the patient makes strenuous exercise, in which case death may come when there is still eight per cent oxygen."[11]

One correspondent, after a failed suicide, wrote, "After everything was done I felt like removing the bags again because I couldn't stand the hot plastic sticking at my nose each time I took a breath."[12] Suggestions for overcoming this minor problem have included a wide-brimmed hat or a spray-painter's mask.

Failures
The Scottish euthanasia society (*Exit*, formerly Voluntary Euthanasia Society of Scotland or Scottish Exit) has received many letters over the years detailing failure in the use of plastic bags for suicide, though far fewer since we issued detailed instructions in *Departing Drugs*. One man said he had attempted, and failed, seven times. A typical letter read: "I put the bags on again, because I wanted to succeed, and then I don't remember anything any more. Subconsciously I must have removed them again, because the following morning I woke up dizzily." Anecdotal evidence conveyed by the Dutch euthanasia society also indicated an alarmingly high failure rate with plastic bags. Some documented cases of failure with plastic bags are additionally recorded in the literature.[13]

The type of plastic used, the size of the bag, the type of drugs, drug dosages, varying metabolisms and medical conditions, and the failure of an assistant to realise that the patient was not in fact dead[14], have all been cited as possible causes. Oversensitivity to carbon dioxide levels in the body's breathing control system can cause sleep apnea (a temporary inability to breathe) in some people with heart failure. Enhanced sensitivity could destabilise breathing during sleep. Normally, carbon dioxide levels rise during sleep, causing breathing to increase slightly to eliminate the excess carbon dioxide. Even among many normal people, if carbon dioxide levels fall too low (as they can during hyperventilation), breathing stops until the levels return to normal. In patients with an oversensitivity to changes in carbon dioxide levels however, rising levels during sleep stimulate an exaggerated response in the form of hyperventilation. Hyperventilation then drives carbon dioxide levels below the threshold where breathing ceases, causing sleep apnea. The result is periodic breathing with recurring cycles of apnea and hyperventilation.[15]

Types of plastic
Plastic bags, even those that seem 'airtight', have both myriads of tiny holes[16] and a degree of permeability to oxygen.[17] The 'permeability coefficient' is the constant relating the rate of transfer of a diffusing substance (such as oxygen) through a unit area of a film or sheet of a given thickness to the concentrations of the substance on either side of the sheet.[18] While the permeability of bags used in attempted suicide is probably small, it cannot be ruled out as negligible. The chemical structure of the plastic is the main factor affecting permeability, although physical factors, such as density, thickness and elements in the manufacture may all influence the degree to which oxygen can permeate the bag and so extend the dying process. Low-density polythene may allow more than seven times as many oxygen molecules through its surface than high-density polythene. PVC allows substantially less.[19]

Sizes of bags, drug dosages and types of drugs

The recommendations as to size of bag in *Departing Drugs*[20] and this book are based on logical arguments relating to the time taken for drugs to immobilise the patient; as opposed to merely putting the patient to sleep. It is not difficult to calculate, from a given volume of air in a bag of a certain size, and the average amount of air breathed in a minute, how long the oxygen portion of the air in the bag will last. The calculations can be checked by experimentation (non-harmful) where an observer looks for first signs of cyanosis (a bluish-purple discolouration of the skin resulting from a deficiency of oxygen in the blood, which may first manifest itself in the fingertips).[21] The speed of action of drugs can also be estimated – not with precision, but with sufficient accuracy to make a broad judgement. The stages of drug action can include a) deep sleep, b) immobility and c) death. If asphyxiation begins before stage (b) has been reached, then the patient may struggle violently, even though asleep. In some cases the patient tears through the bag(s) or effects removal. If the drugs used prove insufficient to cause death then the patient in most cases eventually awakes, with or without additional severe damage depending largely on the drugs taken. In earlier self-deliverance manuals it was only thought necessary to use drugs to put one into a sleep so the plastic bag could have its effect – nowadays we know that additional precautions are desirable: namely, that the bag should be large enough to allow the drugs ample time both to put the patient to sleep and to produce a degree of immobility, and that the drugs in themselves (if possible, though not essential) should be of a more lethal variety.

An exception to the usual recommendations about the size and use of plastic bags has been pointed out in the case of people who are very desperate and so wanting something very quick even at the expense of a short period of discomfort. In this situation it has been suggested that a very small bag can be used so as to minimize the amount of time before oxygen runs out. This method, while having its advantages, does not have the dignity of the more elaborate methods recommended in various manuals.[22]

Advantages of plastic bags

Whether to disguise the cause of death by having an assistant remove the bag afterwards, or for other reasons, the fact that plastic bag suicide in itself leaves little trace of the cause of death sometimes makes it attractive.

> Analysis of the autopsy findings showed no specific features for this method of suicide. In particular, pete-chiae,[23] which are often considered a marker of as-phyxia, were present in only a small minority of cases (3%). Furthermore, the scene investigation rarely re-vealed specific features, other than the plastic bag in place. Thus, if the plastic bag were removed after death, the cause and manner of death would be ob-scure.[24]

Drugs of most sorts are prone to a certain percentage of failures and the plastic bag provides a back-up mechanism to help guarantee success in self-deliverance. Of the drugs where lethality is better documented, many are almost impossible to obtain by most people or else require very careful use to avoid mishap.[25]

Unlike drugs and firearms, plastic bags are, however, easily available.

Disadvantages of plastic bags

Over-reliance on plastic bags as a principal mechanism for achieving death, failure to obtain a suitable bag[26] and possible premature removal of the bag are all disadvantages. The successful deployment of a plastic bag in suicide needs either luck or careful planning. Development of physician-assisted suicide with appropriate safeguards[27] will, hopefully, in the longer term, make such deliberations and dilemmas redundant.

References

1. An early history of self-deliverance guides was published as: Docker C, "A Guide to Suicide Guides" in: Smith C, Docker C, Hofsess J, Dunn B, "Beyond Final Exit" Right to Die Society of Canada 1995, an updated edition of which appears later in this volume.
2. Principal, detailed descriptions are found in:
i) Docker C, Smith C, (North American title:) Departing Drugs: An international guidebook to self-deliverance for the terminally ill. UK title: Supplement to How to Die With Dignity – Departing Drugs. 1993, Voluntary Euthanasia Society of Scotland. North American edition published by The Right to Die Society of Canada.
ii) Humphry D, "Self-deliverance from an end-stage terminal illness by use of a plastic bag" 1993 ERGO! pamphlet.
iii) Humphry D, "Final Exit" 2nd edition, revised and updated, Dell Paperbacks 1996.
3. Feedback should be sent to the author, not necessarily for publication, c/o Exit, 17 Hart Street, Edinburgh UK. Personal experiences as well as scientific data and published accounts are all welcomed.
4. See for instance, Colin Brewer's article "Darkness at Midnight", VESS Newsletter Sept 1987.
5. Or occasionally to facilitate death by lethal gases. A Northern Californian man, attempting to follow the deaths of the "Heaven's Gate" cult suicide victims, placed a bag over his head and inserted a propane hose under the bag and turned on the gas. (Nando.net, Assoc. Press 1997). See also: Avis S, Archibald T, Asphyxial suicide by propane inhalation and plastic bag suffocation, J Forensic Sci. 1994 Jan;39(1):253-6.
6. John Pridonoff, former Director of Hemlock USA, "Meyer Case Exposes Problems With Use of Plastic Bag", Hemlock Timelines Nov-Dec 1994:5.
7. Supra. A not-for-profit booklet available from Exit. Applications can be made by approved members of right to die societies of at least three

months' standing together with acceptable documentary proof and appropriate payment in Sterling currency or by credit card. (The simplest method is just to join Exit. Please note that at the time of writing, the London-based society, Dignity in Dying, will *not* supply the required proof, as they feel this could implicate them in a suicide.)

8. Hamilton and Hardy's Industrial Toxicology 4th edition Asher J Finkel 1983, pp.154-155.

9. The composition of air at sea level is 78.08 per cent nitrogen, 20.95 per cent oxygen, 0.93 per cent argon and 0.03 per cent carbon dioxide.

10. Supra, Hamilton and Hardy.

11. Ibid.

12. Letter from abroad received at the Office of the Voluntary Euthanasia Society of Scotland.

13. Ogden, R, Euthanasia, Assisted Suicide and AIDS, 1994 Peroglyphics Publishing p.83. See also: Jamison S, When Drugs Fail: Assisted Death and Not-So-Lethal Drugs. *In:* Battin M, Lipman A, (eds), Drug Use in Assisted Suicide and Euthanasia, 1996 Hawarth Press.

14. This is not as uncommon as it might sound. One particularly dramatic account can be found in Holtby M, Assisted Suicide – Gone Wrong, Colorado's AIDS Newsletter, Resolute! April 1995.

15. Javaheri S, A Mechanism of Central Sleep Apnea in Patients with Heart Failure, New England Journal of Medicine 341(13) September 1999.

16. Correspondence from Glasgow University, December 1995.

17. Pauly S, Permeability and Diffusion Data. *In:* Brandrup J, Immergut E, Grulke E, et al, Polymer Handbook 3rd edition, John Wiley & Sons 1989. I am indebted to Professor Whitehead of the Science Faculty at Glasgow University for bringing this to my attention.

18. Ibid, Pauly, p.435-436. The permeability coefficient equals P in the equation $F=P(C1-C2)/L$ where F is the rate of transfer, L is the thickness of the sheet and C is the concentration(s) of the substance. The values of P can vary widely depending on the particular gas/polymer being considered. This for oxygen, values vary from 1.3 x 10-18 for polyvinylidene chloride (a barrier polymer) to 205 000 x 10-18 for silicone rubber. Most plastic bags are made of low-density polyethylene (polythene).

19. Ibid, pp.435-449.

20. Supra pp.20-21.

21. Experiments of the International Drugs Consensus Working Party, 10th November 1993, Edinburgh.

22. Humphry D, Self-deliverance from an end-stage terminal illness by use of a plastic bag, ERGO!, 1993. Humphry himself puts forward this method as an alternative for extreme cases.

23. Petechiae are minute discoloured spots on the surface of the skin caused by underlying ruptured blood vessels.

24. Haddix T, Harruff R, Reay D, Haglund W, Asphyxial suicides using plastic bags, American Journal of Forensic Med Pathol 1996 Dec;17(4):308-11.

25. Barbiturates are very difficult to obtain for most people in most countries. Certain over-the-counter anti-malarials, documented in *Departing Drugs,* are difficult to obtain in the USA, and in any case require careful combination with suitable sedatives.

26. This article is not recommending any particular type of bag. It tries to set out the criteria and facts on which readers can make intelligent decisions. Some readers have written to us about the customised 'Exit' bag mentioned in an addendum to Beyond Final Exit, which, in spite of the name, had no direct connection with Exit. The chapter on the that particular exit bag was inserted by the book's editor and without the permission of the book's principle authors.

27. See the model approach in VESS Newsletter Vol.19 No.4 by Prof. S.A.M. McLean for a considered approach to legal reform.

Note that information on permeability and diffusion in plastics can also be found in Polymer Handbook, by Brandrup E, Immergut E, Grulke E et al (Eds.); Wiley, New York, 1999. The relevant chapter is: by Pauly, S, Permeability and Diffusion Data (pp VI 435-449)

The chloroquine controversy

CG Docker & CK Smith

This is a reprint of the ground-breaking article from the April 1993 VESS Newsletter *and from* Beyond Final Exit *and is reprinted here for reference. Readers please note that chloroquine is not readily available in the United States, but otherwise the article contains the necessary scientific information regarding the use of this drug, which requires considerable care and deliberation. Opinions on the use of benzodiazepines continue to fluctuate, although this article seems clear enough is delineating the evidence (as opposed to opinions).*

No universally accepted authority on self-deliverance euthanatics currently exists. Doctors are not trained on this aspect of drugs and the drug companies' interest, like that of medical schools and medical practice, relates only to therapeutic effects. While toxicologists may be able to determine the minimal lethal dose of a drug, they cannot necessarily indicate possible side-effects that might make the drug unsuitable, in some or most cases, as a euthanatic. The drugs involved in physician aid-in-dying, a procedure used in the Netherlands, may not be applicable in cases of self-deliverance. In addition, findings of doctors who have prescribed lethal drugs have not been published, due to restrictive public opposition or illegality.

At least two right-to die societies have advocated the use of chloroquine as a euthanatic,[6,10,26] one of these especially in combination with other drugs.[6] The German society, DGHS, has advocated the use of chloroquine for self-deliverance since 1983.[6] Members of the World Federation of Right-to-Die Societies generally have been sceptical of this use of chloroquine. Widely differing opinions and conclusions have been reached, yet no supportive documentation, to our knowledge, has been put forth to justify them.

In an attempt to encourage further dialogue in a logical manner, we first considered three areas:

i) physiological effects of chloroquine overdose and speed of onset, from published data (theoretical),
ii) observed evidence from case studies (clinical), and
ii) patterns or popularity of use in suicide (sociological).

We obtained data on theoretical aspects by examining some forty published papers from 1964 to 1991, as well as established reference works. Some of these contained no relevant data – e.g., certain papers looked exclusively at long-term therapeutic use. We avoided extrapolation and paraphrased as little as possible. We approached clinical aspects by review of papers that included detailed case studies and we also sought unpublished information on case studies of intentional suicide from the German right-to-die society (DGHS). Our research indicated that chloroquine has been, and still is, a popular suicide agent in several parts of the world – e.g. Africa,[14] Papua New Guinea[28] and Germany.[27] This sociological factor seemed to warrant serious attention, although other considerations, such as distressing side-effects, are of more importance. We visited the staff at DGHS, the German right-to-die society, to learn from their extensive practical experience with the use of chloroquine. Our findings are not final or absolute, and we invite input from any interested parties who have other relevant data that will further discussion on this issue.

What evidence is there to suggest that chloroquine can be lethal?
Eleven of the twenty-seven sources reviewed specifically state that chloroquine can be lethal[2,3,5,7,11,14,15,16,19,24,26] and, one of these, *Toxicology Management Review* (TMR), reports that,

according to published studies, the mortality rate is among the highest in clinical toxicology.[14] Some rare cases of survival following ingestion of large amounts have been reported when prompt, aggressive treatment had been undertaken,[2,5,26] although according to TMR the higher the dose the greater the likelihood of death.[14] While "1.5g (20mg/kg body weight)"[24] is the generally accepted minimal toxic dose, a recent (1991) report in *Intensive Care Medicine* pointed out that "ingestion of more than 5g chloroquine is usually reported to be fatal without effective treatment".[11]

Chloroquine is described as a potent myocardial poison[7] that is rapidly absorbed from the gastrointestinal tract.[26] Although the drug is slowly excreted,[28] toxic effects rarely last more than 24 hours.[26] The drug depresses the heart and lowers the blood pressure by dilating blood vessels distant from the heart.[7] Death is caused by failure of the heart to contract, complicated by a slow and abnormal heartbeat,[7] with eventual cardiorespiratory arrest.[5] At least one study on the effects of chloroquine poisoning on the heart indicated that a person's weight is more relevant than age to the toxicity of the drug.[7]

One problem with some of the papers that we studied was the inconsistent use of the term chloroquine. As a letter to the *New England Journal of Medicine* points out, failure to differentiate between the base equivalent of chloroquine and the entire salt would hinder calculations of the projected amount needed to produce death.[20] Chloroquine base 100mg approximately equals chloroquine sulphate 136mg or chloroquine phosphate 161mg.[19] Tablets commonly prescribed in Britain contain 250mg of the phosphate (approx 155 base), or 200mg of the sulphate (approx 150 base). In the United States they generally contain 250mg of the phosphate (approx 155 base), or 500mg of phosphate (approx 310 base).

How quickly does chloroquine take effect?

Case studies vary, with death occurring in less than an hour[16] to up to twelve hours[5] after ingestion. The studies indicated that a greater number of deaths occurred in two to three hours[14,5] or less.[16] One author stated that "the absence of cardiac effects 4 – 6 hours after ingestion makes survival likely."[22] DGHS literature suggests that death from chloroquine overdose occurs in 12-24 hours.[6]

What evidence suggests unpleasant side-effects can occur with chloroquine?

Possible side-effects include both unpleasant symptoms that might be experienced before death (or coma leading to death) and serious long-term symptoms that might occur in the case of a failed suicide.

The published reports discuss a wide variety of side-effects that may be caused by chloroquine. The most common of these are respiratory difficulty, drowsiness, and cardiovascular symptoms including low blood pressure, low potassium in the blood and abnormal heartbeat.[14] Other common symptoms include gastrointestinal problems,[3,5,16,19,28] hyperexcitability,[16,22,28] convulsions,[3,7,14,16,22,26] difficulty in breathing,[5,16,22,24] headache,[3,19] slurred speech,[5,16,22] coma,[3,22] and visual difficulties.[1,4,14,19,21,26] Interestingly, some individuals may have no symptoms until suffering cardiac arrest.[24] Gastrointestinal problems, including nausea and vomiting, can interfere with ingestion. Chloroquine has a bitter taste[4] which can exacerbate the problem. According to DGHS, these symptoms, which could weaken the effect of the lethal dosages, may be alleviated by taking a few tablets of an antiemetic an hour in advance.[6] In one case of hyperexcitability, the patient became wild and struggling and four persons were required to restrain him.[16]

Regarding long-term effects, opponents of the use of chloroquine as a euthanasic drug have raised concerns about the potential for blindness resulting from a failed chloroquine suicide attempt. This concern may have come about as a result of knowing that quinine may, in fact, cause blindness when taken in toxic doses.[1,14] TMR, however, cites a number of authorities, including the *Bulletin of the World Health Organisation*, in asserting that "Blindness in acute chloroquine intoxication is always transient and recovers without sequelae, in contrast to the retinopathy following long-term chloroquine therapy".[14] One study of long-term use of chloroquine indicated that withdrawal of treatment caused a reversal of side-effects.[9] The possibility of brain damage after a failed suicide attempt is also of concern. We found only one case in the literature of a survivor exhibiting evidence of brain damage.[17] Unfortunately, there was no indication as to whether the damage was long-term or permanent. Conversely, one documented case discussed a patient who took a very high overdose of chloroquine with no related medical problems one year later.[2]

What evidence suggests interactions between chloroquine and other substances?
Evidence suggests that the cardiotoxicity of chloroquine might be decreased by the concomitant administration of diazepam.[14,19] In fact, diazepam is considered to be a treatment for chloroquine overdose, and may significantly decrease the mortality rate.[24] Several authors noted that patients who had taken diazepam along with as much as 5g chloroquine showed no clinical symptoms of chloroquine

poisoning.[14,24] Milk products, antacids, and kaolin decrease the absorption of drugs, including chloroquine.[6,12,19] On the other hand, cimetidine may increase the effects of chloroquine,[18] and although chloroquine is not soluble in alcohol,[19] alcohol may nevertheless have a synergistic effect.[16] Cardiotoxicity is also influenced by the degree of pre-existing heart disease.[3]

References (see also the chapter on drugs, earlier in this volume)

These references generally provide secondary references for further study. In addition, we welcome constructive comments from our readership and see this article as a preliminary for further discussion.

1.Bacon P, Spalton D, Smith S (1988) Blindness from Quinine Toxicity. British Journal of Ophthalmology 72: 219-224.

2.Bauer P, Maire B, Weber M, et al (1991) Full Recovery After a Chloroquine Suicide Attempt. Clinical Toxicology 29(1): 23-30.

3.Britton W, Kevau I (1978) Intentional Chloroquine Overdosage. The Medical Journal of Australia 407-410.

4.Centers for Disease Control (1990) Recommendations for the Prevention of Malaria Among Travelers. Morbidity and Mortality Weekly Report 38(RR-3):1-7.

5.Czajka P, Flynn P (1978) Nonfatal Chloroquine Poisoning. Clinical Toxicology 13(3):361-369.

6.Deutsche Gesellschaft fur Humanes Sterben, 8th ed (November 1992) Medicaments List; 2nd ed p. 17 (1983) Menschenwurdiges und selbstverantwortliches Sterben. Augsburg.

7.Don Michael T, Aiwazzadeh S (1970) The effects of acute chloroquine poisoning with special reference to the heart. Am Heart J 79(6): 831-842.

8.Duncan C, ed (Sep 1992) Infections & Infestations. In: Monthly Index of Medical Specialties. Haymarket, London 167-168.

9.Frisk-Holmberg M, Bergkvist Y, Domeij-Nyberg B, et al (1979) Chloroquine serum concentration and side effects: Evidence for dose-dependent kinetics. Clinical Pharmacology Therapy 25(3): 345-350.

10.Guillon C, Bonniec Y (1982) Suicide Mode d'Emploi: Histoire, Technique, Actualite. Moreau Editions, Paris 231-232.

11.Hantson P, Ronveau J, De Coninck B, et al (1991) Amrinone for refractory cardiogenic shock following chloroquine poisoning. Intensive Care Medicine 17:430-431.

12. Henry J, ed (1991) A-Z of Drugs. In: The British Medical Association Guide to Medicines and Drugs. Dorling Kindersley, London 220.
13. Ivanina T, Sakina N, Lebedeva M, et al (1989) A Study of the Mechanisms of Chloroquine Retinopathy. Ophthalmic Res 21: 216-220.
14. Jaeger A, Sauder P, Kopferschmitt, Flesch F (1987) Clinical Features and Management of Poisoning due to Antimalarial Drugs. Toxicology Management Review 2: 242-273.
15. Kelly J, Wasserman G, Bernard W, et al (1990) Chloroquine Poisoning in a Child. Annals of Emergency Medicine 19(1) 47-50.
16. Kiel F (1964) Chloroquine Suicide. Journal of the American Medical Association 190(4):398-400.
17. Larkworthy W (1971) Acute Chloroquine Poisoning. Practitioner 207: 212-214.
18. Long J (1992) The Essential Guide to Prescription Drugs. Harper Perennial, New York: 311-315.
19. Martindale the Extra Pharmacopoeia 29th Ed (1989) Pharmaceutical Press, London 508-512.
20. Mofenson H, Caraccio T (1988) Letter, Treatment of Severe Chloroquine Poisoning. New England Journal of Medicine 319(1): 50.
21. Potts A, Gonasun L (1980) Toxic Responses of the Eye. In: Doull J, Klaasen C, Amdur M eds. Toxicology: The Basic Science of Poisons. Macmillan, New York 282, 291-293.
22. Proudfoot A (1982) Diagnosis and Management of Acute Poisoning. Blackwell Scientific, Oxford, 90-91.
23. Raines M, Bhargava S, Rosen E (1989) The Blood-Retinal Barrier in Chloroquine Retinopathy. Investigative Ophthalmology & Visual Science 30(8): 1726-1731.
24. Rajah A (1990) The use of diazepam in chloroquine poisoning. Anaesthesia 45: 955-957.
25. Riou B, Barriot P, Rimailho A, et al (1988) Letter, Treatment of Severe Chloroquine Poisoning. New England Journal of Medicine 319(1): 50.
26. Stiff G, Robinson D, Dugnoni H, et al (1991) Massive Chloroquine overdose: a survivor. Postgrad Med J 67: 678-679.
27. Wiedenmann C, von Hoesch H (March 5, 1993) Personal conversations with the authors.
28. Wilkey I (1973) Chloroquine Suicide. Medical Journal of Australia 1:396-397.

Toxic plants

(Being a preliminary review of some poisonous plants with relation to their possible use in rational suicide)

Many authorities have stated that plants are not a particularly peaceful or reliable means of ending one's life, yet right-to-die societies get frequent enquiries about the toxicity and suitability of various plants. Folklore, while containing a grain of truth, has possibly fuelled belief in the potency of plants even to the modern day. I propose to briefly outline the plants of most common interest and their effects, in the hope that this short article will persuade all but the most dedicated plant-lover to use more readily available, more reliable, and less unpleasant methods of auto-euthanasia than that offered by plants. Anyone seriously wishing to use the plants listed below, having read of the unpleasant effects involved, will need some knowledge of plants in order to correctly identify the plants in question: therefore I will omit any detailed descriptions of their appearances (these can be found in the references at the end).

Unless you obtain a drug from a plant under laboratory conditions, you have little control and don't really know what you're getting. The fact that many drugs are derived from plants doesn't indicate that the same effect can be achieved by boiling up the raw materials! Alkaloids and glycosides are amongst the most important chemicals found in plants that can have a lethal effect. When poisonous plants are eaten, the mouth, stomach and then the rest of the digestive system are often the first parts of the body to be affected. The nervous system is then frequently attacked. Fatalities may occur due to heart failure.

Autumn Crocus (Colchicum autumnale)

Autumn Crocus is a popular garden plant, although it appears in the wild in some damp meadows and woods. It has long, tubular, purple or white flowers. Poisonous alkaloids are present in all parts of the plant, but more concentrated in the underground stem and the seeds. The toxicity also remains after drying. Initial symptoms may be delayed several hours and include burning sensations, diarrhoea, difficulty in swallowing, abdominal pain and nausea. Large amounts might cause collapse, convulsions, paralysis and death.

Deadly Nightshade (Atropa belladonna)

All parts of the Deadly Nightshade plant (but particularly the berries) contain a variable mixture of hyoscamine, hyoscine and atropine. Cases of poisoning have been known, for instance, when the leafy part has been cooked and eaten as a vegetable or the berries stewed as a dessert. Symptoms develop within a few hours and may include dry mouth, flushing, rapid pulse, possibly difficulty in breathing, constipation, hallucinations, convulsions and coma. Death may follow in 6-24 hours. Woody Nightshade is sometimes mistaken for deadly nightshade, though less poisonous. The name nightshade is similarly applied to a variety of other plants in various countries.

False Hellebore / White Hellebore (Veratrum species)

This plant should not be confused with true hellebores. False Hellebore is much more poisonous, especially in the rootstock and leaves. Symptoms may include a burning sensation in the mouth and throat, abdominal pain, vomiting, diarrhoea, muscular twitching and cramps. In more severe cases there may be slow pulse, difficulty in breathing, coldness, trembling, collapse and death.

Foxglove (Digitalis purpurea)

Foxglove is a common ornamental flowering plant, used in medicine for its digitalis. It contains glycosides such as digitoxin and digitalin that are potentially lethal; due to the vomiting that the plant induces however, these are rarely fatal. The plant may be boiled, dried or stored without affecting the toxicity. It has a bitter taste. Toxic symptoms may result from drinking tea prepared with the leaves or from eating the leaves or flowers. Symptoms include nausea, vomiting, abdominal pain, diarrhoea, headache and slow irregular pulse. In severe cases there are visual disturbances, trembling, convulsions, delirium and hallucinations. The name probably means Folks' Glove (i.e. Fairies' Glove). In Scotland, its names have included Bloody Fingers and Dead-Men's-Bells, and the German name Fingerhut (thimble) is said to have inspired the botanist and physician Leonard Fuchs in 1542 to employ the Latin adjective digitalis as the designation of the plant. Foxglove tea used to be an "old wives'" remedy for dropsy.

Hemlock (Conium maculatum)

The common hemlock is well known in folklore. Several dangerous alkaloids are present in the plant but much of the toxicity is lost in drying. A number of people have died after eating the plant. It exudes a fetid smell, resembling that of mice, and has a bitter taste. Symptoms can appear between fifteen minutes and two hours. According to authorities, burning and dryness of the mouth is followed by muscular weakness leading to paralysis that eventually affects the breathing; vomiting, diarrhoea, convulsions and loss of consciousness and death may follow. All this differs from the reassuring tale of Socrates offered by Plato. Crito supposedly told Socrates to simply walk about until his legs felt heavy and then to lie down: Plato then describes how cold and numbness spread peacefully from Socrates' feet upwards. The romantic notion was reinforced by the poet Keats, who wrote: "A drowsy numbness pains My sense, as though of hemlock I had drunk." The toxicity of Hemlock varies greatly according to the conditions under which it is grown and the season or stage of growth at which it is gathered. The mature plant is the most toxic, and should be gathered during the flowering period, or later on when the fruits are fully grown. The wild plant growing in exposed situations is said to be more potent than garden-grown samples, and more potent in dry warm summers than in those which are dull and moist.

Hemlock Water Dropwort (Oenanthe crocata)

Hemlock Water Dropwort has leaves that are similar to those of celery and with a similar odour. The flowers have a wine-like scent. Oenanthetoxin is found in all parts of the plant, especially the roots, where its concentration is highest in winter and early spring. These roots have a pleasant taste, similar to parsnip. The toxin remains largely active in the dried plant or after cooking. However, the poisonous juice which exudes from the cut surface of the root deteriorates and loses its toxicity on exposure to air, changing colour from yellow to brown. The plant is poisonous, frequently fatally, even in small doses. Symptoms develop within an hour or two and include nausea, excessive production of saliva, repeated vomiting, diarrhoea, profuse sweating, and weakness of the legs; loss of consciousness and convulsions may occur before death. The plant is also known as Dead Men's Fingers.

Henbane (Hyoscamus niger)

Henbane is a weed that grows on wasteland. It is an unpleasant tasting plant with poisonous seeds that have an action similar to deadly nightshade. Blurred vision and mental confusion may be followed by rapid heartbeat, staggering, extreme agitation, loss of speech, hallucinations, paralysis, unconsciousness and death. The extract has been used medicinally as a sedative; country-folk once smoked the seeds and capsules as a remedy for toothache!

Mistletoe (Viscum album)
This parasitic plant has played a role in superstition even to the present day, though it is no longer generally attributed with sacred or medicinal properties. Mistletoe growing on lime or poplar trees is more poisonous than that growing on apple trees. The leaves and stem are the most poisonous, followed by the berries. It causes serious digestive disturbances. Reactions to mistletoe vary considerably, although fatalities are not unknown. The mistletoe has been revered in many cultures - mistletoe growing on oak especially so by the Druids.

Monkshood (Aconitum napellus)
Monkshood is a very poisonous plant containing aconitine and other alkaloids. Some of the toxins remain after drying or storage. Symptoms of poisoning develop in less than an hour. A burning sensation in the mouth and throat, coldness and sweating, are followed by general numbness, vomiting, diarrhoea, and abdominal pain. A slow pulse may develop, with eventual convulsions, coma and death, all within two hours.

Moonseed (Menispermum canadense)
Like the moon, moonseed has its bright and dark sides. On the bright side, this North American vine's roots furnished 19th century medicine with a drug that was not only an effective diuretic and laxative but was reportedly useful in treating a wide range of ailments from tuberculosis of the lymph glands in the neck to certain rheumatic and arthritic diseases. On the dark side, this plant produces poisonous blue-black berries that can easily be mistaken for wild grapes, and

there have been accidental deaths. Excessive doses bring on an extremely rapid pulse rate and severe vomiting and purging (Also known as Canada Moonseed and Texas Sarsaparilla.)

Oleander (Nerium oleander)

Oleander grows as a greenhouse plant and is native to southern Europe, though growing wild elsewhere in warm climes. All parts of the plant contain glycosides, and the toxicity remains after drying or boiling. Accidentally eating skewers of oleander wood has known to be fatal, as has herbal tea made from an infusion of the leaves. Chewing 8-10 seeds of the yellow oleander is commonly fatal and it has been used in India for suicide. The plant causes an immediate burning sensation in the mouth and a bitter taste. A few hours later, numbness of the tongue, abdominal pain, nausea, vomiting, diarrhoea, and rapid pulse follow. Visual disturbances develop and later on an irregular pulse and fall in blood-pressure can precede death.

Poison Ivy (Hedera helix)

All the parts of this wild, trailing/climbing evergreen have long been considered poisonous, yet treatment is rarely considered necessary. Full recovery usually occurs in a few days. The berries have a bitter, unpleasant taste causing a burning sensation in the mouth and throat. More serious symptoms are uncommon, but might include difficult breathing and even coma.

Thorn Apple (Datura stramonium)

This annual plant has a distinctive unpleasant odour, especially when bruised or crushed. The whole plant (but especially the flowers and seeds) contains hyoscamine, scopalamine and other toxins – the concentration of which varies with the stage of growth and environment. Drying or boiling does not affect the toxicity. Most cases of poisoning have occurred whilst using the plant for its hallucinogenic properties. In Shakespeare's Anthony & Cleopatra, Cleopatra uses it in her wooing of Caesar. Symptoms include nausea, irregular heartbeat, hallucination, delirium, convulsions, coma and sometimes death. The nickname Jimsonweed originated from a poisoning that occurred amongst soldiers at Jamestown, USA, in 1676.

Water Hemlock/Cowbane (Circuta virosa/Circuta maculata/Circuta douglasii)

Circutoxin is present in all parts of this plant, particularly in the yellow juice of the underground parts. It remains active after the plant has been dried. Even a few bites of the plant can cause poisoning and death. Symptoms may start within half an hour. It causes a burning sensation in the mouth, profuse production of saliva, nausea, vomiting, flushing and dizziness. Muscular contractions and convulsions, accompanied by difficulty in breathing, are followed by death, often within a few hours of eating the plant. Reports of the lethal dose range from a whole root to 1 cm of the stem. The smell is that of celery and the taste of sweet potato or parsnip. Death is fairly rapid as a result of the violent neurotoxic effects. Water Hemlock was used by the Iroquois Indians to commit suicide.

Yew (Taxus baccata)

A mixture of alkaloids are present in all parts of the plant. The toxicity is not decreased in fallen branches or hedge trimmings. People have died after eating the leaves or fruits. The fruits are poisonous when the seeds inside them are chewed. Toxic alkaloids are released which can cause symptoms ranging from mild nausea and abdominal pain to coma and death. The latter may be preceded by lethargy, trembling, coldness and convulsions. The alkaloids are rapidly absorbed and interfere with the action of the heart. Surprisingly enough, the evergreen yew, which lives to an immense age, has also been regarded through the ages as a symbol of everlasting life. The poisonous properties were known and referred to by classical writers such as Caesar, Virgil and Livy.

When we are reasonably fit and well, thinking of ingenious ways in which to achieve death may be an interesting intellectual exercise. For the person desperately seeking a way to end his or her own life now, reliability and freedom from further pain are the most important factors. Direct use of plants is not likely to satisfy either the criterion of reliability or that of freedom from further pain, and I urge readers to instead look to the methods described elsewhere in this book. Much more research is needed (research that will be particularly difficult to implement) before we can say that any of these plants definitely causes a peaceful death, or what sedatives would be effective in combination with them to achieve such an end. This chapter will have served its purpose if it helps to avoid, for some, what is no more than the roulette-wheel of possible death using poisonous plants and the unwarranted imposition of needless, further suffering.

References and further reading

- Cooper, M. Johnson, A. Poisonous Plants and Fungi, an Illustrated Guide. London: HMSO 1988.
- Chisholm, H, ed. Encyclopedia Britannica. 11th Edition, Cambridge: University Press 1910.
- Cummins, R. et al. Near-FatalYew Berry Intoxication. In: Ann Emerg Med(Jan 1990) 19(1):77-82.
- Frazer, J. The Golden Bough. .London: MacMillan Press 1922. Knutsen, O. Paszkowski, P. New Aspects in the Treatment of Water Hemlock Poisoning. In: Clin Toxicol (1984) 22(2): 157-166.

- Fox K, A Basic Guide to Herbs – Uses, Side Effects, Interactions and Overdose, Bloomington 2003.
- Lampe, K. McCann, M. AMA Handbook of Poisonous and Injurious Plants. Chicago: AMA 1985.
- Malcolm, I. Routledge, P. Hemlock Water Droplet Poisoning - A Review. In: Clin Toxicol (1978) 12(4):417-426.
- Misra, A. Poisoningfrom Thevetia nerifolia (yellow oleander). In: Postgrad Med J (1990) 66:492.
- Radford, E. Radford M. Superstitions of the Countryside. Ed. Hole, C. London: Arrow 1978.
- Rizzi, D. et al. Clinical Spectrum of Accidental Hemlock Poisoning. In: Nephrol Dialys Transpl (1991) 6:939-943.
- Samal, K. et al. Yellow Oleander (Cerbera Thevetia) Poisoning with Jaundice and Renal Failure. In: J Assoc Phys India (1989) 37(3):232 233.
- Urich, R. et al. Datura stramonium: A Fatal Poisoning. In: J Forensic Sc (Oct 1982) 27(4): 948-954.
- Yersin, B. et al. Fatal Cardiac Arrythmias and Shock Following Yew Leaves Ingestion. In: Ann Emerg Med (Dec 1987) 16(12):1396-1397.

Fasting to death

The arguments on terminal fasting are fairly complex, as this chapter demonstrates. They have been summarised in the *Starvation* chapter earlier for general reading, but anyone seriously contemplating doing without food and water in order to end their life is strongly advised to investigate the facts in considerable detail. Admonitions concerning comfort care are included in the earlier chapter rather than repeated here.

Sitting quietly one day, a month before his 100th birthday, Scott Nearing (the American conservationist, peace activist, educator and writer) said: "I think I won't eat any more." It was 1983. The house, which he had had a hand in building himself, overlooked a quiet bay in Maine. Scott wanted the tranquillity of his life to be mirrored in his dying. For a month he drank fruit juice, then he decided he wanted only water. Lucid, and with no pain, pills, or professional nursing, he was in good spirits. Gradually, his breathing became fainter, as if he were detaching himself. He spoke his last words and died so gracefully that his death inspired a book as a testament of his passing from one who was with him. (Readers of the earlier chapter may wish to note that Nearing was a vegetarian.)

Compare this passing with a very different one . . .

> Another filling came loose. The choking sputter as the prisoner spat it out hurt his ulcerated throat. The conditions first experienced after a fortnight of fasting were much worse. Six weeks into his hunger strike, the IRA prisoner couldn't move his gaze properly without turning his head. He was light-headed and kept vomiting. Later his speech became slurred and his vision failed. Eventually he was going to die - like nine others who starved themselves to death in 1981 in the Maze Prison of Northern Ireland.

Finally we have yet another real life scenario . . .

> The crowds gathered. Some took photographs. Jinen-
> dra Varni, the Jain scholar, sat cross-legged as the
> throngs gazed in awe. He has taken a vow of terminal
> fast and had gradually cut back on solids, then on liq-
> uids. There seemed little evidence of any pain or even
> hunger pangs. Varni abstained from water on alternate
> days until May 23, 1983 when he gave it up altogether.
> Reclining onto his side and exuding a tremendous
> peace and calm, he died the following day.

Different deaths. Different contexts. Different experiences.
Why do some people die a horrible death without food and
water and others experience an almost idyllic departure?
Reports show little consensus. Before considering it as a
method of self-deliverance, this article seeks to establish the
known facts about starvation (or fasting) and dehydration.

The right-to-die debate, as it affects patients and physicians,
has taken a new turn recently in terms of rights, duties and
cooperation. Abstinence from food and drink, as a means to
willed, voluntary death, has been put forward as a solution to a
particular legal and moral stalemate that has persisted between
patients and doctors, right-to-die proponents and 'pro-lifers'.
For we see that:

> . . . educating chronically ill and terminally ill patients
> about the feasibility of patient refusal of hydration and
> nutrition (PRHN) can empower them to control their
> own destiny without requiring physicians to reject the
> taboos on PAS [physician-assisted suicide] and VAE
> [voluntary active euthanasia] that have existed for mil-
> lennia.[1]

This proposal, which seems to many an attractive one, is beleaguered with apparently conflicting evidence about the painlessness of such a course of action. One of the aims in here is to summarise and hopefully bring some cohesion out of widely disparate claims.

In 1993, the International Drugs Consensus Working Party's[2] comment on fasting as a means of self-deliverance was:

> This method is extremely slow, taking two weeks or more.[3] ... As a traditional method, it was practiced by the American Indians. Unpleasant medical complications may set in before death occurs. A little liquid should be taken to moisten the mouth and prevent painful dehydration.[4]

The recommendation seems to discourage fasting as a method of self-deliverance while nevertheless admitting that it has sometimes been successfully employed. Let us expand on and explore the known facts about fasting and dehydration. My tentative conclusion is that it may be a viable method for suitable individuals, but the evidence suggests that, without medical examination of the person undergoing the fast to ascertain suitability, and the provision of palliative care for alleviation of troubling symptoms, it may be an uncertain course for an individual to embark on, especially when suitable drugs for self-deliverance can be obtained without too much difficulty in most countries and so provide an alternative route to dying in dignity.[5]

A principal feature of fasting however, is that it potentially allows the active cooperation of the health care team. Except in limited parts of Continental Europe, or potentially in Oregon USA under Measure 16, medical assistance in accelerating dying is outlawed, but fasting and dehydration, almost through a legal technicality, allow active participation without active medication. Patients have the right to refuse life-support systems, such as forced feeding by gastric tubes and intravenous drips of expensive nutrient solutions. They also have the right to palliative care.[6]

The moral agendas and societal attitudes which underlie such shaky legal divides are nowhere more evident than in the dilemma facing doctors who feel vocationally devoted to curing or comfort care but not to being an active assistant in the death of a patient. Thus:

> . . . there is no disagreement that physicians are morally and legally prohibited from overruling the rational refusal of therapy by a competent patient even when they know that death will result. There is also no disagreement that physicians are allowed to provide appropriate treatment for the pain and suffering that may accompany such refusals.[7]

It is hardly surprising, however, that even in Britain or the United States where medical law is widely disseminated, confusion should arise in the minds of health care workers. Although a competent patient can refuse nutrition and hydration, the incompetent patient may not be afforded the same option. Lord Musthill, for instance, noted that: . . . in 20 out of 39 American states which have legislated in favour of 'living wills' the legislation specifically excludes termination of life by the withdrawal of nourishment and hydration.[8]

In one study:

75 per cent of physicians surveyed objected to the idea of withdrawing intravenous fluids. This is understandable given the widespread emphasis in medical education on acting, on doing something, however futile, even if no real good is brought about for the patient.[9]

This reluctance to permit death to occur by withdrawing fluids is reinforced by popular images of what 'good doctors' do: paradoxically, ignorance of the law may involve breaking it in the false belief that one is staying on the right side of it:

> The symbolic power of 'giving a cup of water to a thirsty person' is almost overwhelming. How much greater is the symbolic power of food and water intervention when nothing else we can do will actually help the dying patient? . . . It must be frankly acknowledged that one reason physicians might use for ordering nutrition for the dying is to avoid a lawsuit . . . . Nevertheless, using the dying patient to protect oneself is a violation of the principle of beneficence upon which medicine rests. It is also a violation of the implied or explicit contract with patients through which the physician must act to care for their best interests.[10]

For a doctor trained in medicine, rather than ethics and the law, the number of situations requiring virtuosity of approach is almost overwhelming:

> Ethical dilemmas in the field of hydration and nutrition cover a wide spectrum, from dehydration due to dysphagia of various aetiologies, through terminal cancer with intestinal obstruction, to the persistent vegetative, state, terminal Alzheimer's disease patients

who are unable to eat, and patients with anorexia nervosa or elderly depressives who deliberately refuse
nourishment to the point of self-annihilation.[11]

. . . not to mention the rational self-deliverance of someone
who has decided to end their own interminable and unrelievable suffering.

Full awareness of the law is necessary before physicians will be
persuaded to embrace such an idea.

When death results from lack of hydration and nutrition, it is less plausible to say that the death was
caused by the disease process - thus someone must be
assigned responsibility for the patient's death and physicians wish to avoid this responsibility. Physicians
who recognize that patients have the authority to refuse any treatment, including hydration and nutrition,
are more likely to avoid unjustified feelings of responsibility for their deaths.[12]

The issue has been further complicated by ignorance as to the
therapeutic value, if any, of nutrition or hydration in terminal
care, and reliance on possibly erroneous assumptions.[13] A
more scientific rationale has been forwarded by Thomasma et
al, who concluded:

Our policy rests on an argument that there is a morally relevant difference about chronic illness, debilita-
tion, and terminal illness that permits us to treat the
patients suffering from these assaults on bodily integrity differently than we would other patients. This
morally significant difference lies in the ratio between
contemplated intervention and possible benefit. The

only medically secure treatment for a dying patient is comfort. That is the only way medicine can benefit such persons. We have argued that nutrition and fluids are optional treatments on this basis.[14]

The goal, or good of the patient, has often been obscured by the immediate medical contingency. Medicine has become enraptured of itself, and dilemmas are solved by what is medically correct rather than what is correct for the patient. Most of the problems connected with voluntary euthanasia, living wills and self-deliverance arise because of this excessively medicalized introversion that has the effect of marginalising the patient. Beneficent paternalism often occurs when the patient is enervated, incapacitated or confused as a result of disease, leaving opportunity for the practitioner to combine medical evaluation and expertise with a sensitivity to the wishes, values and needs of the patient; dogmatic paternalism occurs with increasing frequency when the problem is seen only in the (increasingly complex) language of medical science, and with an ear to medical science for the answer. The lure of professional challenge calls for the best answer - but with little regard to what the patient might reasonably conceive to be best. Even objective standards are easily ignored when there has been a failure to ask the right questions. As Pearlman discovered:

> Questionnaires of clinician beliefs and chart reviews of patients receiving tube feedings indicate that 'medical indications' without major regard for patient comfort or a patient-centered evaluation of benefits to burdens are a major factor in these decisions.[15]

To examine the underlying issues, which include not only medical and physiological problems but ethical and cultural challenges that are themselves surrounded by controversy, it is first necessary, as Justice Butler-Sloss said, to rid ourselves of the emotional overtones and emotive language which do not assist in elucidating the profound questions which require to be answered.[16] The paucity of reliable material and the inadequacy of rigorous research in this area, together with an overdose of popular but possibly erroneous sentiment, has been highlighted by Printz:

> In the literature, the issue of medical hydration and nutrition in the dying patient remains one of the underexplored areas of medicine.
> Articles objectively dealing with this issue are scarce, and documented research on comfort in dying patients is even more scarce. Opinions about this emotionally laden subject, however, abound.[17]

Source material available is in widely differing contexts - differing academic theories and total fasting studies,[18] hydration and nutrition studies in terminal patients,[19] deaths connected with anorexia,[20] hunger strikers,[21] isolated case studies of voluntary and willed death through fasting,[22] famine victims,[23] and deaths through malnutrition during persecution and war.[24] All these areas are emotionally laden in differing ways, and the bias thus implied must be stripped away before any scientific examination of the facts can take place. Even provision of artificial nutrition and hydration to dying patients remains controversial, with opposite practices sometimes being implemented in hospices and hospitals;[25] the mechanisms of anorexia are poorly understood, often arousing irrational responses in the public who unsuccessfully try to differentiate between a mental illness and a physical need; case studies of mystics or unusual individuals who manage to fast to death in a peaceful, serene manner are viewed by right-to-die enthusiasts as definitive rather than as the anecdotal descriptions which they tend to be; pictures of famine victims, with bloated bellies, give a graphic and horrifying picture of starvation and an emotional bias that links the supply of nutrition to a caring attitude - reinforced (rightly in this instance) by relief agencies such as Oxfam; macabre descriptions of the day-to-day deterioration of prisoners-of-war dying of malnutrition reinforce the idea that lack of food and water results in a very unpleasant death. It may perhaps be very easy, though somewhat disingenuous, to choose out-of-context, colourful, and ultimately specious examples to either support or oppose the notion of peaceful death through willed, voluntary fasting;[26] but such arguments should be viewed as dangerous, and the more responsible approach is to set out the benefits, burdens and precautions that seem advisable should any person decide against the more obvious methods of ending one's life and seriously contemplate fasting to achieve such an end.

To fast implies a willed action concerning one's own abstaining from food; starving, on the other hand may imply external circumstances forcing themselves on the individual, or, at least, the connotations of a painful condition or lingering death.[27]

Although much of the physiology may be connected, there are great ethical and possibly other differences between fasting and starvation. Additionally, the differing emotive import of the two words makes it very necessary to avoid using the wrong terms. As Ahronheim (et al) said: "The cruelty and abandonment implied in the word 'starvation' are not relevant to the dying patient."[28] Physicians frequently regard fluids and food to be minimum standards of care for the dying.[29] Siegler said that, "For physicians, provision of ordinary means of comfort and care like food and water demonstrates our personal, professional, and social commitment to the dying patient."[30]

Dehydration is also a state which, for the purposes under discussion, requires definitional analysis. On the first level, it is frequently confused with thirst - a state which it may not, as this article will show, necessarily even parallel. Secondly, there are differing types of dehydration from a physiological viewpoint and, depending on the antecedent cause, the resulting symptomatology may be different.[31]

There is an important difference between being thirsty and being dehydrated. Thirst is an uncomfortable sensation experienced when the mouth is dry. Discomfort from dehydration may be entirely absent as long as the mouth is kept moist.

Various authors agree that there may be very different clinical syndromes for sodium depletion as opposed to pure water loss.[32]

Normonotraemic dehydration, characterised by normal sodium concentration, is a common disturbance of fluid balance and is usually not severe. It is caused when fluid loss and sodium loss occur in equal proportions, such as in mild vomiting and diarrhoea.

Hyponotraemic dehydration, characterised by low sodium concentration, results from depletion of both water and sodium but with salt loss predominating, or when salt and water are lost together but only water is replaced. Losses like this arise from the gut (for example, vomiting and diarrhoea) or from the kidneys (for example, overuse of loop diuretics, diuresis caused by glucose osmosis or severe uraemia, or adrenal insufficiency).

Hypertraemic dehydration, with high sodium concentration, develops when water loss is greater than the loss of sodium and may occur when fluid intake is insufficient (for example, in unconscious patients with no fluid intake) and, rarely, with loss of normal thirst. It also results from increased fluid loss, such as that associated with vomiting and diarrhoea, from the skin and lungs in febrile patients, or the fluid loss caused by burns.[33]

Sutcliffe notes that:

> Dehydration in the terminally ill patient may present as a mixed disorder of salt and water loss and may be caused by normal water losses from the lungs, skin and kidneys, with failure to replace those losses, or there might be abnormal gastrointestinal or renal losses. Normonatraemic dehydration may also occur.[34]

Early rapid weight loss, for instance, is primarily due to negative sodium balance.[35] It is perhaps desirable that, as with any other method of willed death, the subject becomes conversant with the process to understand probable effects, their causes, and how to manage them. It is also important to note these differences because some of the evidence presented here and elsewhere for fasting to death is based, in part, on observing terminal patients. We should be aware that different factors come into play and that terminally ill patients who stop taking food and water are in a rather different category to comparatively healthy people who decide on a terminal fast.[36]

What evidence is there of unpleasant effects when intake of food and water ceases?

Many effects have been listed and observed. Kerndt et al include gout and urate nephrolithiasis, postural hypotension and cardiac arrhythmias,[37] and point out that, "The sense of well-being that may occur during short-term fasting is in contradistinction to that seen during prolonged periods of semi-starvation when mental lethargy, apathy and irritability are common."[38] Miller, in his observations on hunger-strikers notes:

> The net result of these metabolic changes is that the person who consumes insufficient protein and calories will experience progressive loss of both muscle and fat. No body organ is spared. The skeletal muscles atrophy more rapidly than cardiac muscle or kidney, but as protein energy starvation continues, the heart and kidney lose mass progressively.[39]

And goes on to explain:

> Lymphatic tissues atrophy, causing impaired cell-mediated immunity and reduced bactericidal activity of polymorphonuclear leukocytes. There is an increased morbidity and mortality during common infections. Pneumonia is a common cause of death . . . metabolic rate is reduced, and hypothermia is common . . . . On physical examination, there is a drawn appearance of the face, the temporal areas of the head are wasted. The intercostal spaces are fleshless, the skin hangs in folds on the wasted limbs. The skin flakes and loses pigmentation, as does the hair. The patient appears pale. He may be edematous. Skin and decubitus ulcers are common.[40]

Sutcliffe lists the potential disadvantages of dehydration as including extreme electrolyte imbalance (eg acidosis), hypernatraemia, hypercalcaemia leading to apathy and depressive states ranging from lethargy to coma and confusion, and also neuromuscular irritability and twitching, hypovolaemia leading to falls, postural hypotension leading to increased risk of pressure sores, reduced skin perfusion leading to increased risk of pulmonary embolism and deep vein thrombosis, water deprivation leading to headaches, nausea and vomiting and muscle cramps, reduced urine output leading to dysuria and increased risk of urinary tract infection, reduced fluid leading to constipation and gastrointestinal tract pain and discomfort. He adds that clinical manifestations often associated with volume depletion include signs of circulatory insufficiency (such as reduced blood pressure, postural hypotension, cold peripheries, decreased cerebral perfusion), uraemia, hyponatraemia and haemoconcentration. Patients may experience dryness of the mouth and mucous membranes, diminished sweat, decreased skin turgor and neurological complications such as weakness, restlessness, confusion, coma and seizures. He tells us that nausea, vomiting, anorexia and taste loss have been noted in experimental subjects with hyponatraemic dehydration; but notes that these may be contributing causes rather than a result of that condition.[41]

Collaud affirms that symptoms rarely mentioned in the literature include nausea, muscular cramps and hunger.[42] Keys et al. note that gastrointestinal disorders are prominent, such as diarrhoea, nonspecific dysentery, colic, flatulence, and a protruding abdomen, which, they say, are universally recognized symptoms of calorific undernutrition and have been observed wherever man's natural food supply has been seriously curtailed.[43] They also say that there is an increased sensitivity to cold,[44] and that numerous physiological changes ensue with malnutrition which become progressively far reaching as the condition continues;[45] slow heart rate,[46] mild cyanosis, cold skin, increased circulatory time,[47] increased water consumption, salt hunger (subjects will consume several times normal quota of salt if available), edema,[48] depressed libido,[49] looking and feeling older,[50] greater accident proneness, diminishing of tendon reflexes, a sharpening of the senses with vision unlikely to deteriorate and hearing may becoming more acute - but with subjects tending to act dull and insensitive as though unaware of or incapable of feeling many of the ordinary stimuli of sound, sight or touch - are all further possible symptoms.[51] Fainting, is common,[52] and there is general weakness and reduced capacity for work.[53]

Winick, in his book of observations in a Warsaw Ghetto, tells us that the skin becomes pale, dry and scaley,[54] and that initial complaints (on 800 calories a day, comprising 3g fat, 20-30g vegetable protein, and the rest carbohydrate; protein was of low quality and very deficient in certain vitamins and minerals, particularly A, D, K and E, calcium & iron) included thirst, polyuria and nocturia, dryness of the mouth. rapid weight loss, and constant craving for food.[55] The skin is easily trauma-tized,[56] and there is a sensitivity to the sun, readily resulting in redness, swelling, local hyperthermia and fever blisters; temperature response to diseases which usually produce a high fever, such as typhus, is blunted.[57]

What evidence is there of beneficent symptoms (or lack of unpleasant symptoms) when intake of food and water ceases?
Keys et al. tell us that

> . . . academic portraits of so-called classical deficiency
> diseases are idealizations or even rather unreal abstrac-

tions with regard to the actual finding where real malnutrition is endemic or epidemic. Moreover, there is
material for argument against the idea of a progression
from positive, nutritional health through sub-clinical
deficiency to the full-blown disorder, in which the
subclinical state is supposed to be characterised by
vague malaise, fatigue, and so on. Some of the cases
of amblyopia and ataxia developed with little or no
premonitory change in the sense of well-being.."[58]

There is also a considerable amount of well-documented but
apparently contradictory evidence, and possible reasons for
such discrepancies will be examined presently. Firstly, however, let us examine some evidence of peaceful and dignified
deaths by the method under consideration. While there are
individual, anecdotal reports that seem to offer much hope,
two principal sets of data I propose to draw attention to cover
a) voluntary fasting by a particular religious sect and b) voluntary fasting in a hospital (or more usually hospice) setting; with
this second category will also be grouped withdrawal of
nutrition and hydration in competent patients. These groups,
however, may be considered to some extent atypical. The
former covers an ascetic and well controlled graduated fast by
relatively healthy subjects; the second relates primarily to
subjects who are mostly elderly, terminally ill and, most
importantly, have access to adequate palliative care.

Voluntary fasting to death within a religious sub-group appears
to be confined to the Terapantha order within the Jaina
Digambara community,[59] where it is said that several well
known cases occur every year.

The fast is described thus:

In early 1983 a prominent Jaina scholar and writer by the name of Jinendra Varni, then in his early eighties, although in reasonable health, decided that he wanted to fulfil his life's journey through a dignified yogic death (samadhimarana). On 12 April 1983 Varni formally withdrew from his worldly commitments and upon request received from the head preceptor of his order, with due acclamation for his courage, initiation into the vow of terminal fast (sellekhana). He had already reduced his food intake; now as each day went past he cut back on certain vegetables, milk, clarified butter, yoghurt, dried fruits, giving up something every day, but retaining small portions of boiled vegetables and sultanas for one meal of the day. Occasionally he would fast all day long, and break the fast with broth from a boiled vegetable. By the end of the month his fluid intake was reduced as well and gradually given up, with plain water remaining as his only intake, which too was set aside on alternate fast days. On 23 May water was given up altogether. Varni reclined with his body to one side during the last days but there was apparently no evidence of hunger pangs, pain of any other kind (particularly from by-now deteriorating internal organs), barring some coughs and discomfort while sitting upright owing to his frail frame; nor did he show any significant loss of attention and consciousness. On 24th May, exuding a tremendous peace and calm in his general demeanor, Vami closed over his eye-lids and breathed his last.[60]

This reassuringly peaceful death is a far cry from the horrors of starvation recounted elsewhere. Glimmerings that death from starvation and/or dehydration may not be as horrific as often contemplated have filtered through in mainstream medical literature for some time, probably starting with early fasting studies, through to observations in palliative care when hospice workers realized that artificial nutrition and hydration were not necessarily beneficial to terminally ill cancer patients, and finally in recent years amidst the right-to-die debate, advocacy of willed fasting as a means to legal self-deliverance combined with the palliative assistance of hospice care.

In the classic work by Keys et al. on starvation in 1950, it was pointed out that in total fasting studies the hunger sensation almost disappeared after a few days; that ketosis was a typical result of fasting but did not develop in semi-starvation; and that famine edema had never been reported in total starvation.[61] In looking at comfort measures for the terminally ill, Billings went a stage further in noting: " . . . fluid depletion in dying patients should be regarded as a disorder with relatively benign symptoms. Successful treatment of the discomfort of thirst and a dry mouth generally does not require rehydration.[62] By 1988, Printz had publicized the little known situation where:

> . . . a hospice nurse in 1983 noted a correlation between comfort and lack of medical hydration. It appeared to her that terminally ill patients in end-stage dehydration experienced less discomfort than patients receiving medical hydration. The dehydration, resulting from lack of nasogastric or IV fluid, seemed to produce a natural anaesthetic effect, often allowing for a reduction in pain medications.[63]

A study by Andrews and Levine published in 1989 showed widespread support among hospice workers for dehydration in some terminal patients:

Of the hospice nurses surveyed, 71 per cent agreed that dehydration reduces the incidence of vomiting, 73 per cent agreed that dehydrated patients rarely complain of thirst, 51 per cent reported that there is relief from choking and drowning sensations when fluids are discontinued, and 53 per cent agreed that dehydration can be beneficial for the dying patient. Also, 85 per cent of nurses surveyed disagreed with the need for hydration by IV and/or tube feeding when dehydrated patients have a dry mouth. Finally, 82 per cent of the nurses disagreed with the statement that dehydration is painful.[64]

They concluded that, in contrast to the assumption of most health professionals, dehydration was not painful, and that it was therefore a viable alternative to facilitate a comfortable death.[65] Concerning the medical symptoms, they observed that: "With dehydration there is decreased urine output and less need for the bedpan, urinal, commode, or catheterization and fewer bed-wetting episodes. There is a decrease in gastro-intestinal fluid with fewer bouts of vomiting. A reduction in pulmonary secretions is also seen with less coughing and congestion and a decrease in choking and drowning sensations. A reduction in the edematous layer around the tumor resulting in less pain may also occur."[66]

In 1990, Ahronheim and Gqsner concurred: "Withholding or withdrawing artificial feeding and hydration from debilitated patients does not result in gruesome, cruel or violent death.[67] Interestingly, . . . deprivation of fluid rapidly results in further depression of consciousness and then coma and the experience does not appear to be painful. There is also some evidence that impaired thirst may occur naturally with advanced age or neurological impairment, and that there may be endogenous production of substances producing natural analgesia.[68]

Sutcliffe and Holmes listed some benefits of dehydration to the dying patient as: reduced urine output leading to reduced incontinence and a reduced need for catheterization; reduced gastro-intestinal fluids leading to reduced vomiting; reduced pulmonary secretions leading to reduced coughing and choking, reduced drowning sensation, and reduced use of tracheal suction; extreme electrolyte imbalance (eg acidosis, hypernatraemia, hypercalcaemia) and hypovolaemia, leading to analgesia due to states ranging from lethargy to coma; anaesthetic effect of ketone production in calorie deprivation leading to anaesthesia; increased production of opioid peptides in malnutrition and dehydration leading to analgesia.[69]

Bernat *et al* also concluded that, "Scientific studies and anecdotal reports both suggest that dehydration and starvation in the seriously ill do not cause significant suffering" and that " . . . the overwhelming majority of hospice deaths resulting from lack of hydration and nutrition can be managed such that the patients remain comfortable." The consensus of experienced physicians and nurses was that terminally ill patients dying of dehydration or lack of nutrition do not suffer if treated, properly.[70]

Miller and Albright also reported that death associated with dehydration or malnutrition was not perceived as painful.[71]

By 1993, a founding member of the Nutrition Society of Canada and former senior toxicologist at the *Bureau of Human Prescription Drugs, Health and Welfare* in Canada was quoted as saying that self-deliverance by starvation was reasonably fast and that it could be painless, or that therapeutic, non-toxic doses of analgesics could be used if required for any reason to alleviate pain and discomfort.[72]

Further studies showed specific differences with men and women, old and young, or thin and obese.

In an experiment with healthy active elderly men (67 to 75 years old) and seven healthy young men (20 to 31 years old) it was found that the older men were less thirsty and drank less after water deprivation.[73]

Why there should be such striking differences in comparisons with, say, prisoners of war, is largely a matter of speculation, but one can hypothesize that other, concurrent factors could play a very large part. For instance, Phillips et al. suggest that if water intake in the elderly is deficient in the face of physiological need, for example in diarrhoea or fever, it could lead to clinical dehydration requiring hospital treatment in addition to aggravating other conditions (eg, constipation or renal stone disease). [74]

Keys *et al.* even note some possible geographical differences. Retrobulbar neuritis, spinal ataxia, burning feet ('acrodynia') with corneal changes, deafness, a myasthenic bulbar syndrome ('kubigassari') - these conditions, though not uncommon in the Orient, are exceedingly rare in modern Europe. The prevalence of nutritional neuropathies and of disorders of the mucocutaneous tissues is far greater in tropical and semitropical regions than in the temperate and subarctic zones, and any influence from racial factors may be ruled out on the basis of the experience with Europeans in the tropics and subtropics.[75]

Other variations observed are: (Sutcliffe:) Thirst is often absent in hyponatraemic dehydration, as this symptom is

primarily provoked by a raised sodium concentration.[76]
(Kerndt et al:) Lean persons become ketotic earlier than obese
persons, and women become ketotic more rapidly than men;[77]
. . . fasting ketosis develops more rapidly in women than in
men . . . This sex difference, however, disappears with increasing body weight; and . . . little or no rise in hormone growth is
seen after prolonged fasting in obese subjects.[78] (Symptoms of
ketosis include drowsiness, headache and deep respiration.)

It is clear that some individuals have experienced a peaceful
death as a result of stopping food and water. It is also clear
that probably a greater number of these have been assisted
with expert palliative care.[79]

Bernat *et al.* go so far as to suggest:

> A pact should be made with the patient that the phy-
> sician will do his or her best to minimize suffering
> during the dying process and will remain available to
> comfort the patient by physical presence as well as
> skillful treatment of symptoms, including dyspnea,
> and dryness of the mouth.[80]

As death from lack of nutrition alone is a potentially very
lengthy process, a combination of ceasing nutrition and
hydration by some method is likely to be a preferred course.
This area undoubtedly needs much more research. While a
peaceful death by this method seems feasible in some instances, without particularized medical advice and medical
back-up, and/or until more is known about the process of
self-deliverance through fasting, an isolated individual acting
alone would appear to have greater assurance of success by
means of drugs. Abstinence from food and drink as a means
of accelerating death does however have the distinction of

being the only method at the present time in which all sides in the "right-to-die" debate may reach common agreement under the law.

Having tried to separate myth, misinformation and scare stories from well-documented evidence, it is still difficult to say that refraining from food and drink will guarantee a peaceful death. Someone wanting a 100 per cent foolproof method might consider it foolhardy to emulate Jinendra Varni. A young, obese woman who has never followed a healthy diet might be ill-advised to attempt total fasting even in the face of unrelievable distress or a lingering, terminal illness.

But this is an area where a personal medical advisor may be able to narrow the odds and, if things go wrong, keep you comfortable in your dying without violating any laws and thus being branded a criminal.

References
1. Bernat J, Gert B, Mogielnicki R. "Patient Refusal of Hydration and Nutrition." Archives of Internal Medicine 1993; 153:2723-2728, p.2723.
2. The International Drugs Consensus Working Party was convened by the present author to look at research on methods of self-deliverance. The results of its work are published, for lay-persons, in the booklet Departing Drugs (qv infra).
3. Saudek C, Felig P, The Metabolic Events of Starvation, American Journal of Medicine 1976; 60:117-126, pl 17: Considering the total calories available to the normally fed man . . . there is enough to last more than 80 days, even assuming utilization of 2,000 calories/day. See also: Miller W, "The Hunger-Striking Prisoner," Journal of Prison & Jail Health 1987; 6(1):40-61, p.45: Total absence of food and water intake results in death from dehydration within a few days. The normal person with an average supply of fat and muscle may survive total starvation for several months, if adequate water is ingested. During the first week of total starvation, the average adult loses 4 to 5 kg. of body weight. After the first two weeks, the overwhelming desire for food disappears. Stomach cramps end. The skin becomes parched and dry. Fillings drop out of teeth. The throat becomes ulcerated. In the case of the Republican prisoners in the Maze prison in

Northern Ireland in 1981, after almost exactly 42 days of fasting, each person experienced a severe exacerbation of his condition. Muscle control of the eyes was lost, with rapid involuntary horizontal and vertical nystagmus. Continuous light-headedness and vomiting occurred. These symptoms persisted for four to five days, after which they ended, leaving the patient in a state of relative euphoria. Then speech became slurred, hearing diminished, vision failed, smell ceased. Death ensued. See also: Craig G, "On Withholding nutrition and hydration to the terminally ill: has palliative medicine gone too far?" Journal of Medical Ethics 1994; 20:139143, p.140: Even a Bedu tribesman riding in the desert in cool weather can only survive for seven days without food or water. Also: Sherwood L, Parris E, "Starvation in Man" New England Journal of Medicine 1979; 282(12):668-675, p.671: . . . a fasting man need drink very little water, the water produced by metabolism approximating that lost in urine and that lost by evaporation from skin and lungs. Therefore, as long as he is in atemperate and humid environment, his water needs are minimal when he is starving. .

. . Also: Keys A, Brozek J, Henschel A, Mickelsen O, Taylor H, The Biology of Human Starvation I & II, Minneapolis: University of Minnesota Press 1950, 1:14-15: With edema, the actual water content of the body may not rise, but it does not decrease in proportion to loss of tissue, so there is a relative increase in hydration, recognizable as a puffiness of the ankles and face (it may disappear in the final stages of starvation, and death occur in a dehydrated state.)

4. Docker C, Smith C, Departing Drugs, Edinburgh: VESS 1993, p.25.

5. Ibid.

6. Frederick G, "An Easy Alternative to Assisted Suicide" Globe and Mail 23 Sep 1993 p.A19.

7. Bernat J, Gert B, Mogielnicki R, "Patient Refusal of Hydration and Nutrition" Archives of Internal Medicine 1993; 153:2723-2728; p.2724.

8. Airedale NHS Trust v Bland [1993] 1 All E.R. 820, 888.

9. Thomasma D, Micetich K, Steinecker P, "Continuance. of Nutritional Care in the Terminally I11 Patient" Critical Care Clinics 1986; 2(1):61-7 1, p.63.

10. Ibid p.61-62.

11. Craig G, "On Withholding nutrition and hydration to the terminally ill: has palliative medicine gone too far?" Journal of Medical Ethics 1994; 20:139-143,. p.139.

12. Cook M, "The End of Life and the Goals of Medicine" Archives of Internal-Medicine 1993; 153:2718-2719; p.2718. Also: McCann R et al; "Comfort Care for Terminally Ill Patients" Journal of the American Medical Association 1994, 272('16):1263-1266, p:1263: ...it has been

established that legal rationale and precedent exist for respecting a patient's explicit wishes regarding nutrition and hydration. Moreover, there has been wide-spread, although not unanimous support from major religious groups that nutrition and hydration may at times be considered unnecessary form of therapy."

13. "It is argued that the reason dying patients should be given medical nutrition and hydration is that humans have a moral urge to feed the hungry and give drink to the thirsty . . . .the assumption in the argument, that the dying must be hungry and thirsty, has not been proved. Indeed, as has been noted, the opposite is suspected by many who have worked closely with the dying." Printz L, "Terminal Dehydration, a Compassionate Treatment" Archives of Internal Medicine 1992; 152:697-700, 698. Also: Ahronheim J, Gasner M, "The Sloganism of Starvation" Lancet 1990; 335:278-279, 279: "Since the beginning of time, until very recently, people who grew too old, too disabled, too weak, or too sick to eat and drink died without a feeding tube in place. Although superimposed medical illness in such people can now be cured, it is logical to assume that rejection of food is a physiological component of the illness and the dying process."

14. Thomasma D, Micetich K, Steinecker P, "Continuance of Nutritional Care in the Terminally Ill Patient" Critical Care Clinics 1986; 2(1):61-71, p.69-70.

15. Pearlman R, "Forgoing Medical Nutrition and Hydration: An Area for Fine-tuning Clinical Skills" Journal of General Internal Medicine (Editorial) 1993; 8:225-227, p.225.

16. Butler-Sloss LJ, in: Airedale NHS Trust v Bland [1993] 1 All E.R. 821,842.

17. Printz L, "Terminal Dehydration, a Compassionate Treatment" Archives of Internal Medicine 1992; 152:697-700, 698.

18. Keys A, Brozek J, Henschel A, Mickelsen O, Taylor H, The Biology of Human .Starvation I & 11, Minneapolis: University of Minnesota Press 1950, 1:29.

19. eg Miller R, Albright P, "What is the Role of Nutritional Support and Hydration in Terminal Cancer Patients?" American Journal of Hospice Care Nov/Dec 1989; 33-38. Burge F, "Dehydration Symptoms of Palliative Care Cancer Patients" Journal of Pain and Symptom Management 1993; 8(7):454-464. Lichter I, Hunt E, "The Last 48 Hours of Life" Journal of Palliative Care 1990; 6(4):7-15.

20. Keys A, Brozek J, Henschel A, Mickelsen O, Taylor H, The Biology of Human Starvation I & II. Minneapolis: University of Minnesota Press 1950, II:971: Mortality directly attributable to anorexia nervosa is only something like 8 per cent.)

21. Miller W, "The Hunger-Striking Prisoner" Journal of Prison & Jail Health 1987; 6(1):40-61.
22. Albury N, The Natural Death Handbook. 1993 London: Virgin Books. Scott Nearing Maine Times June 28 1991. Eddy D, "A Conversation With My Mother" Journal of the American Medical Association 1994; 272(3):179-181. Bilimoria P, "A Report from India: The Jaina Ethic of Voluntary Death" Bioethics 1992; 6(4):331-355:
23. Keys A, Brozek J, Henschel A, Mickelsen O, Taylor H, The Biology of Human Starvation I & II, Minneapolis: University of Minnesota Press 1950, 1:758-759.
24. Winick M, Hunger Disease - Studies by the Jewish Physician in the Warsaw Ghetto 1979, New York: John Wiley and Son, documents starvation until death. Hunger is divided by Winick (p.38) into three degrees: 1) depletion of fat reserves, 2) aging and withering of patient, 3)terminal cachexia.
25. Sutcliffe J, Holmes S, "Dehydration: Benefit or Burden to the Dying Patient?" Journal of Advanced Nursing 1994; 19:71-76, p.71: It appears that those dying from malignant disease in general hospitals are more likely to receive hydration therapies than those dying at home or in hospices. Haas F, "In the Patient's Best Interests? Dehydration in Dying Patients" Professional Nurse 1994; 10(2):82-87, p.82: In hospital settings, intravenous infusions are often given to dehydrated patients who are terminally ill, without any consideration of whether this is in their best interests. Cf. Andrews M, Levine A, "Dehydration in the Terminal Patient: Perception of Hospice Nurses" American Journal of Hospice Care Jan/Feb 1989, 31-34, p.31: "This study suggests that those hospice nurses who have observed terminal dehydration have a more positive perception of this state than those who have not."
26. Ahronheim J, Gasner M, "The Sloganism of Starvation" Lancet 1990; 335:278-279; 278: In Brophy v New England Sinai Hosp, Inc, a dissenting judge relied on discredited trial testimony and described the painful and gruesome death that would result from removing a feeding tube, telling of the desiccation of each organ in turn; in the event, the feeding tube was removed and the man (who was in PVS) died peacefully, yet the discredited description has been repeated in several other cases and even, almost word for word, on the influential TV program (LA Law).
27. The former is an intransitive verb, emphasising the voluntariness of the action since it implies only the actions of the person fasting; etymologically and by common usage, it often implies a higher purpose, whether for strict religious observance or as a deep expression of grief. The latter can not only be a transitive verb, but its etymology and connotations suggest dying

horribly and contemptibly. Oxford English Dictionary; Skeats W, A Concise Etymological Dictionary of the English Language; Oxford: Clarendon Press 1951; pp. 180 & 516. For a fuller comparison of fasting and starvation see: Encyclopaedia Britannica, 11th edition, Cambridge: University Press 1910; 10:193-198. Note also: Bilimoria P, "A Report from India: The Jaina Ethic of Voluntary Death" Bioethics 1992; 6(4):331-355, p.334: The determination made and the ethical prescription adopted to terminate one's life is known as "voluntarily-embraced death" (prayopravesana and more commonly as santhara). The practice more usually . . . involves undertaking an extended fast, ie a graduated withdrawal from the urges of life and desisting from intake of solids, fibrous substances and fluids up to the moment of death . . . . Sallekhana or terminal fast is intended to result in a peaceful passing away of the encumbent (santi-marana) or, in more ascetic terms, in a yogic or `enlightened' death (samadhi-marana).

28. Ahronheim J, Gasner M; "The Sloganism of Starvation" Lancet 1990; 335:278-279, 279: See also: Derr P, "Why Food and Fluids Can Never Be Denied" Hastings Center Report 1986; 16(1):28-30.

29. Thomasma D, Micetich K, Steinecker P, "Continuance of Nutritional Care in the Terminally I11 Patient" Critical Care Clinics 1986; 2(1):61-71, p.61.

30. Siegler M, Schiedermayer D, "Should Fluid and Nutritional Support Be Withheld from Terminally Ill Patients? - Tube Feeding in Hospice Settings" American Journal of Hospice Care March/April 1987, 32-35, p.35.

31. Billings J, "Comfort Measures for the Terminally Ill: Is Dehydration Painful?" Journal of the American Geriatrics Society 1985; 33(11):808-810, p.808: Dehydration, defined here as a loss of normal body water, is a term that is often used imprecisely to describe conditions with differing causes, symptoms, and management.

32. Ibid p.808 Nadal et al., however, suggested the important notion that quite different clinical syndromes could be associated with two prototypical forms of dehydration: sodium depletion and pure water loss.

33. Sutclife J, "Terminal Dehydration" Nursing Times 1994; 90(6):60-63, 60-61; for all these definitions and descriptions.

34. Ibid p.61. Also note: Sodium depletion is . . . sometimes called volume depletion, a term that also is imprecise but that points to the prominence in this condition of signs of circulatory insufficiency. Billings J, "Comfort Measures for the Terminally Ill: Is Dehydration Painful?" Journal of the American Geriatrics Society 1985; 33(11):808-810, p.808.

35. Kerndt P, Naughton J, Driscoll C, Loxterkamp D, "Fasting: The History, Pathophysiology and Complications" Western Journal of Medicine

1982; 137:379-399,p.379. See also: Derr, P "Why Food and Fluids Can Never Be Denied" Hastings Center Report 1986; 16(1):28-30, p.29: A social decision to permit physicians or health care facilities to deny food and fluids to patients who are capable of receiving and utilizing them, directly attacks the very foundation of medicine as an ethical profession. For Derr, the patient's wish is no justification; and he goes on (p.30) to draw an analogy with a patient who desires a botched hernia repair with massive postoperative morbidity . . . Another commentator draws a differing view: "No matter how simple, inexpensive, readily available, noninvasive and common the procedure, if it does not offer substantial hope of benefit to the patient, he has no moral obligation to undergo it, nor the physician to provide it, nor the judge to order it." Paris J, "When Burdens of Feeding Outweigh Benefits" Hastings Center Report 1986; 16(1):30-32; p.32.

36. Printz L, "Is Withholding Hydration a Valid Comfort measure in the Terminally Ill?" Geriatrics 1988, 43(1 1):84-88, p.86: "The symptoms of dying patients who are not undergoing medical hydration and nutrition are more difficult to evaluate than the laboratory data. The range of sensations, other than those of the primary disease, which have been reported vary from no distress and possible analgesia to lethargy, weakness, dry mouth, thirst, restlessness and nausea."

37. Kerndt P, Naughton J; Driscoll C, Loxterkamp D, "Fasting: The History, Pathophysiology and Complications" Western Journal of Medicine 1982; 137:379-399, p.379.

38. Ibid p.398.

39. Miller W, "The Hunger-Striking Prisoner" Journal of Prison & Jail Health 1987; 6(1):40-61, .p.44.

40. Ibid.

41. Sutcliffe J, "Terminal Dehydration" Nursing Times 1994; 90(6):60-63.

42. Collaud T, Rapin H, "Dehydration in Dying Patients: Study with Physicians in French-Speaking Switzerland" Journal of Pain and Symptom Management 1991; 6(4):230-240, p.235.

43. Keys A, Brozek J, Henschel A, Mickelsen O, Taylor H, The Biology of Human Starvation I & II, Minneapolis: University of Minnesota Press 1950, 1:587.

44. Ibid 1:45.

45. Ibid 1:575.

46. Ibid 1:576.

47. Ibid 1:577.

48. Ibid 1:577-578.

49. Ibid 1:578.

50. Ibid 1:579.

51. Ibid I:581.

52. Ibid 1:635.

53. Ibid at I, Chapter 34.

54. Winick M (ed), Hunger Disease: Studies by the Jewish Physicians in the Warsaw Ghetto, New York: John Wiley & Son 1979, p.38.

55. Ibid p.37.

56. Ibid p.38. .

57. Ibid p.39.

58. Keys A, Brozek J, Henschel A, Mickelsen O, Taylor H, The Biology of Human Starvation I & 11, Minneapolis: University of Minnesota Press 1950, 1:583.

59. Bilimoria P, "A Report from India: The Jaina Ethic of Voluntary Death" Bioethics 1992; 6(4):331-355, p.338.

60. Ibid p.335.

61. Keys A, Brozek J, Henschel A, Mickelsen O, Taylor H, The Biology of Human Starvation I & 11, Minneapolis: University of Minnesota Press 1950, 1:29.

62. Billings J; "Comfort Measures for the Terminally Ill: Is Dehydration Painful?" Journal of the American, Geriatrics Society 1985; 33(11):808-810, p.809.

63. Printz L, "Is Withholding Hydration a Valid Comfort measure in the Terminally Ill?" Geriatrics 1988, 43(11):84-88, p.84.

64. Andrews M, Levine A, "Dehydration in the Terminal Patient: Perception of Hospice Nurses" American Journal of Hospice Care Jan/Feb 1989, 31-34, p.32. (This study sent questionnaires to a total of 127 hospice programs - 41 in New Jersey and .86 in Pennsylvania.)

65. Ibid p.34.

66. Ibid p.31.

67. Ahronheim J, Gasner M, "The Sloganism of Starvation" Lancet 1990; 335:278-279,279.

68. Ibid p.278.

69. Sutcliffe J, Holmes S, "Dehydration: Benefit or Burden to the Dying Patient?" Journal of Advanced Nursing 1994; 19:71-76, p.72.

70. Bernat J, Gert B, Mogielnicki R,"Patient Refusal of Hydration and Nutrition" Archives of Internal Medicine 1993; 153:2723-2728,, p.2725-6.

71. Miller R, Albright P, "What is the Role of Nutritional Support and Hydration in Terminal Cancer Patients?" American Journal of Hospice Care Nov/Dec 1989; 33-38, p.35.

72. Frederick G, "An Easy Alternative to Assisted Suicide" Globe and Mail 23 Sep 1993 p.A 19.

73. Phillips P, Rolls B, Ledingham J, Forsling M, Morton J, Crowe M, Wollner L, "Reduced Thirst after Water Deprivation in Healthy Elderly Men" New England Journal of Medicine 1984; 311(12):753-759, p.757: A thirst deficit in the elderly subjects, as compared with the young controls, was indicated by their remarkable lack of thirst and discomfort after 24 hours of water deprivation.

74. Ibid p.757-758.

75. Keys A, Brozek J, Henschel A, Mickelsen O, Taylor H, The Biology of Human Starvation I & II, Minneapolis: University of Minnesota Press 1950, 1:583-4.

76. Sutcliffe J, "Terminal Dehydration" Nursing Times 1994; 90(6):60-63,p.60-61.

77. Kerndt P, Naughton J, Driscoll C, Loxterkamp D, "Fasting: The History, Pathophysiology and Complications" Western Journal of Medicine 1982; 137:379-399, p.396.

78. Ibid p.388.

79. Printz L, "Terminal Dehydration, a Compassionate Treatment" Archives, of Internal Medicine 1992; 152:697-700, 700(Table 2): Dry mouth can be palliated by offering frequent sips of cold water: no treatment is required for other symptoms of analgesia, lethargy and weakness. Also: Printz L, "Is Withholding Hydration a Valid Comfort Measure in the Terminally Ill?" Geriatrics 1988, 43(11):84-88, p.85: Thirst and dry mouth can be readily relieved with crushed ice or sips of fluids. Nausea can be treated with antiemetics. Also: Lichter 1, Hunt E, "The Last 48 Hours of Life" Journal of Palliative Care 1990; 6(4):7-15, p.12: Thirst is rarely a problem, and careful mouth hygiene prevents dryness of the mouth which may otherwise be a source of discomfort. Small quantities of fluids can usually be administered by dropper, and ice may be given to suck. In this way the patient can be kept comfortable. Also: Bernat J, Gert B, Mogielnicki R, "Patient Refusal, of Hydration and Nutrition" Archives of Internal Medicine 1993; 153:27232728, p.2726: Clinical experience with severely ill patients suggests that the major symptom of dry mouth can be relieved by ice chips, methyl cellulose, artificial saliva, or small sips of water insufficient to reverse progressive dehydration. While these are relatively simple palliative measures, the availability of adequate pain-relief or more aggressive palliation will be an important safeguard, especially in the final days.

80. Bernat J, Gert B, Mogielnicki R, "Patient Refusal of Hydration and Nutrition" Archives of Internal Medicine 1993; 153:2723-2728, p.2727.

A guide to suicide guides

This is an expanded version of an article previously published in Exit Newsletter *and* Beyond Final Exit. *Its purpose it so explain the history of self-deliverance guides.*

Why the need for guides?

Ironically, some of the strongest supporters of voluntary euthanasia are survivors of the Nazi holocaust – while some of the most vociferous opponents, with no experience of life in concentration camps, use such incidents as the Holocaust and the twisting of the word *euthanasia* to suggest that 'right-to-die' legislation will lead to Nazi-type abuses. Perhaps I can begin this chapter by quoting no less an authority than Lord Kagan, who, having survived a concentration camp in Lithuania during World War II, spoke up in the English Parliament in favour of being allowed to end one's own life:

"I witnessed the fears. The greatest fear was not of being killed, it was not of being dead, but the manner of one's death, the timing of one's death, the power of decision leading to one's death and not having the ability to prepare for one's death. It was not dying, it was not death, but that. There was the fear of torture without escape, without limit as to its extent and without a limit on its time.

"The most fervent prayer in the camp was to acquire the means to end one's life, to achieve the death of one's own choosing at the time of one's own choosing and in the manner of one 's own choosing. This became the ultimate liberation and the greatest prize. To achieve this in the camp one was prepared for any sacrifice and to submit to any deprivation. Having it proved to be a great comfort. It did not encourage one to use it, and this is what I should like to bring to your Lordships' attention. Having the means of the decision to end one's own life in one's own way did not encourage people to use it. It gave one strength to carry on fighting because one felt one had the means, ultimately, not to buy or extend survival at any price. It prevented the collapse of courage... It prevented the collapse of principle if one got caught and, under torture, feared one would betray one's friends.

"These are extraordinary circumstances I have witnessed, but cruelty and despair can be suffered not only at the hand of man but at the hand of nature in circumstances of illness, particularly terminal illness. Doctors and priests know more about that. But if the reaction in despair is similar to the one which I have seen and lived with, then is it not time not only to stop making the end of one's life a crime, but to establish it as a right?"[1]

Difficult beginnings

In July 1979, a few years before Lord Kagan's speech, EXIT – The Voluntary Euthanasia Society (Great Britain) decided that a booklet on how to end one's own life would be a good idea, passing a resolution to that effect at their Annual General Meeting in October. After publicly announcing their plans, membership rose, from an initial 2000 members, at a rate of 1000 a month over the next six months while the booklet, to be called *A Guide to Self-Deliverance,* was being drafted. The Society was undergoing a new radicalism and an upsurge in its popularity. Membership, in expectation of such a book from their own Committee, had now risen to 10,000. But publication of the book was contentious within the Committee. Following a motion of no confidence, at their October Annual General Meeting, the membership sacked 11 of the 12 members of the Committee and appointed new people, all pledged to publishing the booklet as originally promised. But four days later, Dr Scott, a testy member of the Society, took out a private injunction to halt publication. In June 1980 two top legal opinions had given contradictory views on the likelihood of prosecution for such a booklet. Amid the controversy, the VES committee, in July, again decided not to publish.[2]

HOW TO DIE
WITH DIGNITY

4204

by
George B. Mair

Original numbered copy of *How to Die With Dignity*
– the first book of its kind to be published anywhere in the world

The Scottish Region Branch of EXIT was appalled and voted on August 16th to publish such a booklet themselves. The next day, Larry Hill, the acting Chairman in England, telephoned George Mair, the Scottish Organizer, forbidding such an action.

George Mair was a hospital doctor who five years previously had published his autobiographical account of grim realities at the end of life. Called *Confessions of a Surgeon,* it had provoked a stormy reaction. Mair, born in Troon, taught surgery at Law Hospital in Lanarkshire, and subsequently became the Director of the Medical Clinic in Central Scotland. Widely travelled, he had led many Royal Scottish Geographical Society expeditions. He was also a former member of the Crime Writers' Association, to whom he attributed a certain 'meticulousness and thoroughness' in research, and in finding ingenious ways of causing death. It should be possible, he said, to at least apply "some method of choice to oneself rather than to another in order to achieve self-deliverance." He was no newcomer to controversy: In Confessions of a Surgeon he had admitted practicing euthanasia.

At an emergency meeting on 17th August, the Scottish Branch declared independence from England in order to go ahead and publish a self-deliverance booklet, even though their kitty was empty.[3] The booklet was called *How to Die With Dignity,* written by Dr George Mair, and published in September 1980 from Scotland. It was the first booklet of its kind anywhere in the world. Based on the knowledge of a single doctor, the information, by today's standards, was rather primitive. Statements about the law were hazy to say the least. But it survived in its original form for 13 years, with minor additions in the form of short supplements. (The Scottish Society struggles on to this day, often with minimal funds, and managed to keep going largely by way of periodic gifts and legacies.)

In March 1981, the injunction against the English booklet was withdrawn, but the Society was forced to pay most of the legal costs.[4] In June, 1981, The English group finally published *A Guide To Self-Deliverance.* This booklet, like the Scottish *How to Die With Dignity,* listed various drugs that were probably lethal. (The two books were unconnected, excepting that they arose from the same initial idea. Authorship and texts were also entirely different, though similar in spirit to each other.) Litigation, or the threat of litigation however would continue. In April 1982, the Attorney General sought a declaration demanding that the English society stop distribution and destroy any remaining copies. The action was contested, and in 1983 the Attorney General's declaration was refused. Mr Justice Woolf, refusing the declaration, also made it clear that knowingly supplying the booklet to someone intending to commit suicide was risking prosecution. The English society said that it would be "inadvisable to resume distribution of the Guide," and soon withdrew the *Guide to Self-Deliverance*. A report on their AGM in 1984 also mentions publishers refusing to publish their proposed booklet 'after taking legal advice.' 8,000 copies had been sold

A big disadvantage facing anyone writing such a book at this time was that very little was known about the dosage of any drug that could be relied upon 100% to cause death. The Guide freely admitted that, "lethal doses given are not based on the sort of careful experimentation which now guides most treatment".[5] Most of the information that we have now was not available at that time.[6] Interestingly, it made some mention of tricyclic antidepressants[7] – drugs that were bypassed by the Scottish booklet and most other guides until the advent of *Departing Drugs*.[8] Similarly chloroquine was not mentioned, or the modern physical methods that use as compression or helium.

Manuals published in other countries
Several booklets appeared from continental right-to-die societies – in France, Germany, Belgium, Switzerland – all with a similar format to that of the short-lived English book, or rather the Scottish counterpart. English-speaking people from abroad joined the Scottish Society to obtain Dr Mair's book, but lack of funds and fear of prosecution had precluded the publicity necessary to inform a wider audience.

Then, in 1982, a French book, *Suicide – Mode d'Emploi* appeared on the bookshelves and caused a furor.[9] The French Society's own, more conservative book, *Autodeliverance,* was published the same year. Unlike the European right-to-die societies who stipulated a three-month waiting period before members could purchase a manual, *Suicide - Mode d'Emploi* was on open sale. Its approach was anarchistic, including details of how to forge doctors' prescriptions for lethal drugs as well as some 50 'recipes' for lethal cocktails. The publishers gave interviews expressing optimism about the massive profits they anticipated and the book quickly found a firm place on the French bestseller lists by that April.[10]

Around the same time, a rather more responsible approach was seen in America, where, constitutionally, there seemed less question of being unable to publish such manuals. Derek Humphry, a journalist who had helped his terminally-ill first wife to die at her own repeated request,[11] had by this time spent years researching dying, especially through case-studies which people had brought to him. Incorporating drug information into the text of a general book might be a way of introducing such information to the bookshelves without the tables and 'recipes' of the other manuals that might so easily be abused by the suicidally depressed, and Humphry achieved this to some considerable degree in *Let Me Die Before I Wake.*[12] Initially sold only to members of the Hemlock Society, the book was eventually extended and made available to the public.[13] Later editions also included an index, making it possible to look up drug references without reading the whole book. Tricyclic drugs are mentioned in passing in *Let Me Die,* though omitted from Humphry's later book, *Final Exit.*[14] Political infighting[15] broke out in America over the publication of *Let Me Die* but sales grew and paved the way for a bestseller, *Final Exit,* in 1991.

In both books Humphry attempted to make use of the best knowledge available in standard medical manuals and further supplemented his extensive anecdotal knowledge by consulting the work of Dutch euthanasists.[16] *Final Exit* quickly became an international bestseller and helped to establish the name of Derek Humphry internationally.

Scientific and multidisciplinary cooperation

At the International Conference in 1992[17] I tried to find out if anyone had scientifically collated evidence on self-deliverance drugs. We were distributing *Final Exit* to our members, as well as *How to Die With Dignity,* yet there seemed to be little or no agreement within the scientific community about what drugs and what dosages could be relied on to cause death. As a young delegate with little authority it was extremely difficult to challenge the status quo, but I found there were indeed several quiet voices who were concerned about the lack of any really scientific research. As an initial project, I invited Cheryl Smith, then staff attorney for Hemlock, if she would like to investigate a drug called chloroquine with me that was mentioned in the German society's booklets but not in any other manuals. This almost backfired two years later. Smith was no longer working for Hemlock when she started work on literature searches and co-editing *Departing Drugs*, but this didn't prevent a senior ex-Harvard lawyer from Hemlock making an attempt to seize the finished manuscript – on the basis that they 'owned' material which Smith had worked on while with Hemlock. The attempt was sternly rebuffed. Fortunately relations with Hemlock otherwise were excellent – one of their directors, Faye Girsch being particularly supportive (Faye went on to receive a Lifetime Achievement award).

There were many strong opinions being bandied around about chloroquine, for and against, but nobody seemed to have any reliable evidence. In the months following the conference, we collected folder upon folder of published research from medical journals on chloroquine. By using good medical libraries and computerised search facilities we were able to uncover a wealth of information – why had nobody looked before now? Debates over chloroquine caused much concern, but could be pursued with considerable intellectual rigour thanks to the vast amount of published information. The project culminated in a scientific paper,[19] which, after professional pre-review for accuracy,[20] was published by both VESS and Hemlock and reprinted in the Canadian magazine, *Last Rights*. (April-May, 1993)

The success of the chloroquine paper was offset by the fact that it not only challenged but disproved conventional ideas about its use for rational suicide. Research also showed that the drugs to be combined with chloroquine to achieve sedation before death needed to be chosen carefully, and the German society, who had initially alerted us to the drug's potential, withdrew their booklet which at that time had only limited information.

Departing Drugs — the first scientific manual on rational suicide
The methods used to research chloroquine could obviously be applied to other drugs. Cheryl Smith left Hemlock after completing the project on chloroquine and I invited her to cooperate on a new drugs book. She had contributed substantially to Humphry's work on *Final Exit*, was well versed in the subject and also aware of the limitations of methodology employed to date. We applied the same techniques of computerised search, repeating our efforts in various leading libraries and using different computer databases, acquiring vast amounts of material that then needed to be sifted through and collated. But published medical information alone was not enough.

What of the cases where people had followed the advice of 'experts' in trying to take their own lives but not been successful? Interviews followed, the most striking being from eyewitness accounts of failed suicides. Weaknesses in earlier manuals were eventually identified with some certainty, and medical hypotheses re-examined with greater scrutiny. Many errors in self-deliverance information result from following doctors' advice. This is a very flawed approach. Doctors are trained and qualified in how to keep people alive, not in what quantity of a drug will reliably cause death. They generally offer little more than educated guesses, and we had to provide meticulously documented evidence to overthrow the opinions of many doctors. Similarly, pharmacists and pharmaceutical manuals give an idea of what quantity of a drug *may* be dangerous or lethal, but not how much is reliably so. This is largely due to two factors: the drugs testing by pharmaceutical companies (aimed, in this respect, mostly to establish the limits of safe doses) and the data provided on this basis. 'A lethal dose', in pharmaceutical terms, simply means someone has died or might die from such a dose, which is very different from saying that no-one taking such a dose will survive. This is why *failures* have always played such a big part in our research, as they allow us to go back to the drawing board and question original assumptions.

A similar reservation applies to knowledge obtained by first-hand observation – either by assisting someone to die or being present. Just because a method has worked well for several people is no proof in itself that it will work in all or even most cases. Our knowledge of failures came from several sources, including letters and phone calls from our own members, but also from the Dutch society NVVE and a counsellor in California, Stephen Jamison, and others. With this data, we were able to refine the advice in the booklet to minimise the chance of failure or make the instructions sufficiently fool-proof to be relied on with confidence. Our final drafts were however checked by medically qualified experts to ensure we had not overlooked anything. The process was largely one of negation, to rule out inaccuracies or unsuitable methods or flaws by a process of subtracting them or re-submitting them until no flaws could be found by any of the scrutinizing processes.

I sent the early draft to over 40 individuals around the world who might have some expertise to add. Their comments were carefully examined. Finally, evidence was forthcoming from the Netherlands[21] which showed that some patients self-administering euthanasia, in a hospital and under clinical conditions, had taken 10g of barbiturate and yet survived in a coma for up to several days. A doctor in the Netherlands in this situation can administer a further drug to speed death, and tests in such circumstances on dextropropoxyphene and orphenadrine (considered usefully lethal by previous self-deliverance manuals) also threw doubt on the efficacy of these drugs. Knowledge of drugs, particularly barbiturates, has evolved considerably, and the properties of different classes of barbiturate are now better understood. The long coma of a person taking barbiturates in the Netherlands is not a problem there, but to isolated individuals in other parts of the world it poses the worry of discovery and resuscitation.

Arguments over the best way to use the 'plastic bag', and what drugs were effective with this method were resolved, but only finalised at the Working Party's meeting in July 1993. Physical calculations were made, based on published data, concerning air volume (and hence bag size); evidence of failed suicides and medical data combined to ascertain drug suitabilities (especially regarding speed of action and depth of sedation), and practical experiments made to confirm comfort in a suitably-sized bag for the given period. The draft was revised and checked several times. Smith repeatedly worked into the early hours of the morning with me after the Working Party Meeting while we checked and double-checked that data was presented accurately. Then the final draft was circulated to the rest of the Working Party for approval with its copious reference lists and glossaries. It contained clear descriptions of methods and drugs, in simple easy-to-understand language, but not omitting precise technical details and references.

An extensive glossary covered hundreds of brand-name drugs and explanations about the most common drugs queries was added. Dozens of drugs were mentioned for the first time in a self-deliverance publication. A country-by-country appendix gave specific brand names for particular countries. There were sections dealing with obtaining drugs abroad, storage of drugs, buying drugs and obtaining prescription drugs. There were step-by-step sections on different methods as well as an 'essentials checklist' and sections covering legal and financial concerns relating to self-deliverance. An extensive bibliography was included to encourage further research into specific areas. Myths on many drugs were exploded. No longer need self-deliverance books be a collection of doctors' opinions or anecdotal evidence.

Distribution and safeguards
Departing Drugs is available to members of right-to-die societies who have been members for at least three months. The Working Party agreed certain conditions to be strictly imposed: i) a 3 months' wait, ii) *Departing Drugs* to be a non-profit venture, iii) absolutely no alteration or addition to the agreed text. These conditions were drawn up into the form of a legal

contract by Smith (who fortuitously combined a law degree with a medical background: a rare occurrence).

To enforce the non-profit condition more stringently and to enable it to reach more readers at minimal cost, the Working Party authorised it to be published and distributed by myself (for EXIT/VESS) in Sterling, by Smith in US dollars and by John Hofsess[22] (for RTDSC) in Canadian dollars. Legal contracts were signed by these distributors but giving no authority to the parent societies: signatories are held individually responsible. Each had the task of distributing the new book with only minimal funds. None of the people on the Working Party received any payment – neither are they allowed to make profit, either personally or on behalf of a society. Societies publishing the book under licence would do so free of charge and without royalties to the original authors. It was with this attitude of self-sacrifice and beneficence that we hoped to continue to evince the services of top experts that had been invaluable so far and could probably never be bought.

German, French and Spanish translations would also be subject to similar safeguards. Why so much fuss? Why not just publish and pass the profits to the right-to-die societies? For one answer, we look at articles such as *Increase in Suicide by Asphyxiation in New York after the Publication of Final Exit* (published in the *New England Journal of Medicine*).[23] A demand for self-deliverance books and their availability in the bookshops may increase public awareness and help to reach those who need them, but it also evokes the criticism of making information available irresponsibly to suicidally depressed individuals who might use it irrationally instead of solving their temporary emotional or psychological problems. We have to take such criticisms seriously if we are to maintain serious respect as a movement. Interestingly, one study noted of plastic bag asphyxia in Scotland noted that, "In contrast with reports from the United States, publicity associated with 'self-deliverance' did not result in an increased number of deaths from plastic bag asphyxia."[24] *Departing Drugs* also went much further than manuals such as *Final Exit,* since it contained information about over-the-counter drugs and easy-to-obtain prescription drugs. So it became even more pressing to have strict safeguards to try to ensure it was properly used. Ironically, although the cooperation from Europe, Australia and New Zealand was warm, and helpful in ensuring that their members could get the book, political problems from several societies in North America hindered sales, and, although *Departing Drugs* is probably the single most important development in self-deliverance (or auto-euthanasia), several world federation right-to-die societies avoided mentioning it.

From 1993 to the present
In Britain, the legality of publishing information that can be used for suicide has never been properly tested in court. The Canadian publication, *Last Rights*, in its *Beyond Final Exit*[25] series, was at the time probably the only regular source of information on new developments in this field that you could read. Most 'good ideas' about methods of suicide are not such good ideas in practice, and the series was fortunately able to expose the shortcomings of such hopes as street drugs or toxic plants. As the available space in *Departing Drugs* was limited for detailed scientific information useful to the lay reader, some of the more technical analysis of the findings encountered in researching that book were still to be published. *Last Rights* eventually ceased publication, but not before publishing the *Departing Drugs* research articles – in a book also called *Beyond Final Exit* (1995).

Exit's dwindling resources meant reassessing priorities, but Exit's governing body saw that self-deliverance was not only the original reason for the formation of the Society but the one area where Exit could still make a vital difference. Self-deliverance updates were therefore published in the Newsletter. Also published in 1993 – although only in Japanese – was a best-seller by Kanzen Jisatsu Manyuaru, unconnected with the right-to-die movement. Called *The Complete Manual of Suicide*, the book was not concerned with dignity, only assessing methods according to pain, effort, lethality and the appearance of the body after death. In 1995, *Mild Death* was published. The author was M.Verzele, a chemist interested in the right-to-die. In style, it has some similarities to Geo Stone's much later and much lengthier *Suicide and Attempted Suicide: Methods and Consequences (1999)*; But its focus on methods that it admits are unsuitable (a great number) makes it more of a curiosity item than a practical guide. There have been two main advances in suicide methods since the 1990's: the use of helium and the application of compression techniques.

Although helium was mentioned in *Last Rights*, its practical use, particularly in the USA, led to the technique becoming more widely accepted. It was dealt with in some detail in the third edition of Humphry's book *Final Exit*[26] and in the article '*Before the Lights Go Out – Revisiting Asphyxia*' in *Exit Newsletter*[27]. A great asset to the development of knowledge both of helium and of compression techniques (where the oxygen supply to the brain is cut off) was a ground breaking book from outside the right-to-die movement in 1999 called *Suicide and Attempted Suicide*[28] and written by a pharmacologist. Exit has largely pioneered the use of the compression technique[29] through its UK-wide workshops. Apart from Geo Stone's book, *Five Last Acts* is the only major self-deliverance work detailing the use of ligatures, tourniquets and compression for rational suicide.

Exit, like the Swiss organisation *Dignitas,*[30] receives no recognition or assistance from the large World Federation of Right to Die Societies[31] and works on a tiny shoe-string, developing the key practices and methods that the larger, wealthier organisations and their members rely on.[32]

In 2006, Philip Nitschke co-authored *The Peaceful Pill Handbook*[33], which included mention of the helium method (the title was derived from the theoretical desirability of a pill for suicide, rather than indicating its existence). The book had a strong emphasis on technical processes, including making one's own barbiturates (wearing protective goggles) or obtaining barbiturates illegally from Mexico. Such lengths are too extreme for most people to readily recommend: the barbiturate-making process is hazardous and difficult (as well as illegal) and obtaining drugs from abroad is fraught with problems, especially considering the straightforward nature of the helium and compression techniques. Yet Nitschke's energy and enthusiasm is unmistakeable – whether or not it is well-directed will be left for the future to decide. The case for obtaining drugs from Mexico, fraught as it is with danger, is put convincingly in his book and with considerable detail.

Since 1993, Exit has received a number of requests to 'update' *Departing Drugs* but the advice contained in it has not really changed. The extensive list of local names of various drugs around the world could be updated, but as generic names are provided with any drugs literature this is easy for individuals to check rather than for Exit to expend the exorbitant time, money and effort obtaining the dispensing information from countries around the world and reprint. The main update needed was not on drugs but on physical methods.

Five Last Acts

First published in 2007, Five Last Acts[34] was the most comprehensive book on self-deliverance techniques to date. Although *Exit Newsletter* has provided necessary updates on self-deliverance methods, ordering back-copies was not an ideal way of collecting all the information in one place. Self-deliverance workshops across the UK over several years have demonstrated that people want to know the *best practical methods*. Additionally some people want to know how to *check the information* by reference to more academic articles. When there are several good, reliable methods available, with relatively easy-to-obtain drugs and equipment, it makes limited sense to embark on a holy grail for (difficult-to-obtain) barbiturates or knowledge of wild and wacky methods. The aim of *Five Last Acts* was to condense everything you need to know in one slim volume, presenting the best, properly validated methods, but with sufficient background material to do your own corroborating research if you desire. Publishing an international book from a tiny, under-resourced office had many problems. When the book came back from the printers, the binders flatly refused to finish the order. One of their man customers was a medical publisher who they felt might be 'offended.' After a desperate last minute search, and the printers wanting to know where to deliver the unbound books, a new binders was secured. Volunteers helped bag the books ready for despatch. Demand was considerable and, especially when one factored in interest from abroad, soon beyond Exit's ability to satisfy fully without a further print run.

Other guides

A number of other books have appeared on self-deliverance. You may want to browse them for background reading and ideas – it will help you think your ideas through – but apart from *Departing Drugs* and *Beyond Final Exit* we cannot vouch for the accuracy of the information and advice. Many of them contain well-meaning and reassuring recommendations that do not stand up to critical examination – just because the author 'knows someone' who used a specific method or is a medical doctor is, in itself, no guarantee. Humphry's *Final Exit* has become a standard and the most widely available book of its kind; but it gives a broad sweep rather than including details of methods such as compression.

A rather less-successful attempt (in our opinion) was a book called *Guide to Self-Chosen Death*[35] by Wozz Foundation. This was a strange mix of excellent work and muddled production. Two of the authors, Chabot and Ogden, produce first-rate right-to-die –related work in their own fields. Chabot's work on self-denial of food and drink added essential field work to theory on this method of self-deliverance. Ogden's first-hand observations of helium deaths provided a number of well-documented cases. But this team of gifted people were nevertheless responsible for wrongly attributing the dangerous chloroquine-zopiclone combination to Exit, basing their conclusions on an illegally and dangerously adulterated copy of *Departing Drugs* that was being distributed by the Dutch euthanasia society, NVVE. (If readers can separate facts that are correctly documented from ones that are not, or conclusions that are barely justified, the slim volume does however have something to offer.) And without its clues on the misappropriation of *Departing Drugs* materials by the Dutch organisation, Exit would probably not have noticed the dangerously misleading breach of copyright. One of the authors privately suggested that it had simply been a case of not being clear over which author would be responsible for checking which sections. For all its flaws, the book helped to stimulate interest in self-deliverance briefly and also provided the Dutch organisation with a self-deliverance manual for their members when

Exit, in view of the bad faith exhibited NVVE, revoked overseas distribution rights for the Dutch translation of *Departing Drugs.*

A slim volume by Boudewijn Chabot entitled *A hastened death by self-denial of food and drink*[36] offered a stepping stone in the much-misunderstood method of starvation ('self-denial of food and drink' also being a more accurately descriptive phrase for the process). Chabot collected empirical data on 110 individuals who had died by this method and expanded on the chapter in the 2007 edition of *Five Last Acts.* Chabot's study added considerable detail on the practical management of this technique. One campaign group, known as Friends At The End[37] (Fate), distributed Chabot's book zealously, as well as a pamphlet on the technique, but soon became embroiled in adverse press coverage as at least one person died horren-dously.[38] The families of two women who consulted Fate for advice on the method described their mothers' deaths as 'horrific.'[39] Friends At The End had splintered off from Exit in 2000 in order to provide a befriending service. Exit believed such a service would create a conflict of duties. Providing self-deliverance information lawfully (using the legal device of *novus actus interveniens*) is technically only possible when there is not one-to-one advice with the person immediately intending to use it. Exit had been formed with the intention of researching and providing reliable self-deliverance information as a priority. The majority of the balloted membership overwhelm-ingly supported maintaining the same solid basis for research, development and publication. The Fate group, led by Libby Wilson and unwilling to accept Exit's priorities, was expelled. Some years later, Wilson was arrested on suspicion of assisting in the suicide of Cari Loder, although the authorities, after lengthy delays, decided that it was not in the public interest to proceed with a prosecution.

Chabot's study patients had died in carefully controlled environments. Self-denial of food and drink, like self-deliverance through chloroquine, is not a method that can be recommended lightly: it requires comprehensive preparation and risks dire results if not completed carefully. Fate's founders were wrong to advocate so publicly the stopping of food and drink as a method to be followed without greater precautions against people dying badly by the method. Chabot's book, like *Five Last Acts*, makes it clear that such a course is a difficult path to take, requiring both understanding and backup. One of Fate's members, Michael Irwin, was more successful in assisting some people travelling to Switzerland for assisted suicide at Dignitas, similarly challenging the DPP to prosecute, and the group's role may be more valuable in terms of important civil disobedience work than providing self-deliverance information. (Dr Irwin has more recently been connected with yet another group, called Soars.)

Updates to Five Last Acts
Frustrated at the logistics and costs of distributing accurate self-deliverance materials, Exit in 2009 published a major update on self-deliverance methods in a bumper edition of its magazine, with eleven pages devoted to helium alone.[40] The moral dilemma of making direct and accurate instructions on self-deliverance hard-to-get (so as not to fall into the hands of youngsters, people temporarily suicidally depressed, or those without capacity) had to be balanced against the danger of people obtaining less reliable information which was easier to access and could prove insufficient, resulting in an even more gruesome death. It wasn't so much a case of making *new* information available (although a considerable amount of supportive methodology had come to light since the first edition): it was making it easier to understand and put into practice safely and securely. Much of the new developments

had come from Exit workshops in the intervening period. If you have nine groups of up to twenty people experimenting, a lot of things come to light. Whether it is how to make an 'Exit Bag,' the simplest way to achieve effective compression with differing neck lengths, or even little practicalities like how to turn a stiff gas tap by small increments. The ins and outs become much clearer when you have many different people of differing backgrounds and physical abilities (or disabilities) all trying them out in dress rehearsals.[41]

The current volume is available through Exit at a reduced price but with the same stringent requirements such as proof of age and discretionary delays to deter the foolhardy. The Internet price is greater, partly to dissuade youngsters who try to order it, perhaps with a parent's credit card. Exit has become a distributor rather than publisher, and is not responsible for Internet sales. (These recommendations were made after much soul-searching by the Exit Board.)[42]

What next?
Developing the frontiers in self-deliverance relies on a very small band of dedicated people, often living and working with little or no pay. Your purchase – whether of this book, a membership of Exit, or donations and legacies – all help that work to happen. Not only is your money going to an excellent, near-unique cause, but as a member you are among the first people to have access to the best expert advice and get the information for peace of mind at the end of life. Exit currently works with just one member of staff (the present author) and frequently can't afford to pay wages. Additionally, I would like to retire at some point! Perhaps most of the work on self-deliverance has been done. Perhaps a bill through parliament allowing assisted suicide and voluntary euthanasia with appropriate safeguards will come to pass and make the work

redundant. Until then, there's still much to be done.

References

1. The passage is taken from his speech in support of Lord Jenkins' attempt to modify the laws on assisted suicide and reprinted in The Euthanasia Review Vol. 1(2) Summer 1986:120-126.
2. Exit. A Guide to Self-Deliverance (1981):32 A Chronology.
3. Minutes of the Executive Committee Meetings 16/17 August 1980. By the date of this meeting, sufficient funds had been donated to make a part-payment to the printers.
4. Exit, supra. *See also:* Kemp N, Merciful release – The history of the British euthanasia movement, Manchester University Press 2002. *See also:* Ferguson P, Killing "Without Getting Into Trouble"? Assisted Suicide and Scots Criminal Law, ELR 2(3) Sep 1998 pp288-314. The case involving the Attorney General's attempt to stop the book was, *Attorney-General v. Able* [1984] QB 795.
5. Ibid.p.19.
6. Chloroquine is a notable exception - hundreds of case studies had already been published in medical journals, but largely overlooked until examined in The Chloroquine Controversy. Correct use of chloroquine was first explained in Departing Drugs, qv infra.
7. For an analysis of the literature on tricyclic antidepressants, see: Smith C, Tricyclic Antidepressants and Suicide (1993) Last Rights No.l0:43-45.)
8. Docker C, Smith C (eds) and The International Drugs Consensus Working Party (Docker C, Smith C, Brewer C, Schobert K, and another). Departing Drugs - the International Supplement to How to Die With Dignity. (1993) Edinburgh: VESS. Reprinted in Victoria BC: RTDSC. (The fifth member of the Working Party, from Netherlands, agreed to give evidence on condition of anonymity).
9. Guillon C, Le Bonniec Y. Suicide - Mode d'Emploi - histoire, technique, actualite. Paris: Alain Moreau 1982. The rather gruesome nonchalance of Mode d'Emploi is repeated even more fully in a new Japanese bestseller called The Complete Manual of Suicide by Wataru Tsurumi, that includes such 'gems' as the location of suitably high buildings or how to lock oneself in the refrigerator.
10. Going Gentle into That Good Night in: Time, March 21, 1983; France's "How-To" Suicide Text Object of Outrage, Brisk Sales by Carolyn Lesh, Associated Press. Both news items were reproduced in Compassionate Crimes, Broken Taboos (1986) Los Angeles: The Hemlock Society, ed. D Humphry.

11. Humphry D. Jean's Way. London/New York: Quartet 1978.
12. Humphry D. Let Me Die Before I Wake - Hemlock's book of self-deliverance for the dying. Los Angeles: Hemlock; Member's draft 1981, First edition 1982.
13. Ibid, from a statement on origins and purposes at the front of the 1987 edition.
14. Humphry D. Final Exit - The Practicalities of Self-Deliverance and Assisted Suicide for the Dying. Oregon: The Hemlock Society 1991.
15. Humphry D, Wickett A, The Right to Die - Understanding Euthanasia. London: Bodley Head 1986: ppll3-114.
16. Such as: Admiraal P. Justifiable Euthanasia - A Manual for the Medical Profession. Amsterdam: NVVE 1983 (English translation: 1984). 11pp. Early drugs-manual issued to doctors in the Netherlands to guide them if they decided to assist dying. Its information is now considered out of date but no update has yet been printed in English.
17. World Federation of Right to Die Societies 9th Biennial International Conference, Kyoto.
18. Deutsche Gesellschaft fur Humanes Sterben, Medicaments List. Booklet of the German right-to-die society. No longer issued.
19. Docker C, Smith C. The Chloroquine Controversy. VESS Newsletter April 1993.
20. Pre-publication review by Dr Colin Brewer MB. MRCS. DPM. MRCPsych, Medical Director of The Stapleford Centre, London.
21. Unpublished research presented at the first meeting of the International Drugs Consensus Working Party, Edinburgh, 10-11 July 1993.
22. Hofsess had supplied me gratis with extensive medical material from Canada, pharmaceutical manuals, and had even promptly researched specifics by phone and fax for me to ascertain availability of Canadian brand-names. His magazine Last Rights demonstrated considerable publishing capabilities and the Working Party had no hesitation in deciding to make him the Canadian outlet for the book. Hofsess and Humphry would later help to develop the 'helium method,' sharing ideas through their 'NuTech' Group in 1999 (*See*: Côté R, In Search of Gentle Death – A Brief History of the NuTech Group, Corinthian Books 2009.)
23. New England Journal of Medicine, 11 November 1993. Observing these criticisms does not minimize the ground-breaking work of Final Exit in bringing the dilemmas of self-deliverance to the attention of the world.
24. Jones L, Wyatt J, Busuttil A, Plastic bag asphyxia in southeast Scotland, American Journal of Forensic Medical Pathology, 2000 Dec;21(4):401-5.
25. Beyond Final Exit was both the name of the series of articles in Last Rights and the name of the Departing Drugs companion work that

gathered the articles together in a single volume. Both are now out of print, but all the key articles have been reprinted or updated in Exit Newsletter. The title 'Beyond Final Exit' was connected with Derek Humphry's book Final Exit inasmuch the editor of Last Rights wanted to extend and refine the Humphry's work by way of the Last Rights series of articles.

26. Humphry D, Final Exit #3 - The Practicalities of Self Deliverance and Assisted Suicide for the Dying, New York: Dell Publishing 2002.

27. Docker C, Before the Lights Go Out (revisiting asphyxia) in: Exit Newsletter Vol 23(1) Edinburgh: April 2003.

28. Stone G, Suicide and Attempted Suicide, New York: Carroll & Graf 1999.

29. Covered in some detail in Exit Newsletters Vol 21(3) (Letters) Autumn 2001 and 24(1) July 2004 (whole edition).

30. Dignitas is the small German organisation that has afforded many people from the UK the chance of assisted suicide at their clinic.

31. The World Federation of Right to Die Societies (WFRDS) is a would-be 'umbrella' group for societies worldwide. It claims to provide "an international link for organisations working to secure or protect the rights of individuals to self-determination at the end of their lives." Exit seceded due to the high WFRDS membership fees and the perception that the WFDS "was not demonstrating it was pursuing efficient means to further the cause of voluntary euthanasia". Exit's motions for improving the basis of the WFRDS by a basic code of ethics, although passed, was not implemented, and Exit noted that at the last Board meeting - admission to which being one of the few benefits of WF membership - the time was spent chiefly on discussion of the internal constitution, and at considerable expense, and that discussion of matters relating to v.e. was shelved. (Comments are taken from Exit's official statements in July 1997 Newsletter.)

32. Departing Drugs is provided on a non-profit basis to members of other societies and is distributed under licence in several languages by foreign right to die societies. Exit Newsletter is sent on a complimentary basis to some right to die societies worldwide.

33. Nitschke P, Stewart F, The Peaceful Pill Handbook, Exit International US Ltd 2006. (Exit International US and other organisations using the name Exit in various forms are not connected with Exit, which is an international organisation based in Edinburgh, Scotland).

34. Docker C, Five Last Acts (1st edition) published by Exit, 2007.

35. Admiraal P, Chabot B, Ogden R, Rietveld A, Glerum J, Guide to Humane Self-Chosen Death, WOZZ Foundation, Macdonald 2006. First edition in Dutch, 2003. "The Foundation was established in 2001 by four

doctors. The WOZZ is independent, but it works with the Dutch Voluntary Euthanasia Society . . ."

36. Chabot B, A hastened death by self-denial of food and drink, Amsterdam 2008.

37. Friends At The End were formed after the membership of Exit voted overwhelmingly to expel retired doctor, Libby Wilson, who subsequently set up her own group and is their medical adviser.

38. 'Terminally ill opt for suicide by starvation,' by Sarah-Kate Templeton, Sunday Times, March 8th, 2009.

39. 'Retired GPs advise terminally ill on suicide by starvation,' by Simon Johnson, The Telegraph, 8th March, 2009. While such guidance might have been ill-advised medically, the principle of *novus actus interveniens* would suggest that there was no danger of legal prosecution. This was not case with Cari Loder, when an arrest was made following guidance on using helium. *See for instance:* McGinty S, Interview, The Scotsman 2nd Oct 2009, http://news.scotsman.com/euthanasia/Interview-Libby-Wilson-doctor.5697694.jp accessed 6 Sep 2010.

40. Docker C, Helium uncovered, in: Exit Newsletter Vol.29 No.3, November 2009. It includes many of the details reproduced in this volume, as well as photographs from te workshops showing participants engaged in making their own helium hoods.

41. The author conducted Exit workshops in Edinburgh, Glasgow, Aberdeen, Manchester, Leeds, Birmingham, Wolverhampton, Derby, Nottingham, Bristol and London. Workshop duration was either one full day or a two-day session.

42. Board recommendations, 2010.

Ethical questions on publication

WHAT ARE THE ETHICAL QUESTIONS TO BE ASKED OVER WHETHER TO PUBLISH SELF-DELIVERANCE INFORMATION?

nb this is not a 'how to end one's life' chapter – it instead aims to put the publication on a firmer ethical foundation. The formatting is changed to make arguments easier on the eye for readers. For readers who wish to skip some of the formal analysis steps, it is also possible to get a brief picture by reading it 'backwards' – skipping forward to the last section (Ethical Decision to Publish) and working towards the earlier sections, through the references provided, to understand the supporting structures, argument and research.

As the final draft of this book drew near, I became ever more aware that, although it is a very important and controversial issue, there has been very little in the way of attempts to analyse the ethics of publishing self-deliverance information. I can't expect to fill that gap. Neither is this essay a purely philosophical examination. But hopefully it may at least perhaps try to break some difficult ground.

Have you ever felt a time when you were so very, very sure of something – and then at the last moment felt a sudden doubt?

A paper was published in the American Journal of Forensic Medicine and Pathology recently entitled: "Suicide By Asphyxiation Due to Helium Inhalation." This is of interest to any researcher on methods of self-deliverance. But as I read the fourth sentence of the abstract, with a completed *Five Last Acts* transcript in my hand, I shuddered:

The 10 asphyxial suicides involving helium identified in North Carolina tended to occur almost exclusively in non-

Hispanic, white men who were relatively young (M age 41.1 +/- 11.6). In 6 of 10 cases, decedents suffered from significant psychiatric dysfunction; in 3 of these 6 cases, psychiatric disorders were present comorbidly with substance abuse. In none these cases were decedents suffering from terminal illness. Most persons committing suicide with helium were free of terminal illness but suffered from psychiatric and/or substance use disorders.[1]

It made me pause. Would publishing this book be irresponsible? Would it indeed be unquestionably the 'right' thing to do?[2] Or could it cause irreparable harm that I would regret the rest of my life? Even beyond that, is there not a duty to set out a defensible ethical position when dealing with something so weighty as to involve potentially the life and death of others? It is not just a rallying cry for the legalisation of physician assisted suicide.

I was under no contractual obligation. I have to seriously question the next step. I imagine someone who dies needlessly. The pain those who care for them will feel. Perhaps even a parent whose teenage child ends their life prematurely. Unlikely? Perhaps. Impossible? No.

---

[1] Howard M, Hall M, Edwards J, et al, *Suicide By Asphyxiation Due to Helium Inhalation,* Am J Forensic Med Pathol, post author corrections, 20 July 2010.

[2] This essay focuses on the rights and wrongs of publishing self-deliverance information. It is beyond the scope here to look at the rights and wrongs of suicide and even euthanasia in general. These have been well rehearsed elsewhere. For instance, Keown J, *Euthanasia examined* CUP 1995. *Also:* Dworkin R, *Life's Dominion,* Harper Collins 1993. *Also:* Donnelly J (ed.) *Suicide – Right or Wrong?* Prometheus 1998. *Also:* Kuhse H (ed.) *Willing to listen, Wanting to die,* Penguin 1994. *Also:* Rachels J, *The End of Life,* OUP 1986.

Exit's previous policy has been to make such information available only via its membership, requiring up to three months wait to dissuade unconsidered suicide, and also requiring formal proof that the person is over 21 years. Although reserving the right to refuse to supply such material, Exit does not generally screen applicants on moral, psychological or medical grounds as to do so would introduce too many variables that could not be adequately monitored, not to mention legal problems.

Now in a position of contemplating wider dissemination, Exit (and the present author) must answer questions about ethical policy. Exit's income is not derived from such books, and its constitution allows it to focus on other areas such as political campaigning and living wills, so it does not have a vested financial interest (Many of its previous self-deliverance manuals were specified, some by legal contract, to be not-for-profit). This 'wider distribution' policy will allow the new edition of *Five Last Acts* to be distributed on Amazon and in bookshops; and it covers not just choosing death through helium but through even easier and more available methods not requiring equipment or drugs.

Five Last Acts goes further than that of *Final Exit* or similar books in that it describes both painless methods that can be used even in hospital and also a thorough examination and warnings on suicide by refusing food and drink which, if done with insufficient preparation, can be horrific.[3]

A further concern is that absence of such information disadvantages several groups of people, persons who have legiti-

---

[3] 'Terminally ill opt for suicide by starvation,' by Sarah-Kate Templeton, Sunday Times, March 8th, 2009. And, 'Retired GPs advise terminally ill on suicide by starvation,' by Simon Johnson, The Telegraph, March 8th, 2009.

mate reasons to seek a peaceful death but do not have access to, or the ability to use, helium:

o Persons who cannot afford to go to Dignitas in Switzerland for an assisted suicide costing thousands of pounds.
o Persons who are not able to achieve a peaceful death by means of their living will /advance directive when ceasing treatment will not result in a desired peaceful death.
o Persons who do not die naturally and peacefully or with the help of increasing palliative doses of lawful medication.

Rights of free speech in publishing, and the rights to determine one's own death must be balanced against duties to protect the vulnerable and even the duty not to cause offence. These to some extent beg the question about what sort of society we wish to live in. The drive towards a 'nanny-state' on this issue is possibly doomed to failure. Not only are high cliffs, bridges, and ropes always easily available, but one could even point out that the explicit detail in the abovementioned article could guide anyone, with or without a psychiatric illness, in the necessary ways of helium suicide upon payment of £40 to download the article from the Internet.

Usually, the way a 'self-deliverance' manual such as this might begin would be by re-capping the needless suffering of someone dying slowly, the inadequacy of palliative care for certain conditions, the unfairness of having to go to Dignitas in Switzerland or a brief homily about respect for autonomy, dignity and so on, interspersed with acknowledgements that such measures as rational suicide are only needed by a few, that hospices do wonderful work, and that if you feel depressed you should call a counselling service.

Suddenly this did not seem enough. I guess I have always 'believed' that these years of research have been the right thing to do. There have been a number of checks and balances – of a sort – when books I worked on were only available through Exit. People have to be a member, supply proof of age, and even then the right to refuse a request for self-deliverance information is reserved if there is a sense of 'alarm bells going off.' Exit has always maintained friendly relations with the police, stayed carefully within the law, and generally avoided the adverse publicity which seemed often to follow Australia's 'Exit International,' America's 'ERGO' and 'Final Exit Network;' or even the other home-grown organisations.[4] If a

---

[4] Exit International: "Plans by Exit International to hold a second UK Voluntary Euthanasia meeting on Sunday 19 October have been cancelled. This is due to four main reasons. 1. Local Councils advised all hotels not to hire a room to Exit. 2. Police Chief Dick Coates erroneously stated that a public meeting would be a crime. 3. Prayer vigils were planned for locations involved, further scaring venue managers. 4. The staunchly conservative VE Society of the UK advised individual members against becoming involved with Exit." (Exit International Website 15 Oct 08 http://www.exitinternational.net/page/Blog, accessed 5 Sep 2010.)

Ergo: a) Gilson T, Parks B, Porterfield C, Suicide with inert gases: Addendum to Final Exit, Am J Forensic Med Pathol. 2003 Sep;24(3):306-8. "These fatalities coincide with publication of an update to a popular right-to-die text in which this method is described. Although right-to-die literature was absent from all scenes, this method was not previously observed in our jurisdiction, and the deaths likely reflect exposure to this information."

b) Cina S, Raso D, Conradi S, Suicidal cyanide ingestion as detailed in Final Exit. J Forensic Sci. 1994 Nov;39(6):1568-70. "Final Exit is an "informational aid" advocating the practice of active euthanasia and describing the proper method for the foolproof commission of suicide. Although it has been directed toward assisting the terminally ill patient who desires to terminate suffering, it has been suggested that the widespread availability of this book may result in its abuse. Specifically, there is growing concern that "do-it-yourself suicide manuals" could bring about the fruition of suicidal ideations that are relatively common among mentally ill patients and impressionable adolescents. Described is the suicidal ingestion of cyanide by a physically healthy 30-year-old man. His diary, found next to the body, contains a recipe for suicide copied verbatim from Derek member was found deceased and with our 'how-to' literature near the body, police would often just ring to confirm the person had been a member – perhaps just to help rule out suspicious circumstances.

But the logistics of supplying the book on an in-house basis have become insupportable. A private print run of such a size was no small undertaking, and there were problems finding a binders who weren't offended by the content. For a small organisation with limited funds, the size of the print run was a

---

Humphry's Final Exit. Although the decedent's history, the scene investigation, and the external examination strongly suggest an underlying psychiatric disorder, postmortem examination disclosed minimal underlying physical disease. This case graphically illustrates the abuse potential of this literary genre."

Final Exit Network: "Final Exit Network members charged with assisting suicide," The Guardian, Tuesday 9 March 2010.

Voluntary Euthanasia Society: See: *A guide to suicide guides,* this volume. After the controversy over whether to publish self-deliverance material, VES (now 'Dignity in Dying') mostly distanced itself from all self-deliverance material, to the present day.

Fate: a) "Terminally ill opt for suicide by starvation," by Sarah-Kate Templeton, http://www.timesonline.co.uk/tol/life_and_style/health/article5864857.ece. Online, Times Online March 8th, 2009 Accessed 5 Sep 2010. "Local GPs administered small doses of morphine to combat cramps and a sedative to relieve "emotional anxiety". One of her daughters, Jenny, 40, recalls: 'That worked well enough until day 18 and day 19. They were two of the most horrific days of my life. Wilson, who was in contact with Lily during the 25 days, added: 'She took a bit longer to die than expected but then we discovered that she had been sucking ice cubes.'"

b) "Retired GPs advise terminally ill on suicide by starvation," by Simon Johnson, http://www.telegraph.co.uk/health/healthnews/4957436/Retired-GPs-advise-terminally-ill-on-suicide-by-starvation.html, Telegraph Online 08 Mar 2009, accessed 5 Sep 2010: "A 75-year-old from Scotland, who had advanced motor neurone disease, took 25 days to starve and dehydrate to death after consulting Fate for advice. As the days turned into weeks, however, she used a communication aid to write: 'You wouldn't put a dog through this.'"

gamble. When delivered, UK orders were deliverable but the cost of overseas postage had been underestimated. Additionally, there was no convenient method for distributing quantities of the book to organisations overseas for their members. Undertaking a bigger run, for an expanded book and operating with just a single member of staff (often unpaid), who was also responsible for all other aspects of running the organisation, was not a viable prospect. Yet removing it entirely from in-house production presents its own problems. New distribution channels would make it much more widely available and where even the nominal checks on applications could barely be applied, if at all. Could the good that might be achieved, outweigh the terrible harm that could also be part-and-parcel of such general availability? The very notion of the guide is based on the idea of a 'least worst option,' in the absence of suitable legal provisions to allow doctors to assist and with proper safeguards. But is it an 'option too far?'

Howard *et al,* in the paper mentioned at the start of the chapter, gathered together a small number of case studies in the literature but without presenting any statistically significant scientific analysis. The suggestions in their paper show an evident concern for vulnerable individuals within which it is temptingly easy to jump to conclusions.[5] Further research is needed on larger samples, combined with logical analysis in interpretation. In allowing books like *Final Exit* and *Five Last Acts* to become available for order on the Internet, their authors incur an ethical responsibility. (In the event of publication, the author of *Five Last Acts* will be monitoring developments so that, if the evidence proves strong enough and burdens can be seen to outweigh benefits, the book can be

---

[5] Eg Kim JH, *Suicide and internet use levels – the evidence is lacking,* BMJ Rapid Responses 21 April 2008 http://www.bmj.com/cgi/eletters/336/7648/800#194029, accessed June 24, 2010.

withdrawn.) In contrast to the implied suggestion in Professor Howard's paper however, evaluation of the current situation, as we shall see, can suggest greater openness rather than less, and even rally public support for open-ended counselling within existing legislation (which might even benefit from being adapted for the purpose).

I did not wish to take the decision lightly and neither did I wish to take refuge in the all too familiar arguments recited by the 'pro-choice' camp. There have been numerous studies on the ethical dilemmas of providing voluntary euthanasia or of a physician assisting a suicide. There have been critiques and responses over publications such as Derek Humphry's Final Exit,[6] usually resulting in keeping the issue 'alive' but not really changing anybody's mind one way or the other. What is the most responsible way of coming to a decision about such things?

DIFFERENT WAYS OF TELLING RIGHT FROM WRONG

Is it just a gut instinct? If not, what sort of processes do human beings have for making such decisions? And when we decide, how do we define 'right' and how do we define 'wrong'? I might begin by examining personal qualities. Integrity and respect for the wishes of others and a desire for their good. The trust placed in me for this work. Hume[7] argued that it is our feelings that move us to action in a way that reason alone cannot do. Yet unless they are analysed in the crucible of reason – or provided with a solid foundation in another way – good intentions alone may not always result in a

---

[6] Humphry D, Final Exit, 3rd edition, Dell 2002, & *vide supra*.

[7] David Hume as referenced in Schneewind J, Modern Moral Philosophy, *In:* Singer P, *Companion to Ethics*, Blackwell 1991, p.150. (Hume D, *Treatises of Human Nature*, 1738.)

favourable balance of good. A careful and rational assessment can go some way to making our actions more understandable to those who sincerely disagree.

What are the common ways we make moral decisions?

Debate

Debate is a time honoured method. Debate still seems to be the most popular way of teaching 'ethics' in schools and extends (with some modifications) right up to the Houses of Parliament. The desire to 'win' motivates each side to find the most convincing approaches, researching facts to 'support' their position. Debates are great fun (they have emotional resonance) and often bring out some interesting points. They can emphasize the development of critical thinking skills, and tolerance for differing viewpoints. We 'listen to both sides of the argument' and 'make a considered judgement.' But are debates in any sense scientific? Skilled debaters excel at spotting local fallacies – and also committing them with impunity. Debate is not about being right, but about winning.[8] It frequently represents the two most extreme positions, ignoring the middle ground. It can turn on whichever side has the most skilled debater. While most people probably have an *interest* in how we die, I would expect the majority of the population are not passionately for or against assisted suicide, for instance. They are the large unrepresented middle ground. Should this edition of *Five Last Acts* be widely available? I can easily construct powerful arguments either way. Does that bring us any closer to finding a middle ground? Probably not. But if debate can be criticised for resulting in the most con-

---

[8] Schopenhauer A, *The Art of Always Being Right* (with an introduction by AC Grayling) Gibson Square 2004, gives a thorough analysis of falsification in debating methods, both conscious and unconscious.

vincing answer at the time (rather than a 'right' answer) then debate alone is not enough.

Personal beliefs – spiritual, personal moral code

Most of us have our own moral code. A set of inbuilt rules by which we try to live. Not all moral codes are the same. We can take a personal pride in a 'virtue' we hold dear. It might be 'telling the truth' or 'respecting someone's wishes.' But if I tell a murderer how to find his victim, that is clearly wrong, even though I am 'telling the truth.' If publication of this book is based on adherence to an abstract moral principle, is that a sound basis for choosing right over wrong? The very fact that two sincere and upstanding people can disagree over what is a right course of action must give us occasion to pause. Persons from different social spheres may also have different, deeply held views on what is 'obviously' right.[9]

In terms not least of our social conscience, many people would admit their sense of right and wrong matures over time.[10] It might be clearer (and less apt to make mistakes) at the age of 50 than at fifteen. Would I, *with hindsight,* make a more justifiable decision than I do now? If so, is it possible to make a *more* right decision now that won't be regretted or regretted less? Developing the best aspects of one's own (moral) character is undoubtedly a powerful tool in trying to discern right from wrong. But in order to apply qualitative analysis (such as used in the moral philosophy exercise later in

---

[9] This point is convincingly developed, for instance in Hare R, Universal Prescriptivism, *In:* Singer, *ibid,* p. 459.

[10] Kohlberg's Stages of Moral Development in: Crain W, *Theories of Development* 1985 Prentice-Hall. pp. 118-136.

this essay[11]), perhaps one of the most important character traits to treasure is a tolerant open-mindedness and willingness to embrace opposing viewpoints. And while it might not be possible to look with certainty into the future, one can at least try to make a *well-reasoned* decision rather than just an inspired one.

Authority: parents, teachers, priests, peers, role models, law

Some authorities give us moral clues. The law can give a useful indication (many court judgements reflect careful analysis based on jurisprudence – the theory and philosophy of law, which in itself is based in formal ethics). The *novus actus interveniens*[12] doctrine, examined earlier in this volume, cuts the cord of causation in law. Of the thousands of self-deliverance books sold, only a tiny proportion is used for suicide. Evidently there must be an additional factor – mere availability of the book does not cause suicide. It would need an exceptionally wide (if not inconceivable) interpretation to say that the book's availability alone is responsible. The legal effect of a successful *novus actus interveniens* plea is to absolve the defendant or original wrongdoer of legal liability or further legal liability. But legal permissiveness does not necessarily equate to moral right. In the case of *novus actus interveniens,* the device can be seen largely as based on policy.

In *Lamb v Camden London Borough Council*[13] Lord Denning M.R. said: "The truth is that all these three – duty, remoteness and

---

[11] Kallman & Grillo, *vide infra.* The Bowling Green State University in commending the exercise, suggests it is most useful when the decision maker can "tolerate ambiguity, complexity or conflict." (http://www.cs.bgsu.edu/maner/heuristics/1996Kallman.htm).

[12] In U.S.: 'superseding cause'.

[13] [1981] QB 625 (CA) at 636.

causation – are all devices by which the courts limit the range of liability for negligence or nuisance. As I said recently '…it is not every consequence of a wrongful act which is the subject of compensation. The law has to draw a line somewhere'. Sometimes it is done by limiting the range of the persons to whom duty is owed. Sometimes it is done by saying that there is a break in the chain of causation. At other times it is done by saying that the consequence is too remote to be a head of damage. All these devices are useful in their way. But ultimately it is a question of policy for the judges to decide." As a limitation of liability device, the onus rests on the defendant to persuade the court that the intervening event 'so overwhelms the original wrongdoing that the original wrongdoer – the defendant – avoids responsibility.'[14] Or, as Singleton L.J. put it in *Philco Radio and Television Corporation Ltd v J. Spurling Ltd,*[15] 'the onus is on the defendants to show that there was a new act intervening which relieves them from responsibility.'

An important point for the issue in question is that an intervening cause does not operate to exempt a defendant from liability if that cause is put into operation by the defendant's wrongful act or omission.[16] The dislocation between publishing the book and an act of suicide based on the information contained in it, is not something put into motion by Exit or by the author or publisher, there being no knowledge of the persons who may actually use the material much less foreknowledge or any action by the defendant that severs what would otherwise be an existing connection.

---

[14] *Mitchell v Rahman* [2002] MBCA 19 para. 31.

[15] [1949] 2 All ER 882 at 886 (CA) citing *Dominion Natural Gas Co. Ltd v Collins and Perkins* [1909] AC 640. This and the preceding examples are quoted in Hodgson D, *The Law of Intervening Causation,* Ashgate Publishing 2008.

[16] *Williams v. Le,* 2008-VA-0611.024 (06/06/2008) S.E.2d--VA

Teachers may have (or not have) a more educated view than the student possesses and so be in a position to guide. I had the privilege of studying under Robin Downie, who used to say that ethics can be learnt but not taught. Many of us will use role models to guide us, whether teachers or parents, asking ourselves, what would *they* do?[17] Yet although occasionally authority will choose to guide or 'protect' us, we are all ultimately individually responsible for our actions.

Experience

We are all deeply affected by our personal experiences. We could even say we are made up of the genetic inheritance each of us carries, together with the experiences that have shaped it, and any will that we bring to bear on circumstances or ourselves. Many readers will have purchased a book such as this after the trauma of seeing a loved one die badly, with no control over their dying days; another person may have a strong commitment to the 'pro-life' position after seeing the apparent miracles that palliative care has wrought in a particular case.[18] It seems to me that both of these scenarios present a partial picture, although there is no denying the power of

---

[17] Carlyle T, *On Heroes, Hero-Worship, and The Heroic in History,* Echo Library 2007 develops this theme and demonstrates that it does not have to be limited to 'real' people. Symbolic representations of virtue, whether from legends or the ancient gods, can serve as well. A more modern assessment is reported in Lynoe N, Löfmark R, Thulesius H, *Teaching medical ethics: what is the impact of role models? Some experiences from Swedish medical schools,* J Med Ethics 2008;34:315-316 which suggested (based on a survey of 409 students) that increased interest in medical ethics was related to encountering good physician role models, and decreased interest, to encountering poor role models.

[18] In Aristotelian ethics, a distinction is drawn between these virtues: experience and maturity is needed for practical wisdom, but not for theoretical wisdom. Additionally, excellence of character is acquired through habitual practice, not instruction.

seeing things from a three-dimensional perspective rather than theorising. What might have been an abstract case becomes 'real' in the light of seeing it happen to someone we love, a real person. This has led some moral philosophers to embrace the arts for scenario-based problem-solving.[19] The 'moral dilemmas' early in this book are a simple exercise in trying to visualise the complexity of a real life situation.

The present author explored this technique during an ethics workshop on euthanasia for 6th formers.[20] We would take a simple scenario – say a person dying in hospital – and allocate different roles. A patient wanting to die, a relative wanting them to have every life-prolonging treatment possible, a nurse caught in the middle as patient-advocate and so on. After acting out the scene with intensity (teenagers can produce extremely passionate and emotionally-charged performances!), I would re-allocate the roles. In this way, during the course of the workshop, participants would experience the very different emotions associated with opposing characters' viewpoints. This was to facilitate each person experiencing a different moral position rather than merely learning about it in an intellectual fashion. Real-life ethical decisions rarely occur in a sealed enclosure of theoretical niceties. There may be very little time to make a decision. Future visualisation may help us, especially if we have had limited experience of opposing views. But although such exercises broaden our knowledge and maybe let us see paradigms we might otherwise miss, can even broad experience provide a basis for a defensible and robust course of action?

---

[19] Using Literature in the Arts, *In:* Downie R, Calman K, *Healthy Respect – Ethics in Health Care,* OUP 1994:143-148. Also: Downie R, Macnaughton J, *Bioethics and the Humanities: Attitudes and Perceptions,* Routledge-Cavendish 2007, Chapters 6 & 7.

[20] Swanshurst School, Birmingham UK (Ethics Conference).

Philosophical medical ethics (moral philosophy)[21]

This is the area that I intend to focus on for the rest of this essay. How can one take all those differing views and ways of reaching them, and place them into some sort of structure. A method of weighing everything in the balance. A rational process that, if our life depended (or depends) on it, we can say with some certainly that we at least followed a clear and rational course of action.

I wanted to examine the question of whether to publish, and to do so from as many different angles as possible. This would include:

- looking to see if further guidance can be gleaned from the law;
- listening to my instincts;
- looking at formal guidelines discussed with Exit; and also my duties as Exit's Director;
- looking at general rights & duties (deontological approach)[22]
- looking at my personal duties and values, and my professional ones

---

[21] Gillon R, *Philosophical medical ethics,* John Wiley & Sons 1995. After a preamble explaining what it is not, Gillon speaks of philosophy as being, "the critical evaluation of assumptions and arguments," and of moral philosophy as being "philosophical inquiry about norms, values, right and wrong, good and bad, and what ought and ought not to be done." Gillon then uses the similar term, 'medical ethics' or medical moral philosophy as denoting "the analytic activity in which the concepts, assumptions, beliefs, attitudes, emotions, reasons, and arguments underlying medico-moral decision making are examined critically."

[22] Deontology (from the Greek δέον meaning obligation or duty; and -λογία, logia). Immanuel Kant, for example, argued that the only absolutely good thing is a good will, and so the single determining factor of whether an action is morally right is the will, or motive of the person doing it (assuming it does not interfere with the will of another). It is frequently contrasted with *Utilitarianism* – which examines outcomes.

- Looking at possible consequences (utilitarianism)
- Looking at questions of consistency and respect, and asking if it would be acceptable for everyone to act like this (Kant's Categorical Imperative);
- Using a 'four principles' approach of beneficence, avoiding harm, justice, and respect for autonomy.[23]

I can hear some people at this point perhaps saying that such deliberations are intellectual conceits. That it is 'obvious' (one way or the other, depending on their strong feelings no doubt.) But that is exactly why the exercise is so necessary. Many people have strong but contrary feelings of what is right. As part of society, and inasmuch as our actions affect others, isn't it appropriate to try to get an overall picture? One that finds logical solutions that can be accepted by all, even if not everyone can support them 100 per cent? These strong feelings about what is right and wrong are personal morals rather than universal ones. So the first thing to do is decide on a house into which we can place all these divergent opinions and moral judgments. It might not result in the one 'right choice' capable of satisfying everyone, but the process may at least help us to find the 'least worst choice.'

METHOD

Many models of ethical analysis are either specific to particular types of situation[24] or else outline principles without necessarily indicating how to apply them. The analysis model I selected, for its breadth and methodical way of exploring avenues in order to reach a logical decision, was that of

---

[23] Beauchamp T, Childress J, *Principles of Biomedical Ethics* OUP 2008.

[24] Saarni S, Hofmann B, Lampe K, Lühmann D, Mäkelä M, Velasco-Garridod M, Autti-Rämöa I, *Ethical analysis to improve decision-making on health technologies,* Bulletin of the World Health Organization, August 2008, 86 (8), for instance.

Kallman & Grillo.[25] Kallman & Grillo present their analysis structure as a series of workbook exercises over several pages which proceed towards a conclusion. It is not, as far as I am aware, online, but readers can get some idea of its nature by referring to the outline published on Bowling Green State University's website,[26] which also houses an excellent collection of ethical analysis working models.[27] BGSU describe the Kallman & Grillo model as, "Notable for its completeness, for focusing equally on action and inaction, for trying to prevent recurrence, and for doing what-if analysis at 'pivot points'."

Additionally, I used a technique espoused by Robin Downie and touched on briefly in the *Moral Dilemmas* chapter of this book, implied in the introduction to this essay, and described briefly in the section, *Different ways of telling right from wrong*. It involves extending imagination to deepen our sympathies from different viewpoints and hence be able to appreciate a wider spectrum of feelings than otherwise might be the case from an abstract or purely intellectual manner.[28] In this way, greater sensitivity for conflicting points of view can be developed, bias tamed, and perhaps even the possibility of a more successful outcome increased.

[25] Kallman E, Grillo J, *Ethical Decision Making and Information Technology – An Introduction with Cases,* McGraw Hill 1995.

[26] http://www.cs.bgsu.edu/maner/heuristics/1996Kallman.htm Accessed 6 Sep 2010.

[27] http://www.cs.bgsu.edu/maner/heuristics/toc.htm Accessed 6 Sep 2010.

[28] Using Literature in the Arts, In: Downie R, Calman K, *Healthy Respect – Ethics in Health Care,* OUP 1994. Pp143-148. Also: Downie R, Macnaughton J, *Bioethics and the Humanities: Attitudes and Perceptions,* Routledge-Cavendish 2007, Chapters 6 & 7. For a more in depth examination of the use of literature in ethics, *see:* Nussbaum M, *Love's Knowledge – Essays on Philosophy and Literature,* OUP 1990. For art images and dying, see Carmichael K, *Images of dying,* Exit Newsletter 2007 27(1).

Perhaps the single most common shortcoming of both the 'right-to-die' movement and the 'pro-life' movement is an abject failure to identify effectively with the formative images typical of the ones which shaped the views of people on 'the other side.' Take two scenarios. Imagine you have personally known someone whose prognosis looked very bleak indeed. He was only narrowly persuaded to live on – yet against all odds he found he had a lot more life he wanted to enjoy; and did. That will be a very strong memory that will probably shape the way you think about things, all textbooks aside. Now consider a case of someone with degenerative disease. They are fully aware of their condition. It is unbearable and has been for some time. It *might* not get worse quickly; but it is scientifically impossible to recover. They have no hope of improvement to look forward to. Then they are granted an exit strategy. It might be a promise of help if required from Dignitas. It might this book. That knowledge, that there is someone prepared to do their bidding if needs be. Or show them how to take matters into their own hands. The relief is very tangible. Or imagine it was someone that never got that kind of help. Instead they died screaming. Or withering away like an abused animal. (The end stages of some diseases can be terrifying and even today not all suffering can be relieved.) Witnessing that happen will scar someone's brain with the memory. It is the reason why a very large proportion of members of right-to-de societies joined up. They don't want it to happen to them.

Both these types of experiences involve dramatic events, ones that form strong images in a person's life history. Each is as real as the other. Recalling such images can generate a barrier to understanding that 'it doesn't always happen like that.' The psychological process of recalling such images was well described by Susan Sontag in a discussion of the power of photographs: "Photographs lay down routes of reference, and serve as totems of causes: sentiment is more likely to crystallize around a photograph than around a verbal slogan. . . . Ideologies create substantiating archives of images, representative images, which encapsulate common ideas of significance and trigger predictable thoughts, feelings."[29] Evoking contrary images is a way of balancing one's 'viewpoint,' and making it less susceptible to being thrown off by dramatic and emotive arguments (usually ones that suit one's own predilection) during the course of serious analysis. This is especially important when one has developed strong biases over a period of time that would predispose towards a specific course of action.[30] The present author has a historical commitment to self-deliverance information to deal with, yet must still do his 'honest best' to examine the question of whether to publish in such a way that is as unbiased as possible: if for no other reason than the philosophical analysis (by means of the Kallman & Grillo framework) is undertaken to find an answer, not as a mere intellectual exercise.

A further 'side' and one most relevant to the dilemma of whether to publish self-deliverance information is suicide prevention. For someone steeped in 'right-to-die' literature, dramatic evocation of ill-judged suicide helps to take such tragedies with the seriousness they demand.

A BRIEF HISTORY OF FACTORS RELATING TO ETHICAL CONSIDERATIONS IN EXIT'S POLICY

---

[29] Sontag S, *Regarding the pain of Others*, Penguin 2003, pp76-77.

[30] Tobler P, Kalis A, Kalenscher T, *The role of moral utility in decision making: An interdisciplinary framework*, Cognitive, Affective, & Behavioral Neuroscience 2008, 8 (4), 390-401. *See also:* Baron J, Ritov I, *Protected Values and Omission Bias as Deontological Judgments*, Psychology of Learning and Motivation 2009, Vol 50, Chapter 4.

REGARDING PUBLICATION OF SELF-DELIVERANCE INFORMATION

(n.b.: I have printed some key considerations in bold, for ease of referring back through the text.)

1980 The Society was formed to fulfil a specific need for self-deliverance information after strong evidence of great public demand. Its then parent organisation, the Voluntary Euthanasia Society, after publicly announcing plans to produce the world's first 'suicide guide', saw membership rise, from an initial 2000 members, at a rate of 1000 a month over the next six months. Publication was halted at the last minute, and the Scottish section, now Exit, broke away in order to publish and satisfy that demand, which was then estimated at 10,000 members.[31] The Society's first booklet[32] was published with a number of provisions: **a)** Each booklet carried a number which was identified on Scottish Exit's **central register** of members with the name of the purchaser. **b)** An inside cover warning stated: "Should a booklet find its way into non-member's hands the original purchaser will be readily identified and MAY – under certain circumstances – such as the forwarding of the booklet to England or certain other countries, be liable to possible arrest by the authorities of these countries." c) Applicants had to be listed on the Society's Scottish register. d) A number of exhortations were included. e) A (waivable) **90-day waiting period** was introduced.[33] These provisions were continued through several updates and 'Supplements.' The original purpose of issuing 'supplements,' rather than revising the booklet, was to preserve the integrity

---

[31] These details taken from Minutes of the Executive Committee Meetings, 16 & 17 Aug 1980.

[32] Mair G, *How to Die With Dignity*, Scottish Exit Committee 1980.

[33] See illustration at end of chapter.

of George Mair's original even after he had left the Committee and passed away.

1993 When a new (and larger) booklet, *Departing Drugs*[34] was devised, the numbering system was eventually dropped as impractical. The 90-day waiting period was maintained. Expert multidisciplinary advice and peer review ensured greater **accuracy** of recommended self-deliverance methods and a firmer **legal** basis. The result of an international project, the book was further protected by legal contract, specifying that sales at home or abroad were to be a) **non-profit;** b) subject to a minimum **90-day waiting period** (The basis for this was formalised with the advice of a leading consultant psychiatrist, that ill-considered and acute suicidal ideation would be more likely to pass after such a period); c) That translations must retain the exact sense of the original without extrapolation or addition. Original authors retained **copyright** to protect accuracy (overruling one committee member who objected to certain drugs but without any evidence to back up his objections). Purchase from Exit was **at discretion** (as before). It could be purchased by **members only**, either members of Exit or members of other recognised right-to-die societies on production of approved documentary evidence of membership. To overcome perceived objections, particularly legal or political ones, Individual organisations licensed to sell the booklet (including Exit), could use a different title should they so wish. In spite of reassurances, Exit decided to issue it under the title *1993 Supplement to How to Die With Dignity,* wanting to **minimize any public attention** that the release of a new book might bring. The 'year' was included since the Committee Minutes noted that there was already considerable confu-

---

[34] Docker C, Smith C (eds) and The International Drugs Consensus Working Party (Docker C, Smith C, Brewer C, Schobert K, and another). *Departing Drugs - the International Supplement to How to Die With Dignity* 1993 Edinburgh: VESS.

sion over the number of different 'Supplements' to the 1980 booklet.

2000 Exit formally adopted the *Carver Policy Governance Model,*[35] a paradigm shift that structures an organisation's goals, the means of attaining them, and the ethical limits an organisation wishes to set in achieving those aims. (This brought to an end a period of confusion and internal unrest within the running of the Society from the mid-90's and ending in 2000.)

2003-2009 Exit looks at precise wording regarding the provision of self-deliverance information *(nb: numbers indicate minuted Board decisions; bold type is for ease of reference but again not used in the originals):*

a) (2003, No.5) 46-49: "In the event of Chris Docker producing a new booklet, he would retain sole copyright, authorship and **intellectual property** (in other words, the EC, for Exit, may choose to publish / distribute etc or not, but would not have any right to change the finished document other than accepting or rejecting it.)"

b) (2003, No.6) 27-35: "With regards to self-deliverance, Exit seeks to provide appropriate information to appropriate persons by appropriate means (and within its resources). This may, from time to time, include publications or workshops on self-deliverance. Exit reserves the right to use its **discretion to decline** to provide such information to any individual(s) or group at any time. Grounds for declining may include legal or moral considerations."

---

[35] Oliver C, Getting Started with Policy Governance: Bringing Purpose, Integrity, and Efficiency to Your Board, Jossey-Bass, 2009. *Also:* Carver J, Boards That Make a Difference: A New Design for Leadership in Nonprofit and Public Organizations, Jossey-Bass, 1990; 3rd edition, 2006.

c) (2006, No.1) 25-42: "Exit works for the practice, enactment and beneficial working of measures to enable people to avoid suffering and to die peacefully. Specifically, this includes, within strictly defined limits self-deliverance information. Exit supports generally facilitating the diffusion of information on the subject in order to enable members to make an **informed choice** as to the options which are or might be made available. **Avoidance of suffering**, in Exit's specific remit, covers **mental and physical illness and injury**, when it is **unrelievable and unbearable, whether terminal of itself or not**. It does not include suffering due, for instance, to lack of support from social services, suffering of a seemingly temporary nature (such as that induced or exacerbated by drug or alcohol abuse, romantic disillusionment, exam failure, financial problems). Although persons may have every right to end their lives due to reasons outside of Exit's remit, or for no reason, it is not Exit's mission to support these cases as there are other services better placed to tackle such problems."

"Exit also works within a remit of **'least worst options'** since there would be less need (or no need) for self-deliverance information if there was ready access to medical assistance for suicide. Exit needs to **balance the need to provide information** to those for whom it is intended against the need to **reduce the likelihood** of it falling into the hands of those that would use it in a way not intended by Exit, and to do this within Exit's resource limitations and reasonable **legal obligations**."

d) (2006, No.1) 43-48: "The Booklet will continue to be provided with discretion to members **over 21** who have fulfilled the requirements of the application process. For the time being, self-deliverance information and especially information updates will continue to be **provided in the Newslet-**

ter where necessary to communicate it to the members. When resources allow, such information can in the future be restricted to a booklet or updated booklet and provided to members who provide **proof of age**. At such time this policy could be reviewed and refined."

e) (2009, No.2) 18-19: "The Director shall not accept at face value **membership** applications of persons **under the age of 21** unless he feels persuaded that they actively support the aims of Exit."

2007 Publication of the first edition of this book largely followed principles established since 1980. The conditions under which information was imparted were explained more specifically. Conformance to the *novus actus interveniens* principle was included under 'reasonable legal obligations.' Explicit workshops followed the same principles. When information was sometimes included in the Newsletter (received by all members), Exit tightened up on age requirements as a precaution.

2010 (2010, No.2) 66-67: "Exit supports Five Last Acts but is not prepared as a Society to publish and distribute the book without **existing safeguards**. Exit sees no problem in Chris Docker publishing the book on his own accord."

This policy decision was arrived at specifically to address the dilemma of the 'how' and 'if' to make the book available to the general public through normal bookseller outlets, whether bookshops or online ordering (of hard copies, not electronic downloads). Excessive restriction could limit the ability to see the book published at all.

It would mean that Exit would be able to distribute the book from the Office with existing age checks, a 90-day provision and any other checks it wanted to enforce from time to time. Exit would be able to acquire the book at cost, for re-sale to members. Exit would not be formally associated with sales outside of the Office and the book would not be printed as an 'Exit' book.

It was further recommended that a considerable price increase should be implemented to deter purchase by children (for copies purchased outside of the Office). Other comments from Board members included, "mindfulness of both the need for information and for the need to protect minors;" and one member spoke of her "faith in the responsible image of Exit" and how "the upright stance of making it quite difficult to get the book" had particularly impressed her when she joined the Society.

Is it hypocritical for Exit to both condone the book and refuse to take responsibility for the general sales that make it possible? Not necessarily. By maintaining the safeguards, Exit stays within its original remit.[36] The author is not bound by that remit, but must decide his own moral position on whether to publish. Should he decide not to, Exit would not however have the book to distribute to its narrower target membership.

APPLYING THE KALLMAN & GRILLO 4-STEP APPROACH

(This is a condensed account of the workbook applied to the current question of whether to publish, and the formulation of a decision.)

---

[36] Further benefits of this separation of responsibilities are listed under Section III (D), below.

Step I: Understanding the situation

A. Numbered list of the relevant facts

i) Exit has published and distributed self-deliverance information since 1980. It is considered a 'leader in the field' of self-deliverance information. The new book includes material and safeguards not readily available elsewhere.

ii) Practical issues involving time, money, resources and distribution make in-house publishing no longer viable.

B. Which of these raises an ethical issue? And why? What is the potential or resulting harm?

Benefits/harm is an ethical issue in (ii) above.

i) A benefit is that dying or seriously ill people who are suffering unbearably and unrelievably would have the choice to take matters into their into own hands by using the information to end their life painlessly.

ii) Benefit is the sense of hope and courage that having such information can bring (as attested to by many letters) even if the information is never used. An incidental benefit might be pressure for law reform,[37] so that individuals can seek assistance from doctors or clinics similar to the Swiss 'Dignitas' (but without the heavy expenses of using that clinic).

---

[37] Wolf S, *Final Exit – The End of Argument,* Hastings Center Report 1992, 22(1). In discussing the pressure and momentum for physician-assisted suicide, Wolf suggests: "Derek Humphry's publication of *Final Exit,* billed as a suicide manual for the terminally ill, has played no small part in fuelling the current swirl of activity."

iii) A further incidental benefit might be that it increases pressure for better palliative care.[38]

iv) A potential harm is that the information, while freely available and can be collected from newspapers, journals and online, could be used to facilitate an unnecessary suicide.

v) Exit and/or the author might feel anguish if the material was misused in that way.

C. List the stakeholders involved.

i) Persons with unrelievable and unbearable suffering.

ii) Persons who fear that they might one day be subjected to unrelievable and unbearable suffering.

iii) Exit, as an organisation that has committed itself to providing such information.

---

[38] Exit euthanasia blog, *Euthanasia & hospices: the unexpected link,* July 14 2010, http://exiteuthanasia.wordpress.com/2010/07/14/euthanasia-the-hospice-uneasy-deathbed-mates/ Accessed 10 Sep 2010. Draws on information from: The Economist Intelligence Unit, The quality of death: Ranking end-of-life care across the world, 2010, http://graphics.eiu.com/upload/QOD_main_final_edition_Jul12_toprint.pdf Accessed 10 Sep 2010. " . . . pressure brought on policymakers over these issues can be a catalyst for the improvement of palliative care services – as in Australia, where the federal overturning of a Northern Territory euthanasia law in 1996 led to increased national funding for end-of-life care." Countries with 'right-to-die' legislation also featured high in the rankings of quality of death, even though such legislation itself was not allowed to affect the rankings. Similarly, Robert Byock, writing in The Hospice Journal, called Final Exit a 'A Wake-Up Call to Hospice.' (The Hospice Journal, Volume 7, Issue 4 March 1992 , pages 51 – 66).

iv) Exit members, present and future, who look to Exit to provide the best information available on such matters.

v) The present author, who has invested many years of his life developing such information, and may therefore have an interest in seeing such work come to fruition, even if there is no financial incentive.

vi) Society at large, that may or may not wish that such information can be obtained.

Step II: Isolating the major ethical dilemma

What is the ethical dilemma to be resolved NOW?
State it using the form: Should someone do or not do something?
Note: Just state the dilemma here; leave any reasoning for Step III.

Answer (the 'action'): Should the new self-deliverance information (*Five Last Acts, 2ⁿᵈ edition*) be published in a way that means it can be bought by members of the public without the additional checks made by Exit?

Use informal guidelines

a) Is there something you or others would prefer to keep quiet?

No. Publishing self-deliverance information was a concern of the Committee in 1993, mostly due to fears of prosecution, which would render it unreachable by those that needed it. This is seen to apply less now, with the clearer understanding of the law that is possible.

b) Does it pass the 'Mom Test': Would you tell her? Would she do it?

My gut feeling is, yes, I would tell her. I'm proud of the work. Would she publish? She might be more inclined to say, you go ahead and do it if you think it's right – but on your own head be it.

c) Does it pass the 'TV Test': Would you tell a nationwide audience?

Yes. The publicity would benefit many people.

d) Does it pass the 'Market Test': Could you advertise the policy to gain a market edge?

Yes and no. The contents would have a market edge if marketed successfully; the policy under question (wider availability) could be seen as damaging the more 'careful' approach. But the inclusion of a clear and robust ethical analysis might give it a small edge over a policy of lesser, more restricted, distribution, and even an edge over 'similar' publications that omit any attempt at thorough ethical self-examination.

e) Does your instinct tell you something is wrong?

No, but it does tell me to exercise caution in case there are factors of which I am not fully aware and cannot predict (such as whether young persons might avail themselves of it without proper cause.)

f) Does it pass the 'Smell Test': Does the situation 'smell'?
It passes this test! It feels right to publish – partly on account

of the erroneous information available elsewhere that people might use with disastrous results. There is some concern however over the reaction that often seems to occur within the movement, particularly from groups that are not operating to the highest standards, and proving particularly troubling at times. Attempts to minimise this include openness and transparency, and a genuine desire to assist sister societies wherever possible, irrespective of any past differences.

Apply formal guidelines

a) Does the act violate corporate policy?

No. Corporate policy has specifically allowed for it to be published on the basis currently being considered. (See *History*, 2010 (2010, No.2) 66-67, above).

b) Does the act violate corporate or professional codes of conduct or ethics?

No. Higher standards of professional ethics devised and implemented for publishing such material generally would be desirable. *Five Last Acts*, as with previous Exit publications seeks to stay at the forefront with accuracy, ethical transparency and accountability. The Policy Governance System adopted by Exit in 2000, puts in place required compliance with acceptable ethical guidelines as standard.

c) Does the act violate the Golden Rule?[39]

---

[39] Roughly speaking, in various forms, the 'Golden Rule' says, 'What you do not want others to do to you, do not do to them' (Would you be willing to accept the consequence of your action if you were the one affected?). It can be found as a general ethical principle in Confucianism and in the scriptures of nearly every

I disagree with Kallman & Grillo that this is a genuine 'formal guideline,' as it struggles to uphold the formal logic associated with formal guidelines – I see it more as an informal one that is at the base of many religious systems and feel it is a gross oversimplification of Kant's (later) Categorical Imperative[40] ("Act only according to that maxim whereby you can at the same time will that it should become a universal law.") Kant pointed out that, under the Golden Rule, a criminal for instance could dispute with judges. A constructive variation was made by Karl Popper, who said, "The golden rule is a good standard which is further improved by doing unto others, wherever reasonable, as they want to be done by."[41]

But does publishing violate the Golden Rule in the ordinary sense? In my case no, as I would keenly want others to publish this type of information should I ever wish to use it and, as a responsible citizen, like to know about the scientific accuracy of such things and whether they can be relied upon.

Would a man who is temporarily unbalanced and planning to commit suicide want such information as *Five Last Acts* to be freely available? (Using Popper's definition.) This is harder to answer. If he was seriously intent on suicide come what may,

---

major religion since. It can be argued that it does not follow the stricter logic of moral philosophy unless it is modified – for instance to include taking into account your neighbour's tastes as you would that he should take yours into account.

[40] Kant I, *Groundwork of the Metaphysic of Morals,* CUP 1998. The Categorical Imperative is discussed more fully later. See also: Beauchamp T, Childress J, *Principles of Biomedical Ethics* OUP 1994, p.57: "The categorical imperative, then, is a canon of the acceptability of moral rules – that is, a criterion for judging the acceptability of the maxims that direct actions. This imperative adds nothing to a maxim's content. Rather, it determines which maxims are objective and valid."

[41] Popper K, *The Open Society and Its Enemies* (Vols I & II), Routledge 2002.

then presumably he *would* prefer to know how to achieve it painlessly rather than painfully (the latter being the case with popular spontaneously chosen methods, such as hanging that does not involve the professional executioner-determined 'drop,'[42] or extreme paracetamol (Acetaminophen)[43] overdose.)

But what if someone is less seriously inclined and the availability of information 'pushes him over the edge' as it were? Perhaps I would not want the information available in that case. But the evidence to suggest whether availability of means affects suicide (rather than just the method chosen) is sketchy. In many cases, no such link has been demonstrated.

The question of access by minors is particularly emotive and worrying. Would a child (or young teenager), with some suicidal ideation of any degree, and if they could look back in hindsight, want such information to be readily available to them? This is where I struggle with Kant. Can it be said that publishing will be in line with the Categorical Imperative? I tend to take refuge more in Popper's maxim, 'as far as is reasonable;' together with such small safeguards as can still be maintained; and together with such scientific evidence as may be available now or in the future to determine whether

---

[42] Capital Punishment UK website, *Hanged by the neck until dead! The processes and physiology of judicial hanging.* http://www.capitalpunishmentuk.org/hanging2.html Accessed 8 Sep 2010. "It should be clearly understood that suicide by hanging is likely to be very painful as there will hardly ever be sufficient drop to break the neck." The comment applies to 'short drop hanging' such as when individuals hang themselves from a light fixture.

[43] Sheen C, Dillon J, Bateman N, Simpson K, MacDonald T, *Paracetamol-related deaths in Scotland, 1994–2000, British Journal of Clinical Pharmacology* (54)4. *See also:* Defendi G, Tucker J, Toxicity, Acetaminophen, eMedicine http://emedicine.medscape.com/article/1008683-overview updated Apr 16, 2010, accessed 6 Sep 2010.

undesirable outcomes require my 'reasonable' to be re-evaluated.[44]

Minimal safeguards include devices such as credit card or in-store purchase. Although it is not impossible for a minor to obtain a credit card, it must be linked to the account of a responsible adult. But age verification systems are imperfect. They can be penetrated by a technically competent minor. And many of the fears of abuse of self-deliverance information focus on those who are already of sufficient age. (The technicalities of the book would to a large extent make it difficult for a young child to follow. In the case of choke holds used in choking games, children discover these by word of mouth when playing with other children.[45] Knowledge such as contained in *Five Last Acts*, if anything, is likely to alert them to the serious dangers more than encourage them.) A further safeguard suggested by Exit is to have a relatively high price for Internet sales to help dissuade youngsters. The publishing question does not include downloads or *e-books*, which might be a more ready danger. Publishing *Five Last Acts* as an e-book is not being contemplated at this stage.

---

[44] Another theoretical tool for interpreting the Golden Rule is through what John Rawls termed, 'the veil of ignorance.' If one were ignorant as to whether one would be in the position of a person justifiably needing the self-deliverance information, or a confused and vulnerable youngster who had come across it at the wrong time, then one can assess with greater impartiality the option of making it available. Rawls J, *A Theory of Justice,* Belknap Press, 1971.

[45] Macnab A, Deevska M, Gagnon F, Cannon W, Andrew T, Asphyxial games or "the choking game": a potentially fatal risk behaviour, Injury Prevention, 2009;15:45-49. "Of 2762 surveys distributed, 2504 (90.7%) were completed. The mean (SD) age of the responders was 13.7 (2.2) years. 68% of children had heard about the game, 45% knew somebody who played it, and 6.6% had tried it, 93.9% of those with someone else. Forty percent of children perceived no risk. Information that playing the game could result in death or brain damage was reported as most likely to influence behaviour."

Finally one can consider the reasonableness, especially for older teenagers and young adults exposed to such materials. Knowledge of helium use in suicide is widespread. It is not complicated and the rough method can be construed by any intelligent young person by reading news reports. Insufficient statistics are available, but as there is a slight danger of serious brain damage (such as when one might be interrupted after a few minutes of anoxia resulting from helium self-deliverance), knowledge of how to do it properly, and with proper precautions (as explained in this book and others), might arguably be better than reliance on second-hand information. A further (hypothetical) consideration of reasonableness might suggest that road and rail deaths could be prevented, including those of youngsters or persons temporarily unstable, by banning such means of transport altogether. In this example, the reasonable solution is to place more emphasis on the prevention by caring, whether it be the caring of parents or by social and psychiatric workers. This would argue that the cause of death is not the presence of the lethal means (cars and trains) but the lack of proper responsibility by individuals or those caring for them.

Step III: Analysing ethicality of Step II alternatives.

Consequentialism

A. If the action in Step II is done, who, if anyone, will be harmed?

Answer: Persons without capacity that have not been protected sufficiently by competent guardians.[46] Such persons

---

[46] I use this sentence in the broadest sense rather than just someone who legally or medically requires a guardian. One is not always 'competent' to decide what one really wants. If, with the benefit of hindsight, one would have preferred not to have been exposed to such material, can one say that the latter autonomous wish

might end their lives needlessly with the help of the information. It is possible, of course, that such persons might 'slip through the net,' even with the three month waiting period and age checks that apply if the information is obtained through Exit. But there are several other manuals available without a waiting period from other sources which they could buy, so the difference is probably small. I am not completely happy with relying on this idea of competence. It suggests a qualifying factor, rather than a default state of being. A slightly different approach is suggested by James Rachels in discussing Tom L. Beauchamp's definition of suicide, hinging on *freedom from coercion*. Following this path, one simply has to ask whether the book, subtly and unintentionally, could bring about a degree of influence tantamount to coercion.[47]

B. If the action in Step II is not done, who, if anyone, will be harmed?

Answer: Persons who rationally seek an end to unbearable and unrelievable suffering. Persons who wish to escape the fear of the same when facing an unknown future. An examination of existing literature suggests flaws that could result in undignified or less than successful attempts at self-deliverance – with

---

is more competent than the former? The reverse situation, in an argument for 'benevolent paternalism' is allowed for under Israeli law when a doctor can overrule the wish of a competent patient to refuse treatment in exceptional circumstances *if the hospital ethics committee feel that, if the treatment is imposed, the patient will later give his consent retroactively.* Glick A, *The morality of coercion*, JME 2000;26:393-395.
Citing: Patient's Rights Act, 1966.

[47] "A person commits suicide if: (1) that person brings about their own death; (2) others do not coerce him or her to do the action; and (3) death is caused by conditions arranged by the person for the purpose of bringing about his or her own death." Although Rachels himself is not entirely satisfied with this either. Rachels J, *The End of Life*, OUP 1098, p.81.

traumatic consequences.[48] Exit members awaiting the (promised) revised edition of the book.

C. Which alternative results in the least harm, A or B?

Answer: In view of the earlier analysis, publishing (A) appears to result in the least harm, although this should continue to be monitored.

D. If the action in Step II is done, who if anyone will benefit?

Answer: Persons who rationally seek an end to unbearable and unrelievable suffering. Persons who wish to escape the fear of the same when facing an unknown future. Exit maintains a degree of moral separateness by not being directly involved. If the author died, the integrity of the content is preserved, and the same control over distribution largely maintained.[49]

---

[48] Mail Online: *Terminally ill doctor survived suicide pact which killed wife because bag used to suffocate himself was too small.* http://www.dailymail.co.uk/news/article-1304427/Terminally-ill-doctor-survived-suicide-pact-wife-bag-small.html Accessed 21 Aug 2010. Failure with anoxic methods can cause brain damage. Injudicious use of chloroquine or starvation as a method can cause painful or distressing symptoms before death occurs. Failure with drugs no longer recommended can cause burning of the stomach or permanent damage to internal organs.

[49] This largely avoids the possibility of distribution of corrupted material not authorised by the author, as happened with a Dutch version of *Departing Drugs;* or the possibility of it being promoted in an arguably dangerously misleading way, as may have happened with Chabot's book, *A hastened death by self-denial of food and drink.* Public availability also increases transparency, reducing the likelihood of errors, including errors of attribution, not coming to light straight away. Something of this nature happened with the Wozz book, *Humane Self-Chosen Death,* which wrongly attributed misleading text to the authors of *Departing Drugs* further to relying on the corrupted Dutch edition. The Dutch book has been withdrawn and Wozz say they are correcting errors in any future editions. (See *A Guide to Suicide Guides,* this volume, for historical information on these instances.)

There is an additional, much larger, group that benefits from the knowledge in books on self-deliverance. In more than fifteen years of working at Exit, the majority of letters about such books are not saying how they will use it, but how it gives them courage to face an unknown future. The size of this group is supported by statistics (of the many thousands of sales, only a tiny proportion commit suicide); and the law – the principle of *novus actus interveniens*[50] means there must be a causal link between supplying the information and the resulting act that involves foreseeability and immediacy. Evidently in the majority of instances, there is not. In terminally ill patients, the relief is even more palpable – the mere knowledge seems to provide a sense of control, and a bulwark against hopelessness.[51]

Exit as an organisation will be able better to fulfil its promise and obligation to its members.

The publication of an ethical template, in relation to publication of self-deliverance material, may also benefit other writers in the field.

---

[50] Literally 'a new act intervening.'

[51] This in turn can increase a person's desire to live as long as possible. Hopelessness is a strong predictor of suicidal ideation in persons who are terminally ill. *See:* Chochinov H, Wilson K, Enns M, Lander S, *Depression, Hopelessness, and Suicidal Ideation in the Terminally Ill,* Psychosomatics 1998; 39:366–370. Some comparison might be made with Dutch requests for euthanasia which are granted and later withdrawn – which one study puts at 13%: van der Weide M, Onwuteaka-Philipsen B, van der Wal G, *Granted, Undecided, Withdrawn, and Refused Requests for Euthanasia and Physician-Assisted Suicide,* Arch Intern Med. 2005;165:1698-1704.

E. If the action in Step II is not done, who if anyone will benefit?

Perhaps persons without capacity that have not been protected sufficiently by competent guardians.

F. Which alternative results in the maximum benefit, C or D?

Answer: In view of the earlier analysis, publishing (D) appears to result in the most benefit, although this should continue to be monitored.

Right and Duties

G. What rights have / could be abridged (if the book is published)? What duties have been or could be neglected? Identify stakeholders, rights, or duties. When listing a right, show its corresponding duty and vice versa.

Rights and duties is a complex area that could of itself fill a book. A right generally presupposes a duty of someone else not to interfere with the performance of that right. The law is murky inasmuch it appears to admit the 'right' of someone to commit suicide yet without a corresponding duty not to interfere with that right. If we go back to even more fundamental principles – say before there were any laws or civilised communities or even many people – then the idea of 'enforcing' one's right to life might seem fatuous when there was no-one conceivably threatening it. It might be more appropriate to ask, what do I want to do with my life? what do I want to achieve? how can I maximise the possibilities? One can imagine *a duty to oneself* to do certain things one wanted to do. As we start to interact with others, we would afford them the same, as long as it did not interfere with our own duty (or right) to pursue our own ends. Immanuel Kant formularised this underlying principle as the *Categorical Imperative* – the formula could be expressed in a number of ways, one of which was to *treat people as an end, never as means.* We should treat others with dignity and respect, reflecting the inherent value of that person (and also their right to pursue their own ends) and never use a person as a mere means to an end.

Our Categorical Imperative immediately finds fault with the notion of suicide. To commit suicide, Kant says, is to use one's life not as an end in itself but as a means to the alleviation of misery.[52] The problem is not with the principle but perhaps with Kant's interpretation of it – or so it might appear. The law has provided us with some examples of how theory can in this case perhaps be equated with the morally desirable course of action. *Airedale NHS Trust v. Bland*[53] concerned a young man who was left in a persistent vegetative state after a human crush at Hillsborough football stadium in which 96 people died. There was no hope of recovery and he could have no 'interest' in life or further life (as he was permanently unaware of what was happening to him). But it is clear that everyone has, at some point, a legitimate interest in how they are (and how they will be) remembered, and how their body is treated after death. If this were not so, we would not treat the dead with the respect that we do at funerals.

Let us imagine a situation where a person has led a long and glorious life and brought much to themselves and others. Let us now imagine a situation arising where their dignity would be stripped from them, their achievements regarded as little, perhaps even their family bankrupted and falling into depression with the strain of caring for them. Imagine a society where such a thing was commonplace and the nobility of

---

[52] Kant I, *Duties towards the body in Regard to Life, Lectures in Ethics,* reprinted in: Donnelly J (ed.), *Suicide Right or Wrong?* Prometheus 1990.

[53] *Airedale NHS Trust v. Bland* [1993] 2 WLR 316.

mankind lowered by the need to keep everyone alive indefinitely. Suicide in such a situation might be regarded as heroic. We slowly arrive at the position adopted by Kant a short while later where he treats Cato[54] as an exception and an 'exception' to the rule. Cato ended his life in 46 B.C. heroically, to preserve his honour and to thwart Caesar: "... if he could not go on living as Cato, he would not go on living at all." There was no high-tech medicine in 46 B.C.. Examples of a hero's death were few and far between. But it is likely that Kant, on his own reasoning and contrary to claims otherwise, would find many – if not all – a modern-day rational suicide, 'death with dignity,' acceptable. The implication is that Cato had both a right and a duty to himself,[55] and his action was in accordance with the Categorical Imperative.

The judgment in *Bland* and the justification of Cato's suicide, both point to an interpretation of the Categorical Imperative that treats a person's life in its entirety, the person's wishes not only during life but how they will be remembered and the effect their life will have. Whatever they truly will with their life, that is to be respected both by the individual and by others.[56] From this, all other rights and duties stem.

---

[54] Campbell R, Collinson D, *Ending Lives,* Basil Blackwell Inc 1988, pp.22-23

[55] As Hinton notes, "Most societies admire those who meet their death willingly and bravely, but disapprove strongly of suicide. . . . People can be intensely hostile towards those who attempt to kill themselves, if they think the reasons are insufficient or cowardly." Hinton J, *Dying,* Penguin 1967, p.32. Kellehear suggests persons seeking assisted death may also be regarded as 'heroes; and persons ending their life by their own hand as 'anti-heroes.' Kellehear A, *A Social History of Dying,* 2007, p.231.

[56] In the *Bland* judgment, there was consideration of the wider interests including: the lack of dignity for him to continue to be subjected to such invasive measures; a desire to be remembered as cheerful, carefree, gregarious, and not as an object of pity; and the ordeal that the treatment involved for his family.

Ronald Dworkin comes to a similar conclusion when he says, "A person's right to be treated with dignity, I now suggest, is the right that others acknowledge his genuine critical interests: that they acknowledge that he is the kind of creature, and has the moral standing, such that it is intrinsically, objectively important how his life goes. . . . (Understanding that dignity means recognizing a person's critical interests, as distinct from advancing those interests, provides a useful reading of the Kantian principle that people should be treated as ends and never merely as means. . . .)"[57]

If we turn to the critical interests of someone who is mentally unstable for some reason (though not necessarily ill) – the sort of person that is sometimes labelled as 'vulnerable' in the face of access to self-deliverance literature, at what point do we have to cease to respect their ability to decide for themselves? Dworkin considers a concept of 'integrity' thus: ". . . if his choices and demands, no matter how firmly expressed, systematically or randomly contradict one another, reflecting no coherent sense of self and no discernable even short-term aims, then he has presumably lost the capacity that it is the point of autonomy to protect." [58] At that point, we still owe that person beneficence, and it is hoped that someone will look after his best interests and protect him from self-harm. How should such beneficence be applied? The law might be considered too blunt an instrument. The majority of people taking their own lives needlessly are neither easy to identify nor likely to be put under forcible protection for their own

---

[57] Dworkin R, *Life's Dominion – An Argument about Abortion and Euthanasia,* HarperCollins 1993, p236. For an opposing view of Dworkin's concept of 'critical interests,' see: Keown J, *Euthanasia Examined – Ethical, Clinical and Legal Perspectives,* CUP 1995, pp.50-53.

[58] Ibid. P.225.

good. Our attention must turn to suicide prevention – for those who have lost their ability, possibly temporarily, to determine their critical interests to the point where they might endanger their life.

There is a small potential for harm to acutely depressed individuals who might not take their lives by using the methods outlined were they not to have access to the information. This harm may well be more alleged than proven, and there are corresponding harms related to withholding the information. Several of the persons in Howard's study had suicidal ideation. Would they have committed suicide if the self-deliverance information had not been available to them? Initial reactions to early criticisms of *Final Exit* and suicides using a plastic bag, including a paper quoted by Howard *et al,*[59] had been countered in the journals by indicating that there had not been a corresponding rise in suicide rates.[60] Although there is insufficient evidence to prove this is always the case, there is sufficient to hypothesize that it is so rather than the reverse. When one method (such as the availability of North Sea Gas in the UK, or easy access to barbiturates) is removed, persons intent on committing suicide may often simply choose alternative means. A retrospective study conducted in Scotland and published in the same journal[61] also found a large proportion (59%) had chronic psychiatric illness rather than chronic debilitating or terminal physical illness, yet noted that publicity associated with 'self-deliverance' did not result in an increased

---

59 Marzuk PM, Tardiff K, Hirsch CS, *Increase in Suicide by Asphyxiation in New York City after the Publication of Final Exit,* N Engl J Med. 1993; 329:1508-1510.

60 Humphry D, Marzuk PM, Tardiff K, Hirsch C S, *Suicide by Asphyxiation after the Publication of Final Exit,* N Engl J Med 1994; 330:1017, Apr 7, 1994. Correspondence.

61 Jones LS, Wyatt JP, Busuttil A, *Plastic bag asphyxia in southeast Scotland,* Am J Forensic Med Pathol. 2000 Dec;21(4):401-5.

number of deaths from plastic bag asphyxia. Many of the deaths were difficult to predict and hence prevent. All such deaths – where they could have been prevented with appropriate psychological or psychiatric support – are deeply regrettable; but persons intent on suicide, whether for arguably justifiable or unjustifiable reasons, have a potential to go through with the act. Statistics for both the US and the UK indicate that helium suicide, the prominent method detailed in self-deliverance manuals, is low on the scale of choices. Hanging (UK) and guns (US) are consistently the main choices.

Suicide among young people has become an increasing concern. In America, it is the third leading cause of death for people aged fifteen to twenty-four, yet analysis of the predictors has thrown new light on whether it is an 'impulsive' act among vulnerable individuals.[62] Recent research demonstrates that most suicides are not attempted impulsively. Smith, Witte, Bender *et al*[63] analyse metadata to demonstrate that such popular media representations are incorrect,[64] and that there is

[62] Smith A, Witte T, Teale N, King S, Bender T, Joiner T, *Revisiting Impulsivity in Suicide,* Behav Sci Law 2008; 26(6):779-797. This age range also suggests a limit to the usefulness of making special provisions for persons under 21 (rather than under 24).

The researchers quote a figure of 30,000 total suicides in the United States each year, and later mention over 1,000 college students die by suicide every year. Statistics from Centre for Suicide Research http://cebmh.warne.ox.ac.uk/csr/profile.html Accessed 12 Sep 2010: "In the UK there are approximately 5000 suicides per year, and considerably more deaths from suicide than from road traffic accidents".

[63] Ibid.

[64] Carey B, *Making sense of the great suicide debate,* The New York Times 2008. http://www.nytimes.com/2008/02/10/weekinreview/10carey.html?_r=2&ref=us&oref=slo gin&oref=slogin. Accessed 12 Sep 2010. The paper claims that, "Suicide is an intimate, often impulsive decision that has defied scientific understanding."

considerable knowledge available about suicidal ideation. The authors suggest that while impulsiveness *as a general personality characteristic* is one of the factors present in many suicidal individuals, impulsiveness *at the time of self-harm* is less important. They call this second type of impulsiveness, 'state impulsivity' (impulsiveness at the point in time of the suicide), which was previously believed to predicate suicides, has little influence.[65] The data also suggest that the acquired expertise to accomplish the suicide is quite separate from the desire to die by suicide. Knowledge alone, such as contained in this manual, is not in itself sufficient to trigger a suicide. While there are many risk factors associated with suicide (including depression and substance abuse), the majority of people displaying such factors do not go on to commit suicide. 95 per cent of individuals testing positive for suicide risk will not die by suicide.

A number of suicide prevention programmes have been implemented in both the U.K. and abroad. There is some evidence that sound suicide assessment has the potential to save lives. Evidence that withholding suicide information makes any impact on suicide figures is less than convincing. If the factors predisposing to suicide are all present, the individual will likely make some plan or other, with or without the

---

[65] On the other hand, " . . . three proximal, jointly necessary, and sufficient causes must be present before a person will die by suicide; these are: 1) feelings of perceived burdensomeness, 2) a sense of thwarted belongingness, and 3) an acquired capability to lethally self-harm. Perceived burdensomeness occurs when a person believes his/her death is worth more than his/her life to others. In essence, a person experiencing burdensomeness feels that others would be better off if s/he were dead. Thwarted belongingness results when one of the basic human needs, to be connected to others, is not met. Both perceived burdensomeness and thwarted belongingness are theorized to contribute to the desire for suicide (cf, suicidal ideation), and elevated levels of both perceived burdensomeness and thwarted belongingness have been found to significantly predict suicidal desire.") Smith, Witte *et al, supra.)*

availability of self-deliverance manuals. This suggests possibly a more effective way of protecting the rights of vulnerable individuals than reducing the flow of reliable data on methods.

Before leaving the issue of rights, it is worth mentioning that many philosophers put the phrase 'right-to-die' in inverted commas to emphasise that it is not technically a right in any sense of the word.[66] It is arguable that one cannot demand a right to something that will happen anyway. One might seek a right to determine the time, or the manner. Talk of 'rights' tends to belong to current use of political rhetoric rather than any philosophical demand.[67] The rights commonly sought by pressure groups (to end someone's life or to have one's life ended) do not exist in our society and are not established merely by asserting them.[68] Reform of the law on murder, on the other hand, to allow assisted suicide in exceptional circumstances and with proper precautions, is both possible and desirable.

---

[66] Talk of rights often tends to polarize issues that are already confrontational. Arguably imprecise use of the language in phrases such as 'a right to die' has been ably called into question both by advocates and opponents of living wills. See: Fletcher J, *The Right to Choose When to Die*, Hemlock Quarterly, January 1989 p3; Kass L, *Is There a Right to Die?*, Hastings Center Report, 1993 Jan-Feb 34-43; Miller P, *Death With Dignity and the Right to Die: Sometimes Doctors Have a Duty to Hasten Death*, Journal of Medical Ethics 1987 13:81-85.

[67] For a concise introduction to the use of rights-based language in morality, law and political rhetoric, see: Brandt R, *The Concept of a Moral Right and Its Function*, Journal of Philosophy 1983 80:29-45; Palley C, *The United Kingdom and Human Rights*, London: Sweet & Maxwell 1991 especially pp.71-78, 'Human Rights Talk - Rhetoric and Enforcement Devices.'

[68] Pollard B, *Euthanasia – Should We Kill The Dying*, 1989 Mount Series, p.32-33.

Stakeholder:	Right:	Duty:
'Right-to-die' society	Publish self-deliverance info	Responsible attitude to suicide prevention
Exit members etc	to purchase / receive suicide info	to use it wisely, and without passing it on
Society in general	to know such info is available	protect those at risk;
Author	freedom of speech	minimize harm; be accurate; be practical; 'least worst option;' pull publication if harm develops.
The unbearably ill	assistance from those willing (in the form of information)	not to implicate others

The rights and duties suggested for this formal exercise are identified simply with a view to finding a right and justifiable ethical outcome.[69] While the law uses rights-and-duties in the sense of contract, a moral sense may involve duties that do not

---

[69] Omitting, for brevity, correlative rights such as, 'if the book is offered at £x, a buyer has the right to purchase it at that price and the seller has a correlative duty to sell it at that price.'

involve the same degree of obligation. As John Stuart Mill pointed out, "No-one has a moral right to our generosity or beneficence, because we are not morally bound to practice those virtues towards any given individual."[70]

Kant's Categorical Imperative[71]

H. If the action in Step II is done, who, if anyone, will be treated with disrespect?

Answer: those who might be vulnerable, at risk of irrational self-harm (or feel subtly coerced) by the availability of the literature. This may be more an irrational concern than a reality given the data and understanding about suicidal ideation. It may not be a factor at all - vulnerable persons likely to attempt suicide will make a plan, with or without self-deliverance information. The fear of pain, which may have been a disincentive in the past, is probably less so now. Most people understand that dignified and painless suicide is possible with helium, just as the 'car exhaust and hose pipe' method was common knowledge in the days before catalytic converters. The main difference that self-deliverance information is likely to make would be reducing botched suicides.

There is evidence to suggest that the *promise* of a peaceful end, whether through the promise of a physician offering to grant a

---

[70] Mill J, *Utilitarianism* (in Collected Works), as discussed in Beauchamp T, Childress J, *Principles of Biomedical Ethics* OUP 1994, p.74.

[71] Kant formulated the Categorical Imperative in three ways: 1)Act only according to that maxim whereby you can at the same time will that it should become a universal law. 2)Act in such a way that you treat humanity, whether in your own person or in the person of any other, never merely as a means to an end, but always at the same time as an end. 3)Therefore, every rational being must so act as if he were through his maxim always a legislating member in the universal kingdom of ends.

euthanasia request or through the knowledge of reliable self-deliverance techniques, can trigger hope and courage; but one cannot assume that this will always be the case or that, of itself, it can suitably address clinical depression. Neither does depression have to be treated with a view to changing suicidal ideation, even if an expressed wish for early death may add some urgency to the proceedings. Studies have stressed the importance of managing clinical bias (in attitudes to assisted death) when treating depression.[72] A desire for death is not a state that needs to be treated as if it were itself 'depression' until such a desire goes away.[73] It is enough that the depression is managed. Exit's "90-day waiting period" may seem over-cautious in view of the psychological mechanisms described by Smith *et al* *(Revisiting Impulsivity in Suicide),*[74] and even delay things to the point where the person dies before having the opportunity to assimilate the self-deliverance material. A major difference is involved where persons may or may not quite reasonably have a desire for rational suicide, even if the mechanisms are similar. The issue becomes one of establishing

---

[72] Ganzini L, Leong G, Fenn D, Silva J, Weinstock R, *Evaluation of Competence to Consent to Assisted Suicide: Views of Forensic Psychiatrists,* Am J Psychiatry 2000; 157:595–600): "The ethical views of psychiatrists may influence their clinical opinions regarding patient competence to consent to assisted suicide. The extensive evaluation recommended by forensic psychiatrists would likely both minimize this bias and assure that only competent patients have access to assisted suicide, but the process might burden terminally ill patients."

[73] Dutch experience suggests desire for hastened death is not normally associated with depression. ". . . in our experience, requests for euthanasia are mostly well considered and commonly not associated with depression. Terminally ill cancer patients who request euthanasia often do so from a position of acceptance of their impending death, rather than being driven by an underlying psychiatric disturbance." van der Lee M, van der Bom J, Swarte N, Heintz A, de Graeff A, van den Bout J, *Euthanasia and Depression: A Prospective Cohort Study Among Terminally Ill Cancer Patients,* Journal of Clinical Oncology 2005 23(27):6607-6612.

[74] *Supra,* III (G) footnote.

capacity, or ensuring the person her or himself re-establishes a capacity to make a rational decision, especially after an initial prognosis and any unsettling effect which that may have triggered. Ideally, this might be facilitated with a routine but expert assessment, yet it should not be beyond the mature individual to consider the "proximal, jointly necessary, and sufficient causes" mentioned by Smith *et al*,[75] to consider the degree to which she or he is able to relate to their 'critical interests' that we have described previously, and assess (or foresee) the point at which they will be able to make a competent decision.

Some people suggest that allowing people to take their own life in a rational way, even in the face of unbearable and unrelievable indignity or suffering, sends out a 'wrong message' which implicitly undermines the sense of security felt by those of a different mindset. Dworkin[76] has argued powerfully against such a position. "But though we may feel our own dignity at stake in what others do about death, and may sometimes wish to make others act as we think right, a true appreciation of dignity argues decisively in the opposite direction – for individual freedom, not coercion, for a regime of law and attitude that encourages each of us to make mortal decisions for himself. Freedom is the cardinal, absolute requirement of self-respect: no one treats his life as having any intrinsic, objective importance unless he insists on leading that life himself, not being ushered along it by others, no matter how much he loves or respects or fears them. Decisions about life and death are the most important, the most crucial for forming and expressing personality, that anyone makes; we

---

[75] *Supra,* III (G) footnote.

[76] *Ibid.* p.239.

think it crucial to get those decisions right, but also crucial to make them in character, and for ourselves."

A limitation of self-deliverance manuals is that some persons – for instance, a person who is quadriplegic – will still be treated unequally since they have hardly any physical capacity.

I. If the action in Step II is not done, who. if anyone, will be treated with disrespect?

Answer: those for whom the information is intended. The many members to whom this update has been promised. Members of the public who legitimately require such reliable and accurate information for peace of mind and possible self-deliverance. In particular (information not available in other manuals), the withholding of detailed information on helium, including the simple methods of adjusting gas flow; responsible provision of starvation safety information; more detailed and simpler explanation of the compression method (together with greater evidence to reassure and give confidence); rebuttal of misinformation about Exit's earlier booklet *(Departing Drugs)* from misinformed sources, correcting what could be needless and upsetting apprehension over the reliability of Exit material.

Two further, controversial categories, must be persons who end their life simply because they are old and 'tired of life;' and then those that do so as part of a loving agreement (or 'suicide pact') with a long-term partner or someone of a strongly kindred spirit.[77] Even given that there may be no overt or

---

[77] James S, *Suicide Pacts: Some Say Ultimate Act of Love,* ABC News 20 Aug 2010 , http://abcnews.go.com/Health/suicide-pacts-rise-elderly-act-love-bad-economy/story?id=11439411. See also Tears G, *Love letter that sealed a death pact,* Observer   7   October   2007

subtle coercion, these categories remain difficult. They are perhaps included in the 'noble' exceptions countenanced by Kant[78] and which do not directly involve illness. They are difficult to understand for many. Yet they would seem to satisfy the 'critical interest' test submitted by Dworkin, to which one might add that people should be free to seek their own critical interests in their own way. A person who fails, as one of the parties within a justifiable suicide pact, could be said to have been let down by not having clear information available.[79]

Exit was formed in 1980 with the specific remit of publishing such material after strong evidence of great public demand. Its then parent organisation, the Voluntary Euthanasia Society, after publicly announcing plans to produce the world's first 'suicide guide', saw membership rise, from an initial 2000 members, at a rate of 1000 a month over the next six months. Publication was halted at the last minute, and the Scottish section, now Exit, broke away in order to publish and satisfy the demand, which was then estimated at 10,000 members.[80]

J. Which alternative is preferable, H or I? [x] H [   ] I

The evidence arguing for non-publication appears quite flimsy upon analysis. But given the seriousness of even one ill-judged

---

http://www.guardian.co.uk/world/2007/oct/07/france.books Both items accessed 13 Sep 2010.

[78] *Vide supra,* the death of Cato.

[79] Exit euthanasia blog, *Heartache of a death not shared – a helium suicide fails,* http://exiteuthanasia.wordpress.com/2010/08/21/heartache-of-a-death-not-shared-a-helium-suicide-fails/ 21 Aug 2010 Accessed 13 Sep 2010 (Death and attempted prosecution of Angela and William Stanton).

[80] Minutes of the Executive Committee Meetings 16-17 August 1980.

suicide, vigilance should be maintained. If evidence arises that the book is a factor that causes ill-judged deaths, then it should immediately be re-considered together with the option of limiting sales. The proposal to make it more expensive when purchased via the Internet or bookshops, compared to a heavily discounted price for members of Exit could further reduce the likelihood of it being purchased by those whose 'critical interests'[81] it could offend.

K. If the action in Step II is done, who, if anyone, will be treated unlike others?

Answer: It initially seemed that those persons with capacity will be treated unlike those persons without capacity. But this is probably not the case. The availability of the information for rational self-deliverance is there for all at such time as it might be used sensibly, including (at a future time) those persons who previously lacked capacity but subsequently regained it. A price differential (plus a three month wait, age checks and any other conditions introduced by Exit) will mean that Exit members will be treated 'unlike' non-members, but membership is generally open to all adults subject to those same conditions.

L. If action in Step II is not done, who, if anyone will be treated unlike others?

Answer: Those who cannot die gently and/or on their own terms compared to those who can afford to go to Dignitas in Switzerland; those whose condition enables them to die through the prescribing of increasing doses of drugs under the

---

[81] *Vide supra* under 'Rights and Duties.'

doctrine of 'double-effect;'[82] those for whom a naturally peaceful death will not occur and for whom palliative care will not bring them dignity or freedom from suffering in their dying days. It can be argued that it is very unfair that some people have the means to a peaceful, painless, and dignified death and others do not. People with some diseases that yield to palliative care. People who can afford to go to Dignitas.[83] People who can simply ease their death through refusing treatment (in an advance directive).[84] They receive 'special' treatment at the hands of circumstances. Not making the information available would fail to reduce the disparity.

M. Which alternative is preferable, K or L? [x] K [ ] L

Not publishing (L) would seem to involve treating people unequally.

---

[82] In medical cases the doctrine of double effect can be used as a defence. As was established by Judge Devlin in the 1957 trial of Dr John Bodkin Adams, causing death through the administration of lethal drugs to a patient, if the intention is solely to alleviate pain, is not considered murder even if death is a potential or even likely outcome. Double effect technically applies to the law of England & Wales: in Scotland a not dissimilar outcome is arrived at legally by consideration of motive.

[83] Among the reasons (underlying diseases) of people going to Dignitas: "Thirty-six of the 114 unnamed Britons had various forms of cancer, 27 had motor neurone disease and 17 had multiple sclerosis," quoted from: Campbell D, *Suicide clinic challenged over patients who could have lived 'for decades,'* http://www.guardian.co.uk/society/2009/jun/21/dignitas-suicide-clinic-britons Guardian 21 June 2009 Accessed 13 Sep 2010. Dignitas costs are included at http://www.dignitas.ch/WeitereTexte/AProspekt_DIGNITAS_E.pdf on the society's English brochure.

[84] Docker C, Advance Directives/Living Wills, In: McLean S (ed.), *Contemporary Issues in Law, Medicine and Ethics,* Dartmouth 1996.

N. Are there benefits if everyone did the action in Step II (c)?

Answer: Yes, with the general availability of self-deliverance information, society might feel prompted to take greater care to protect any who might be more vulnerable as a result (certain people are already vulnerable since suicide information of varying quality is readily available on the Internet, in newspapers etc.) It could also increase the likelihood of improved palliative care and/or just law reform (*as per Section I (B) ii & iii*).

This promising approach is related to possible reform of the law for allowing assisted suicide in exceptional circumstances. A recent world study of quality of dying raised the idea that palliative care improves where there is pressure for assisted suicide.[85] Careful legislation and greater openness might encourage persons seeking suicide to come into contact with the necessary professional support during their quest and so reduce the overall suicide rate. Such monitoring could also identify when a labelling of 'psychiatric illness' as warranting exclusion from justifiable suicide is little more than paternalism.[86]

---

[85] Economist Intelligence Unit:
The quality of death - Ranking end-of-life care across the world 2010,
http://graphics.eiu.com/upload/QOD_main_final_edition_Jul12_toprint.pdf
Accessed June 24, 2010. *See also:* Exit Euthanasia Blog: *Euthanasia & hospices: the unexpected link,* 14th July 2010,
http://exiteuthanasia.wordpress.com/2010/07/14/euthanasia-the-hospice-uneasy-deathbed-mates/ accessed June 24, 2010.

[86] Freia A, Schenkerb T, Finzenb A, Kräuchib K, et al, *Assisted suicide as conducted by a "Right-to-Die" society in Switzerland: A descriptive analysis of 43 consecutive cases,* Swiss Med Wkly 2001;131:375–380.

O. Are there benefits if nobody did the action in Step II?

Answer: No.

P. Which alternative is preferable. N or O?   [x] N   [   ] 0

Step IV: Decision making & implementation

A. Making a defensible ethical decision.

Based on the analysis in Step III, answer the question in Step II. Indicate the letters of the categories that best support your response. Add any arguments justifying your choice of these ethical principles to support your decision. Where there are conflicting rights and duties, choose and defend those that take precedence. (Note: Just make and justify your choice here; leave any action steps for parts B and D below.)

The major ethical dilemma is that by publishing the book in a way that it can be purchased other than through Exit, the nominal checks which Exit applies can not be applied, such as the age of the applicant/purchaser and also the three month waiting period. Should the book be published?

Response:

ETHICAL DECISION TO PUBLISH

A difficult decision has been made easier by calm analysis; and, although the facts point to a clear response, it is not a decision that is undertaken lightly.

Each of the ethical tests applied suggests a clear choice one way rather than the other, and all gravitating in the same direction. Yet the responsibilities involved also suggest that the decision should only be implemented with a clear degree of accountability and control, such as can be achieved.

These factors argue in favour of publication; they are overall determinative and so the decision is to go ahead:

Respect for the critical interests of any individual, and a person's innate right to determine, in his or her own way, the critical interests that define his or her own life and everything that it stands for: respect for this right elicits a duty to publish such information which can support that and which one is able and capable so to do, should one wish to. To be valid, such publishing needs to be accurate, to be practical, and to be accessible.

Objections, based on the potential for harm to vulnerable individuals are, on the basis of available evidence and expert analysis, demonstrated to be over-estimated and, even given that they might have theoretical weight as yet to be established, are not a valid reason for limiting access to information by those who, in their own judgement and on a rational objective basis, have a genuine need of it.

Every person is unique. In some instances a person's critical interests may be hidden from themself. In such a situation, we could call that person 'vulnerable' as they are unable to assert their critical interests, whether through dementia, other mental impairment, temporary mental/emotional upset, or through not having reached an age of maturity whereby he or she has yet to be able to assess such critical life interests. Such a person might even act in a way that is contrary to those interests. Protecting such persons from harm is a difficult task, whether one uses a 'best interests' test, a 'substituted judgment' test[87], or other tests, some of which might simply be based on beneficence, but they are best entrusted to suitably qualified and appropriate persons, such as guardians, parents, psychologists, and those empowered by suicide-prevention outreach programmes – this being far more effective than any minimal measures of very doubtful impact and influence, such as stemming the flow of otherwise needed and harm-reducing information on suicide techniques.

In cases where vulnerability is particularly difficult to assess, the requirement to allow each individual to seek out their own interests in their own manner is very important. For without this, life itself can be reduced of meaning.

n.b.: Letters and Roman Numerals at the end of paragraphs that follow, indicate sections of the chapter supporting each statement.

Harm resulting from inadequate knowledge of safe techniques (and these can include, at worst, serious long-term physical

---

[87] "Best interests is not a test of "substituted judgement" (what the person would have wanted), but rather it requires a determination to be made by applying an objective test as to what would be in the person's best interests." Mental Capacity Act 2005 http://www.legislation.gov.uk/ukpga/2005/9/pdfs/ ukpgaen_20050009_en.pdf

damage), can be minimized by making the book more widely available. **III (B)**

Additional benefits include: peace of mind to those who fear an undignified death, reassuring them with the knowledge of how to achieve dying in a dignified and painless manner should all else fail. A sense of control and sometimes the courage to live longer sometimes occurs in persons who are terminally ill, as a sense of control brings with it a sense of hope (in being able to determine one's own fate). **III (D) & III (I)**

This in no way devalues successful and unbiased treatment of depression following a diagnosis of terminal illness. **III (H)**

Greater safeguarding of the accuracy of the material – important to limit mishaps – is enhanced by separation of authorship and originating society (Exit). **III (D)**

The idea that vulnerable persons could be harmed is difficult to substantiate and more likely to have arisen from coincidental circumstances. Persons do not, as previously believed, commit suicide impulsively, even if they are impulsive by nature. Committing suicide will often be by the most convenient method, or the method believed to be most pain-free, rather than a choice between doing the act and not doing it. Suicide prevention is therefore most effective at preventing people from feeling suicidal; not from restricting the means. Current psychological studies tend to be supported by cross-disciplinary statistics. **III (E) & III (G)**

Publication supports the individual's essential interests and dignity. **III (G)**

It might be argued that a vulnerable person's dignity is compromised by the publication, or that the publication sends out a 'wrong message;' this is a misapprehension of the situation and the means of according respect to a person's dignity. **III (H)**

Is it fair? As a service, the book is primarily for those with unbearable and unrelievable suffering and /or indignity. Vulnerable persons are not treated unfairly since it could be of service to them should they in the future gain or regain capacity. **III (K)**

The terms of publication favour those who have already supported Exit (by offering it to them at a reduced price). Rather than justify this by saying their subscription has already helped to make possible the research and publishing (which it has), one can say their need is more established and persistent. **III (K)**

Why not just let people find out from existing sources? The book corrects a number of sources of error in popular thinking about suicide (and particularly, self-deliverance) methods – some of these misapprehensions could lead to disastrous results. **III (B)** & **III (I)**

Finding information on ending one's life is not so difficult; but it may not inspire confidence or offer reassurance when facing an unknown future unless from a trusted and established source. **III (I)**

The book does not encourage suicide – it simply reduces the chance of further pain and suffering for persons who have made an enduring decision to end their life. **III (I)**

Can't people just go to Switzerland? This is a costly option. It means such freedom from worry and a dignified death are only available to those who can afford it, and discriminates against those who cannot. **III (L)**

But surely doctors can just give increasing doses of morphine? And what about living wills? Again, these two options unfairly discriminate in favour of persons who can be assisted through the doctrine of double effect or cessation of treatment. It discriminates against people whose suffering and indignity frequently falls outside those categories. **III (L)**

General availability of information of this kind is likely to increase pressure for improved palliative care, equitable law reform, and even enhanced suicide-prevention programmes for those seen as vulnerable. **III (N)**

It is hoped that this use of Kallman & Grillo's ethical template, and the processes, data and conclusions uncovered in the course of the analysis, might also benefit others working in the field, by placing such publishing on a more robust ethical footing. **III (D)**

The analysis, originally aimed at answering the question, *is it ethical to publish?* has not only answered in the affirmative but, in this case, translated into an obligation. More research is still needed on suicide prevention, as well as further research into reliable, painless methods of self-deliverance, and perhaps responsible legislative reform that could address perceived need for assisted suicide as well as inequalities posed by travel to Switzerland for assisted dying. Use of this book as an aid in the dying process does not rule out loved ones being at the side of someone ending their life by their own hand; but in the UK there is the fear of prolonged and traumatic police enquiries, required by law, even when no prosecution results. This also needs to be addressed.

B. List the specific steps needed to implement your defensible ethical decision.

o   Finalise manuscript for publication with the inclusion of this defensible ethical decision chapter.
o   Enable Exit to purchase copies at cost-price for internal distribution with added purchase-requirements.
o   Monitor accuracy and usability of information and update as necessary.
o   Reserve right to cease publication and distribution if untoward results demonstrate clear cause and effect.

C. Show how the major stakeholders are affected by these actions.

o   Persons with unrelievable and unbearable suffering will be able to read ways of ending one's life in a peaceful and dignified manner on purchase of the book.
o   Persons who face an unknown future that might include unrelievable and unbearable suffering will be able to read ways of ending one's life in a peaceful and dignified manner on purchase of the book and so receive hope, courage and reassurance.
o   Exit will be able to better fulfil its commitment to its members.
o   Vulnerable persons are unlikely to be affected.

D. What other longer-term changes (political, legal, technical, societal, organizational) would help prevent such problems in the future?

o   Legislation to permit assisted suicide in exceptional circumstances could make use of the book in its present form largely redundant (though not the research into methods). Such legislation would, however, present ethical challenges of its own.

E. What should have been done or not done in the first place (at the pivot point) to avoid this dilemma?

Earlier research might have generated productive decisions earlier. Moral philosophy can generate the right questions, yielding a more fruitful and clearer way of working. Legislation to permit more aid-in-dying would have reduced the need for publication, but also facilitated even greater transparency, openness and cooperation.

WARNING

This book is distributed subject to the following conditions:—

1. It is available only to members of Scottish Exit of at least 90 days duration or to Exit members in other countries where it is legal to give advice concerning self-deliverance (suicide). This may include members of HEMLOCK our 'opposite number' in the U.S.A. as the legal situation within the U.S.A. becomes clear.

2. Each booklet carries a number which will be identified on Scottish Exit's central register of members with the name of the purchaser. Should a booklet find its way into non-member's hands the original purchaser will be readily identified and MAY—under certain circumstances—such as the forwarding of the booklet to England or certain other countries, be liable to possible arrest by the authorities of these countries. Applicants must be listed on our Scottish register.

3. Having noted the essential content which interests a purchaser the booklet should be stored in a secure place such as a safe deposit or bank until further reference is required.

4. It is issued (sold) subject to the clear understanding that the purchaser bears total responsibility for 'abuse'.

5. Scottish Exit retains the right to refuse to sell the booklet to any person whom they judge, through knowledge of their background, to be either irresponsible or of unsound mind.

6. © 1980 by Scottish Exit Committee and George B. Mair Chairman.

7. All rights are reserved. No part of this publication may be reproduced, stored in a retrieval system, or transmitted in any form or by any means, electronic, mechanical, photocopying, recording or otherwise without permission of the Copyright owner.

8. Persons using self-deliverance are asked to destroy this booklet before doing so.

9. Exceptions to the 90 day restriction may be made at the discretion of the committee.

10. **DESPITE UNAVOIDABLE PUBLICITY LINKED TO PUBLICATION, AND DUE TO CIRCUMSTANCES BEYOND CONTROL OF THE AUTHOR AND OF SCOTTISH EXIT COMMITTEE, THIS BOOKLET IS RESTRICTED TO PRIVATE CIRCULATION WITHIN A PRIVATE ASSOCIATION OF LIKE-THINKING PEOPLE FROM EVERY WALK OF LIFE.**

5

The original 'warning' page from the 1980 booklet, *How to Die With Dignity*.

Recommended general reading

- Departing Drugs. Docker C, Smith C, and the International Drugs Consensus Working Party, Voluntary Euthanasia Society of Scotland (EXIT) 1993. This is a cornerstone book on methods of suicide. Readers should bear in mind it was published many years ago, but it is still useful and recommended reading. There are various restrictions on its purchase: buyers must be established members of Exit or show a minimum of three months membership of another recognised right-to-die society on the official application form.
- Suicide and Attempted Suicide. Stone G, Carroll & Graf 1999. Much of this book is available online free of charge at http://www.suicidemethods.net/
- How We Die. Nuland S, Chatto & Windus 1994.
- British National Formulary. Pharmaceutical Press, PO Box 151, Wallingford, Oxford, OX10 8QU, and also online at https://www.pharmpress.com. (You may find an equivalent drugs manual more suited to the country you are living in if outside the UK, but failing that the BNF carries much useful generic information.)
- Martindale – The Complete Drug Reference. Pharmaceutical Press, London. Martindale provides professional and comprehensive information on drugs and medicines used throughout the world. It is an expensive volume, so you may wish to consult it by going to a good library.
- The Natural Death Handbook. Rider & Co; 3rd Revised edition (6 Nov 2003). An invaluable resource to many aspects of death and dying, all types of UK funeral advice including green burials and diy funerals, practical preparations for dying, home care, grieving.

About EXIT workshops

Note: *there may be a number of people and organisations offering 'workshops' and using the Exit name in some form. Make sure you get the full information from the best source. Genuine Exit workshops, described and referred to here and elsewhere in the book, are organised UK-wide through EXIT, 17 Hart Street, Scotland U.K. Unless you book the workshop using this postal address, it is not a genuine Exit workshop.*

There are many strands to the background of *Five Last Acts*. Endless hours of collating and scrutinising data, practical experiments, analysing suicides and feedback. But one aspect has been unusual. During the travelling 'hands-on' workshops where the material is presented in and used in an easy-to-follow format, one thing becomes apparent: many of the participants have prepared, thought long and hard about the techniques, and have both useful questions and dramatic insights. Such as how people cope with limited physical mobility can cope with equipment. These ideas are examined and disseminated, but often form a source of practical help that could not have easily been envisaged otherwise. But aren't they morbid? On the contrary! Knowing answers to these things seems to release a tension valve. Once the knowledge has been assimilated, people find they have made new friends and usually the sessions are punctuated by laughter and great good spirits. But to a person who hasn't encountered them, the idea may still sound a bit threatening. So this last section is to let the reader see into the atmosphere that allows such constructive communication on what is after all still a 'taboo' subject.

"It was very cathartic to meet a few like-minded nice people," says a lady from Devon. And of course, it's not just a social gathering, or a 'sermon to the converted'. We are sharing and overcoming some of our deepest fears about how we will control the uncontrollable.

These workshops are more than a classroom experience. How often do you learn something technically only for it to go out of your head at the critical moment? So we make them a journey of experience. We make the final moments vivid. We come to terms with the bewildering array of circumstances that could arise and work out how to cope. "I feel much more competent than I did 24 hours ago, both technically and emotionally," says a participant from Durham.

There is no 'one size fits all,' and the workshops stress familiarity with several methods in case you change your preferences or circumstances change them for you. "The helium method seems great, but my arthritic hands might struggle to cope." You may have a supply of pills, but what if your ability to swallow becomes impaired? And then the ever-common question of what to do if stuck in a hospital or nursing home. There's no 'one best method' – but having an array of ways at your fingertips allows you both to plan and to improvise effectively.

Feedback during the workshops benefits everyone. "I particularly appreciated getting details of where to buy the various items," says a lady from Caithness. Some contributions become permanent features, such as the information on disability-aids (tap-turners) that can help you turn the helium valve.

The hotels we choose vary but most have gone out of their way to make us comfortable. Advance preparation and experience helps, but there is always the unexpected. On one occasion, building works meant there were no restaurant facilities inhouse or nearby. But after a quick discussion we reached a consensus – send out for pizzas! And in spite of the seriousness of the subject, there is often much shared laughter. A comment echoed by many: "I wouldn't have believed that learning this could have been so much fun!"

Expectations about the workshops range from, will it be explicit enough to will it be too shocking. Hopeful it is neither. "Your call on Sunday evening made it feel less daunting," wrote one Edinburgh woman. Whereas someone else said, "I feared you would beat about the bush . . . but you showed us equipment, invited us to handle it, and demonstrated how to use it."

The challenge we often use at the start of a workshop is, "If you are just in your hotel room, now, could you get everything you need for a successful self-deliverance in half an hour?" By the end of the session, the answers are 'yes.'

Exit workshops are one-day or two-day intensive, interactive sessions covering the main methods of self-deliverance. They cover the information in this volume in a 'hands-on' way. Participants are limited to about 20 to 25 people to allow for plenty of time to convey techniques in ways that each person understands. There are demonstrations, and at different points in the workshop, the participants will work in teams or individually to make sure they have mastered the material (although no-one is forced to join in more than they want to.) Moral, emotional and legal practicalities are covered as well as the nitty-gritty of drugs and assembling equipment. In spite of the responsibly handled serious subject matters, most participants find them great fun, as well as uplifting. The aim is to empower; and by the end of the day participants will *know* how to handle end-of-life situations if the need arises, not just refer to a set of instructions.

Exit subsidises these workshops so that people are not prevented from attending due to cost. They are held in different parts of the UK based on perceived demand and may be taken abroad in the near future. They are not connected or similar to the seminars produced by an Australian group of a similar name operating occasionally in the UK. Exit workshops are 'low profile' and conducted in such a way as to avoid the sort of publicity that risks venue owners refusing permission at the last minute.

They might be small things, but the workshops are a sharing experience. Here's some examples from a recent tour and some of the ideas, both human and technical, so readers can see how people cope with self-deliverance challenges just as they do with all the other challenges and practicalities of life.

The story of a workshop tour

Leeds
An unlucky event unearthed things we hadn't thought of. A postal strike around the time we were sending out confirmations of places raised warning bells. People couldn't get to the workshop if they didn't get the notification! Hence what was expected to be a routine phone-around to make sure people were informed in time. Some people were worried about coming. As if taking such a 'big step' was sealing their fate. Some were worried it would be too 'explicit' and some that it wouldn't be explicit enough. A friendly chat soon put minds at rest.
We can't always get everything right about venues – most are booked by remote. But with the Leeds one we had struck

lucky. A modern, custom-designed hotel included the most forward-thinking features without sacrificing a touch of luxury. Big comfy sofas made relaxing easy and the well-designed meeting room was simplicity itself being on the ground-floor. The atmosphere was so convivial, most of the group even agreed to a photo (which was used in the magazine).

Nottingham

Here we weren't so fortunate. The hotel turned out to be less than easy to find for many people. The city centre neighbourhood looked rather unappealing as an early evening approached. It was a bigger group than in Leeds and problems with getting room details right were an administrative headache. One ray of sunlight was an extra canister of helium, sent free of charge by the balloon company as they thought the tap on the first one might be too stiff. This was helpful as it allowed two smaller groups of participants to get to grips with the 'kit'. One early suggestion had been to 'make a tape' of the proceedings for those unfortunately unable to attend a workshop. This was soon seen to be impractical though. Workshops are an experience rather than seminar or lecture format. Most of the value would be lost on an audio tape and would be hard to capture on video. (Video is still a possibility but it will take some time to work out the details.) A nice surprise was a lady's 'suicide kit' which she proudly showed to the rest of the group. Admirable in that it only took up a small space in her handbag and would excite little unwanted attention. These kits are based on the compression method and becoming increasingly common as an emergency backup that people can carry anywhere with them (You make them yourself – we don't supply them!)

Some discussion covered the new travel enquiry form that some chemists such as Boots are asking people to complete before supplying anti-malarials such as chloroquine. They are basically just a way of covering Boots legally, and if you decline their advice to buy more expensive drugs (which are also generally better at preventing malaria).

Plymouth

After eternal train delays and hold-ups on damp platform between Leeds and Nottingham, the admin worries over the long trip to Plymouth were mounting. But it couldn't have been more pleasant. A long journey that included sunrise at Berwick on Tweed and sunset over Newton Abbott and the River Teign, and the train ran on time and with the efficiency of India's robust railways.

One of the greatest contributions at this workshop was the suggestion to recall positive memories of loved ones when writing farewell notes. One member suggested how much more effective still would be individual notes, remembering special shared moments with the recipient. (This principle is well illustrated in the film *The Hours*)

Several people contributed dramatic stories. Including someone who has personally had malaria three times, and a woman who movingly recalled the trauma of refusing treatment to a relative. The practice of phoning round beforehand (which we'd implemented for the rest of the tour) yielded some stranger results. Someone slammed the phone down thinking it was an unsolicited call to sell double-glazing! But another person recalled how their fears had been calmed by the friendly call.

Manchester

There were no travel problems – the hotel was very easy to get to – but the hotel was also very unresponsive. Just getting them to supply coffees resulted in confrontations! But we'd hired a large suite rather than a function room, and the convivial surroundings helped to bond us as a group.

In the practicals with the plastic-bag-and-drugs method, one person discovered how much easier it was, given the types of bags being often used, to put the rubber bands around a large bag before putting it on. This sounds counter-intuitive (and counter the advice in most manuals that say put the rubber bands around the neck first) but actually works quite well – but depending on the plastic and type of bag you have. Experimentation and dress-rehearsal, as always, is the key.

Glasgow

The overnight sell-out of the Edinburgh workshop meant we transferred a few people to the Glasgow one, which in turn then also sold out quickly. We went to great lengths to try to supply a hearing loop for one member – something we had not encountered before. In practice though, anyone just slightly hard of hearing can generally arrange to be close to what is being said. Why two helium tanks, someone asked? The answer of course is that one is quite sufficient. But a second one is a back-up, just in case there is anything wrong with the first one! One suggestion included using plumber's sealant or Araldite, especially if the exact size of tubing couldn't be obtained, and someone else suggested softening tubing in hot water to get it to fit easier. We're not entirely convinced by these suggestions, but feel free to try them if you wish. If you cannot get the right sized tubing at one hardware store, it is maybe worth shopping around though. Someone pointed out that helium can sometimes be obtained from florists. One person asked where to buy gadgets, so we now include suggestions. Members also compared the ease of inflating a bag with helium first if they find it easy to get over their head (this is increasingly becoming popular – we call it the 'scrunch method'). Finally, in reference to writing farewell notes, Kay Carmichael touched hearts by stressing the importance of making peace with oneself before making peace with others.

Edinburgh

This workshop sold out almost overnight and frantic last minute arrangements were made for a second one. Please keep second choices in mind if booking Edinburgh! The room was slightly cramped but close to rail and coach stations, as well as many facilities. One person raised the question of diapers (appeals to some very tidy and thoughtful people as the bowels relax after death – others rely on having the stomach empty save for a small meal to settle the digestion of any pills). These can be obtained from the same supplier as the tap turners mentioned in the inset of this article. If your helium-kit tubing is slightly larger than the gas outlet, you can use clamps (often sold next to the tubing). But the screw-clamps can be difficult to manipulate. One member suggested looking out for butterfly clamps, which are much easier to tighten. One of the simplest accessories for the compression method is a long toothbrush. Others suggested elastic for the plastic bags method simply as it wouldn't rot if kept for a long time (as rubber bands do). Another thoughtful suggestion referred to when self-deliverance was in a hotel. As bank accounts are closed at death, one should really pay the bill in advance.

Bristol

A mix-up with deliveries created a slight emergency, Usually we arrange to have helium delivered to the hotel so that people can practice fitting the connections and become acquainted with the features of the tank. On this occasion the balloon company had sent it to a hotel with a similar name. Fortunately for us, the staff at the hotel went beyond the call of duty and searched Bristol until they found some helium. It was a non-disposable tank – not the sort we generally recommend (it's very heavy for a start, and the window of opportunity is small as the companies want the tanks back!) But it was good to put our brains in gear and work out how to accommodate the different fittings.

One lady was very critical of the workshop. She interrupted a lot and wrote to us to say she didn't get much from us. This is the only time this has happened and we are very sorry. We really do try to adapt them for every individual and run things democratically. On this occasion, our best efforts were sadly in vain. The more the unsatisfied individual insisted on dominating proceedings, the more agitated the rest of the group became. Leading a workshop like this the objective is to enable as many people as possible and usually that means everyone. But I'm sure she would have been lynched if the majority wish to proceed hadn't been followed. From a facilitator viewpoint, there is only so much time to get all the information across. The pace can be adjusted, but if it is adjusted too much then things become very difficult. It taught us that group workshops are ideal for most people but not for everyone.

London
This workshop booked up so quickly. Overnight we had almost double the places available. A second workshop was hurriedly convened (with a bit of hotel jugglery) so they ran on consecutive days. (A big thank you to the lady who brought me a fruit cake – a kind and unusual gesture that touched me – ed.) London participants were the most intense and well prepared group. People seemed to have read everything on the subject, expressed their questions clearly and concisely, and were adept at cooperating in a group situation. One lady

brought along an inaccurate self-deliverance book from another organisation – we were able to demonstrate this through some open analysis and put her mind at rest.

One unusual guest was Naomi Richards, an anthropology post-graduate student who had registered to better understand approaches of people to death. She took part the same as any member (with the consent of the whole group) and also interviewed some members privately who didn't have to rush off afterwards.

What people say . . .

To get a feel of the responses, here are some of the comments we have received in letters from people who have attended workshops:

From Warminster, Wiltshire:
I just wanted to thank you for all the care and detail you put into the Workshop that took place on Saturday 17th December in London. I was very sorry that I was unable to stay until the end and so missed two of the subjects - but I find the other two very helpful and the whole day was extremely interesting and thought provoking.

Sheila M Jones

From Wimbledon, London:
It is hard to say how great an impact the Workshop I attended in December last has had on me. I've been a member of EXIT on and off since 1975 but never before had practical hands-on information. The workshop was conducted in a friendly manner and at the right level, assuming little or no previous

knowledge or expertise. I enjoyed very much the presence of others of like knowledge. The practical experience of actually using materials "hands on" is invaluable and should always be emphasised. As you say, we think, 'OK, I've got my "stuff"' - I'll just go when I'm ready - but the details could be difficult to overcome when push comes to shove.

Hazel Sherrington

From Edinburgh:
At the workshop in Glasgow in November, you asked for feedback. I'd like to break down my comments into sections:

a) Organisation: I thought the choice of venue was good – I'm not familiar with Glasgow but, knowing that it would be near the stations made me happier about booking. I also appreciated the fact that reasonably priced food was available on the premises – it made it easy for us to get into conversation at lunchtime in a way that wouldn't have been possible if we'd been wandering the street looking for a café. I also felt the size of the group was good: small enough not to be intimidating but, I would think, large enough for those who didn't want to speak to feel comfortable.

b) Content: I expected to find it informative (since I knew nothing to start with!) but I particularly appreciated the practical details you included: where to buy things, what to ask for, etc.

c) Presentation: I was impressed with the way you handled questions and comments, and with the way in which you varied your 'teaching' techniques in the course of the day. (I have the attention span of a gerbil but was kept interested throughout!)

If the above sounds like I am easily pleased, I want to assure you that the reverse is true! I've just retired from 30 years of teaching, and specialised in work with 'difficult' teenagers, so I know that keeping an audience – even one of willing adults – engaged all day is quite a challenge. Also, through my job, I've had a lifetime of sitting through conferences and courses where I felt my time was being wasted due to poor presentation or preparation on the part of the speaker. I've filled countless evaluation sheets with negative comments, so I'm actually a very demanding participant!

So, overall, I'd like to thank you for a very productive day.

Jane Colkett

From Aberystwyth, Wales:
Here is my endorsement of your workshop project, as invited. Attending the Birmingham workshop was a revelation. It made me realise how much this is hands-on work which requires hands-on training. It's too important to rely on the more fallible method of just reading it up. Moreover, working with an experienced trainer gave me much greater confidence and assurance in the methods. And the fellowship of the other workshop participants was heartwarming and supportive. I couldn't have wished for more sane and good humoured companions.

Ken Jones

From Glos:
I wish to thank you for coming down to London last week to conduct a self-deliverance workshop. Although I have been, and still am, a member of various voluntary euthanasia societies in different countries, I have never had the opportunity to attend a workshop. In fact, very few societies offer such a practical workshop.

It was interesting and helpful to me, and I am sure also to other participants, to receive an explanation and assessment of different methods of self-deliverance and their 'pros' and 'cons'. The group discussion helped individuals decide which method(s) were most suitable for their individual needs and preferences. It was helpful to be able to discuss matters freely among a group of like-minded individuals without fear or apprehension. The whole atmosphere was supportive. I congratulate you on the running of the workshop. (Contribution enclosed.)

Christopher John Aeschlimann

From Bedford:
For some time I had been looking forward to learning how to apply the techniques that I'd read about in the Exit Newsletter, having missed several previous workshops. The resulting day exceeded my expectations in every way, and proved to be a most valuable experience. Many small details were covered that could not be included in written articles, and these might make all the difference when using self-deliverance methods. The following list summarises some of the benefits I found attending.

Having the opportunity to actually try out and handle equipment such as bags, helium cylinder and the ratchet tie-down brought out practical differences in their ease of use that couldn't possibly be had from reading about them.

Trying the methods for myself gave me more confidence that I would be able to use them in practice. It became clear why completely different sized plastic bags were needed when used with helium, compared to without, and the reasons were understood.

I found where my own carotid arteries are for the first time, having looked for them in vain at home before the demonstration. Being shown how to connect a helium cylinder made it much more likely that I wouldn't make mistakes. I found that some methods needed physical strength that might be demanding if I was frail or ill. However, the variety of methods demonstrated would allow one to be chosen that was suitable for most circumstances.

Interaction between workshop members helped to bring out some aspects that I wouldn't have thought of on my own. Chris concentrated on methods that were accessible to most people, avoiding, for example, those drugs that are hard to obtain. It was valuable to meet other members and have the opportunity to talk freely about topics that are taboo among my usual friends.

Like some other attendees, before the workshop I had some apprehension that it might be overly delicate, or rather morbid. In fact, it was a thoroughly pleasant experience, with free and natural discussion in a friendly, relaxed atmosphere. Chris dispelled any artificial formality and led the workshop in a light-hearted, humorous way, while always recognising that we were discussing one of the most important decisions that any of us will have to face. He allowed us to participate fully and interrupt with questions as necessary. At one point he even left us on our own to fathom out the helium connections, since we were more likely to remember what we'd learnt if we had to do it unaided. In spite of the freedom to question and discuss, Chris kept to his timetable and managed to cover all the topics fully. In a lunchtime discussion with several other members, we agreed that this was one of the best-led workshops of many we had attended, including those of our professional lives.

C.C. of Bedford (full name withheld by request)

From Tonbridge:
This is to thank you for a great value-for-money workshop yesterday. A sordid way of putting it. 'Value for time' would have been better. Or perhaps, for the more physically handicapped, Michelin's 'vaut la visite' Would be the most appropriate.

I have been to many meetings/workshops of Exit over the last fifteen years since I joined. My late wife and I were both members, but she was the breadwinner and I had time to take part. I can summarise by saying that a day's workshop has always been worth a month's reading the literature. The literature is fine. Keep it coming. It is there to fall back on. But the workshops provide a hands-on experience which most of us need.

For example, you provided a splendid presentation of the helium method of asphyxiation with a clear series of OHP images. The session which followed reinforced the simplicity of all this but also brought out the small but important difficulty for some of us in opening the rather stiff taps on the cyclinder - and suggested ways of coping with it.

The level of presentations was just right. Neither talking down to children nor up to the techies. There was enough time for pertinent questions, but not for anecdotal stuff which, though interesting, would not have moved us forward much.

Exit members really should make every effort to come to the workshops. Those who do not come have no idea how much they are missing. I know it is difficult for some disabled members to get to a workshop even if it is within possible distance. I myself am held together with all sorts of external tubing and leg bags and live in perpetual apprehension of the plumbing coming apart somewhere where on-the-spot repairs would be difficult, but I don't regret having taken the risk yesterday at all.

A suggestion. With the endless appearance of new proprietary drugs it is often hard to know what sort of an animal a zolpidem or a temazepam might be. Having worked in the third world most of my life, where drugs appeared from many sources in the pharmacies, I thought it worthwhile to buy once a year a copy of 'BNF' the British National Formulary. You can get it 'over-the-counter' at many bookshops or supplied by the publisher, Pharmaceutical Press, PO Box 151, Wallingford, Oxford, OX10 8QU, https://www.pharmpress.com. The ISBN changes with each edition, but usually begins with 9 85369. It gives the generic names of most of the proprietary drugs and lists them all by category (e.g. hypnotics / anxiolytics / antidepressants . . .) But you must have known this already. My suggestion is that readers of the Newsletter should be made aware of it.

Michael Dobbyn

From London:
I would like to thank Chris Docker and Exit for an excellent workshop on Saturday. It was practical, informed, well-paced, thorough, sympathetic and pertinent. Chris Docker was reassuring and amusing and very much in control of his material. The venue was comfortable and the whole day relaxed and easy.

Kim Lewis-Lavender

From London:
I have been a member of Exit for almost 20 years. I joined because I feel very strongly that it is a basic human right to be

in control over when and how your life should end. Back then, I focussed on the principles and I wasn't too concerned about the practicalities. Recently I have attended one of Exit's workshops, and found it excellent. It gives such comfort to know how to end your life in a painless and dignified way, if and when the need to do so arises.

Per-Olof Larsson

From Gloucestershire:
We would like to take this opportunity to thank you for the brilliant workshop you ran last Saturday. Both Tom and I gained a great deal of information and came away feeling enlightened and so much happier. We feel that we can now enjoy the rest of our lives secure in the knowledge that we have the necessary information we need to end those lives in dignity as and when we decide to do so - thank you so very much. We did not really know what to expect - there was some apprehension and trepidation - but you put us all at our ease and the whole experience was good. You managed to look at and tackle a very difficult and serious subject with rationality, compassion and even humour at times - not an easy task - well done!

A very pleasant and informative day! If anyone out there would like to go on a similar workshop but is feeling what we initially felt, ie doubt and hesitation, we urge them to attend - they will find it invaluable and very, very comforting. None of us knows what fate has in store for us and in a perfect world we should have no fear of death, but it is the manner of that dying that is of the greatest concern. To be able to control your own leaving of life is a great source of solace and peace. We are so grateful for receiving this knowledge.

Jan & Tom Edwards

From Somerset:

I would like to take this opportunity to say how very helpful the information gained in the Self-deliverance workshop was, both at the meeting but probably even more so in the time spent thinking things over since. The content and the way in which you conducted the meeting filled me with the conviction that should I ever need to use this information I would not have fears of not being able to end my life the way I wish to and when I wish to. The opportunity to meet like-minded people who were not afraid to talk openly with great feeling and, thank goodness, humour, was especially uplifting. Having nursed many people at the end of their lives, both family and friends and professionally, I know for sure that if only many had had forethought, knowledge and support they would have been spared so much suffering. Without doubt the ability to communicate one's fears and practical doubts and to receive straight unemotional and solid information must be the best help of all. Thank you so very much again. I have to say that I really enjoyed myself.

Pauline Macmillan

From Edinburgh:

The day was extremely valuable for many reasons. The technical content was enormously helpful and it was a tremendous relief to know that the various methods of self-deliverance had been so thoroughly researched. The workshop also made me face up to the actual mechanics of self deliverance and the need for meticulous and early preparation, rather than postponing the planning to some indefinite date in the future. It was extremely comforting to be sitting in a room with twenty seemingly rational people discussing self-deliverance with seriousness but with such good humour. It made me feel much less isolated and neurotic!

Ruth Malcolm-Smith

From Thurso:

Thank you very much for the workshop in Glasgow. Everything was so well organised – not a minute of our time was wasted as far as I was concerned. Thank you for your patience – all my questions were answered. It helped a lot that we were able to try out (within limits!) the helium and compression methods, and I particularly appreciated getting details of where to buy the various item. I feel much more confident now that I can choose when and how I wish to die – hopefully not for many years yet – and this is a source of comfort.

Margaret Smedley

From Dunfermline:

I had a great day at the workshop, which I found to be very informative. Hands-on experience with the various methods has certainly boosted my confidence and attitude to deal with one's chosen source. I am now in a much happier and settled frame of mind in what I intend to do. Thank you.

Tom Cairns

A big thank you to all the participants at workshops these past several years - for your warmth an fellowship, your ideas, for everything you have brought to the sessions, and the feedbacks that help us and other members to spot difficulties before they arise and face the future with knowledge and confidence.

Some frequently asked questions

Exit has so few resources that letters are often not answered very quickly. Other things (like producing this book) have to take priority. It seems unfair that people have to wait a long time to get an answer to common questions that sadly have a fairly standard response, so we include some of the common ones here.

Estimating dosages – how do I know how many sleeping tablets I should take?

This varies from person to person. Usually the sleeping tablets are not the cause of death but taken in combination with the plastic bag or chloroquine to ensure a good sleep until the end. (For exceptions to this, see the chapter on Drugs.) The general rule is to see how many tablets you need for eight hours daytime sleep and multiply by ten. This will ensure you are in a sufficiently deep sleep not to wake up. The 'daytime' consideration is so that it is at a time when you wouldn't just fall asleep anyway.

I'd like to visit you in the Office to discuss a few matters

The Exit office is not generally open to the public. Usually when people say 'discuss a few matters' they mean ask advice about methods of suicide. This one-to-one advice is prohibited in the current legal environment. We can answer questions in the book or workshops for general information on self-deliverance and suicide, but more personal advice leaves us open to charges of assisting. So we don't discuss it, and a visit to the Office would not yield the result sought. (If there's further questions after reading this book, do sign up for one of the workshops – these are held around the UK and may be taken abroad in the future.)

But can you meet me or come to see me for a confidential chat – no-one need know about it?
I'm afraid the answer is the same. We work within the letter of the law, officially and unofficially. Many years ago, an official in one right-to-die group went further and advised and helped people in person. To make matters even more serious, in some of the cases it transpired that the people were not as seriously ill as had been supposed. Such situations would lead to Exit being shut down and no longer being able to help anyone. Exit is very clear about what it does and doesn't do.

Did you know that you can commit suicide by . . .
Exit receives on average one letter a month detailing a new or weird and wonderful way to die. Occasionally they lead to further research and reliable new methods (such as happened with, which we first started investigating after an anonymous letter from a judo practitioner). But mostly they fall into one of a number of categories. There are methods that work but frequently produce unacceptable consequences to others, such as jumping from very high buildings. There are methods that have an unacceptably high risk-factor of unpleasant consequences with failure. There are methods that can cause death but not reliably cause death (there are very, very many that fall into this bracket). Then there are methods that we simply don't know enough about (in any scientific sense of being able to assemble sufficient data to recommend them). Research is time-consuming and costly. Saying to you, "I know someone who committed suicide by such-and-such method," doesn't mean it would work for you. This 'anecdotal' evidence is related in many right-to-die books as if it were reliable, but it is a long way from scientifically connected discourse, meta-analysis and peer review that forms the basis of the books published by Exit. If you have confidence in a particular

method then by all means use it if you wish – it is your life and your death.

The last category is methods that are only available to a few people, such as doctors or people who can obtain drugs or equipment not commonly available. You could read a whole book on barbiturates, but to little avail if you cannot get hold of them. Concentrating on such methods draws most readers away from practical methods.

I'm very ill. Can you process my Exit application more quickly please?
Exit cannot offer an 'emergency' or 'fast-track' service. This is partly to do with resources, as explained above. Secondly, it is not up to Exit to be a judge and jury to screen people for urgency and need – and doing so could present legal problems of the sort already mentioned. We supply information for future reference, not for use now. But there are also more practical reasons. Preparing for self-deliverance generally requires ample forethought, possibly a stockpiling of drugs, and generally putting things carefully in place while you still have physical and mental health. It is hard to do once you are very ill. With a very short amount of time available and no previous preparation and knowledge, putting one's efforts into getting good palliative care is often more sensible.

Can you tell me where I can go abroad to get euthanasia or assisted suicide from a sympathetic doctor?
Yes and no. Forget about the Netherlands, Belgium and Washington and Oregon – they can only offer help to their own people. Switzerland is more sympathetic but the process is far from simple. Only one organisation (at the time of writing) will help foreigners, and that is Dignitas. Their website is http://www.dignitas.ch and includes some information in

English. You can also email Dignitas at dignitas@dignitas.ch or write to them at Postfach 9 - CH 8127 Forch. There are certain costs involved, detailed in a brochure in English, available on the website, and which also explains much of the procedure. Costs include a registration fee, an annual minimal fee and, if you receive assisted suicide with their help, the associated costs of travel to Zurich, the fee for preparing an assisted suicide, and a fee for Dignitas managing everything with the authorities in relation to burial and matters after the suicide. Dignitas will require a personal letter and also a copy of the person's medical records. The total cost will come to several thousand pounds. Some critics of UK legislation against assisted suicide have pointed out that it is 'available' already for the lucky few who can afford the fees of Dignitas. Assisted suicide is specifically prohibited to non-residents in the case of the American states that allow the possibility for their citizens. The Dutch and Belgian provisions have a not dissimilar effect inasmuch that the preconditions and procedure of the law clearly establish the principle of a strong doctor-patient relationship. Outside of this long-standing personal contact, it is not possible to consider conducting legal euthanasia.

Where can I get drugs on the Internet

Although we don't recommend this as a primary means (see chapter on Drugs) it is possible to get some drugs on the Internet. As Internet addresses change from time to time and as we do not have the resources to vet them or test the drugs supplied by various Internet pharmacies, we do not recommend specific Internet sources. The main concern is fake drugs, or drugs of an unreliable strength. It is also illegal to import drugs to which you are not entitled. This includes lethal barbiturates.

What about living wills?

Living wills (advance medical directives) are a formal way of *refusing* treatment and recognised in law in many countries including the UK. In terms of a deciding when your own death will be, they can benefit only those people who will die when treatment is withheld.

I don't live in the UK – is there any chance you will be doing some workshops where I live?

Yes, but obviously it needs to be coordinated. The best way is to ask the right-to-die society in the country where you live to request one. They are in a position to advertise it and gauge the demand.

Now I have the book, do I need to join Exit?

As you find yourself wanting to understand more and more about the process of self-deliverance, you may find it will come naturally to you to join the organisation and be the among the first to hear of any new developments.

I've heard Philip Nitschke of 'Exit International' does workshops with helium. Are they the same thing?

Not really. Exit International, an Australian group not connected with Exit in any way, does a workshop that is more along the lines of a seminar. The helium section of an Exit International workshop is described in a BMJ blog: "Dr Nitschke had assembled most of the components of the apparatus on a shopping trip that morning, including a helium canister bought from a well known card shop to demonstrate the technique. The audience was given a detailed step by step guide by 'Betty' who cheerfully demonstrated the process in a series of video clips." This is very different from the Exit workshops. Participants at Exit workshops assemble the equipment themselves, discovering the ins and outs, problems, and how to overcome them. Watching a video clip does not give the same hands-on experience. Additionally, Exit provides expert advice on UK law, and a full range of methods, as covered in this handbook. (The rest of the BMJ report also suggests the two types of workshops are very different in tone and content. See *BMJ Blogs, Lee W, on Nitschke, 17 Oct 08 BMJ Group*).

Can I have a video copy of one of the workshops please?
Unfortunately, at the moment, the answer has to be no. Firstly the workshop is not a demonstration, but a journey of discovery for each person there. People learn at their own speed and the facilitator goes over essential details by means of a Power-Point summary. Members work out how to make a helium hood, experiment with equipment, find their carotid arteries and learn how to apply pressure comfortably, examine the various pills that can be used. A video could be made in the form of a professional documentary, interviewing persons if they are willing and interspersed with assistance from the facilitator or a voiceover to look at things like tourniquet tension and getting the feel of how to adjust a helium tap. But such a documentary would be costly to make. We'd also need to work with participants to look at issues such as confidentiality and anonymity. But I do recognise there is a need for such a film. Two possibilities suggest themselves for the future. One would be if someone makes a very sizeable donation so that a private documentary like the one above described could be made. The other avenue is making one ourselves. We're working on this, and already have a number of video clips to illustrate various procedures. I think it's important to show ordinary people doing them, not a facilitator who has been doing them for years. But it is an ongoing project and takes time. Sacrificing the time of participants to make a film wouldn't be right either. So we have to slowly build it up. But

the advantage is that the workshops come up with different ways of explaining things, and this in turn has been incorporated in this book. Just as we go over everything several times in the workshop, you may find yourself re-reading this book from time to time. Making sure that the knowledge is inside you rather than just on a particular page.

Five Last Acts

Joining Exit

If you wish, you can photocopy this page or copy the details for applying to Exit for membership. Please check current membership rates by telephoning 0131-556-4404 (recorded message) or connecting to the Internet and going to http://www.euthanasia.cc/new_app.html

At the time of publication, annual membership rates are £30 for UK addresses and £50 for overseas. Exit usually has no paid staff so delays may be inevitable. Membership not only furthers research but entitles you to living wills and a magazine detailing the latest updates on self-deliverance information.

Name ....

Address & postcode ....

....

Telephone number (optional)..

Email address (optional)...

Date of birth & proof of age enclosed ....

Amount enclosed (cheque) ....

Or credit card details ....

Expiry date and three digit security code ....

Send to Exit, 17 Hart Street, Edinburgh EH1 3RN (Scotland) UK

Five Last Acts

Do not resuscitate - do not dial 999

In the event that I am discovered unconscious but still alive, whether by medical personnel (including emergency services) or anyone else, I hereby, in advance, explicitly refuse consent to medical treatment, resuscitation, or any measures that might revive or prolong my life. These instructions are my declared wishes as a competent individual – persons disregarding them may be rendered liable to criminal prosecution and I hereby authorize anyone to sue, on my behalf, any persons disregarding them.

My decision was made over a period of time and was not carried out in acute desperation, nor is it the expression of a mental illness. I have consciously, rationally, deliberately and of my own free will taken measures to end my life today, to put an end to incurable and unbearable suffering, and I offer my thanks to anyone finding me for respecting my wishes as expressed in this note.

Full Name ....

Signed ....

Date ....

Five Last Acts

My wishes

Name ....

Date of birth ....

If someone has assisted you in completing this form, please fill in his or her name, address, and relationship to you:

Name ....

Address ....

Relationship ....

What would you like to say to someone reading this document about your overall attitude towards life?

....

....

....

....

....

How satisfied are you with what you have achieved in your life?

....

....

....

How would you describe your state of health at the end of your life?

....

....

....

What would you like others (family, friends, doctors) to know about this?

....

....

....

Have you made any arrangements for family or friends to assist in making after your death? If so, who has agreed to assist in making decisions and in what circumstances?

....

....

....

What general comments would you like to make about the personal relationships in your life?

....

....

....

....

What is your spiritual/religious background?

....

....

How do your beliefs affect your feelings towards serious, chronic or terminal illness?

....

....

....

....

How does your faith community, church or synagogue
support you?

....

....

....

....

What general comments would you like to make about your
beliefs?

....

....

....

What would you like to say about doctors and your other
caregivers?

....

....

....

....

What general comments would you like to make about illness, dying and death?

....

....

....

What general comments would you like to make about your funeral and burial or cremation?

....

....

Have you made your funeral arrangements? If so, with whom?

....

....

....

How would you like your obituary (announcement of your death) to read?

....

....

....

Write yourself a brief eulogy (a statement about yourself to be
read at your funeral).

....

....

....

....

....

....

....

Appendixes: My wishes

Important persons to be informed

Name, address and phone number of my doctor (G.P.)

....

....

....

My solicitor's name, address and phone number

....

....

....

Name and address of my bank

....

....

....

Sort code ....

Account number ....

Address and phone numbers of my other affairs, building societies, mortgage, life assurance policies and any other ongoing arrangements

....

....

....

....

My birth certificate, marriage or civil partnership certificate, NHS medical card, and pension and benefits books can be found:

....

....

Names and contact details of a friend, family member, or someone close to me, who should be contacted now please:

....

....

....

....

Five Last Acts

Three steps to a good death

As a parting summary, here's what I'd call 'three steps to a good death.' It should include not just the self-deliverance techniques, but writing letters to relatives, seeing that relevant forms, banking and insurance details are accessible for instance; also an appreciation of getting good palliative care where appropriate – not instead, but as well as being prepared to take matters into your own hands if necessary.

o   Visualise it. See it in your mind's eye and feel the emotion of having everything in order.
o   Focus on the end goal. Think of nothing else while you work out the details. Do the dress rehearsals until you know without a shadow of a doubt that you are completely capable and confident.
o   Be persistent. Work out the details in practice as well as in your mind's eye. Revise them annually.

Your notes

Reponses to criticism

On the use of zopiclone with chloroquine:

It was alleged by *Wozz* that the authors of *Departing Drugs* had recommended the use of zopiclone as a suitable sleeping drug to be taken for self-deliverance in combination with chloroquine.[88] A case of a person using this combination and experiencing a painful death was quoted.

Response: The quotation was inaccurate and misleading. The authors of *Departing Drugs* had never made such a recommendation. It transpired that the allegation was based on a version of Departing Drugs which the Dutch society (NVVE – of which one of the Wozz authors is an honorary member), had reissued in their own version and with unauthorised text. NVVE had made the recommendation to use zopiclone with chloroquine, not the authors of Departing Drugs.

On the use of benzodiazepines with chloroquine:

The Wozz authors[89] criticised the Exit/Departing Drugs claim that benzodiazepines are not the best choice of sleeping drug for use with chloroquine.

> "Diazepam is indeed used to counteract chloroquine poisoning. But this does not allow us to conclude that diazepam is an antidote to the lethal effect of chloroquine on the heart. Tests on animals have confirmed this. Also on theoretical grounds diazepam would not be expected to prevent cardiac arrest brought on by chloroquine. In our view, diazepam has been used by

---

[88] Admiraal P, Chabot B, Ogden R, Rietveld A, Glerum J, *Guide to Humane Self-Chosen Death*, WOZZ Foundation, Macdonald 2006. Page 57-58.

[89] Ibid.p.56

clinicians in emergency cases against chloroquine poisoning because it suppresses muscular contractions and epileptic seizures. It is also exactly these contractions and seizures that one will want to suppress in the case of a chloroquine overdose for a humane self-chosen death."[90]

The Wozz authors go on to recommend a sleeping tablet combination comprising either a) barbiturate, or b) a combination of short + long-acting benzodiazepine[91], irrespective of the fact that most of these drugs are almost impossible to obtain.

In support of the idea that benzodiazepines do not interfere with the lethal effect of chloroquine – an idea contrary to mainstream clinical practice – the authors curiously quote a retrospective study by *Demaziere et al,* [92]yet that very study states:

"No statistically significant difference was found between either the control and diazepam groups or between subgroups, concerning the distribution of age, sex, amount of chloroquine supposed to have been ingested, delay in hospital admission and death rate. **However, there was a higher death rate in the asymptomatic subgroup not treated with diazepam than in the diazepam group.**"

---

[90] Ibid. pp.56-57.

[91] Ibid.p.59

[92] Demaziere J, Saissy JM, Vitris M, Seck M, Ndiaye M, Gaye M, Marcoux L. *Effects of diazepam on mortality from acute chloroquine poisoning,* Ann Fr Anesth Reanim. 1992;11(2):164-7.

Response:

Wozz quote two other old studies (out of the many, many studies available on chloroquine poisoning), but the findings are inconclusive. One, for instance, speaks of a number of treatments including diazepam and concludes that, "these elements, either singly or in combination, do not appear to have a truly antidotal effect in acute chloroquine poisoning."[93]

A third speaks of a trial involving diazepam in the treatment of chloroquine poisoning involving less than 4g of chloroquine, well below the recommended dose for self-deliverance, and makes the conclusion that, "Diazepam, at the dose studied, does not appear to reverse the chloroquine-induced membrane-stabilising effect in acute moderately severe chloroquine intoxication,"[94] an observation which might be of rather limited relevance to the use of chloroquine in large doses.

It is clear that there is room for debate on the issue of diazepam's interaction with acute chloroquine overdose. Even the Wozz authors' claim that the theory is backed up by experiments with animals is strongly contested, especially if we examine more up-to-date material than that quoted by the Wozz authors. For instance, we find, "Studies in animals and humans suggest that early aggressive management of severe chloroquine intoxication has a cardioprotective effect and reduces the fatality rate."[95]

[93] Clemessy L, Taboulet P, Hoffman R, Hantson P, Barriot P, Bismuth C, Baud F, *Treatment of acute chloroquine poisoning: a 5-year experience,* Crit Care Med. 1996 Jul;24(7):1189-95.

[94] Clemessy J, Angel G, Borron S, Ndiaye M, Le Brun F, Julien H, Galliot M, Vicaut E, Baud F, Therapeutic trial of diazepam versus placebo in acute chloroquine intoxications of moderate gravity.

[95] Brent J, *Critical care toxicology,* Mosby 2005, p.675.

And in enumerating the specific types of aggressive management, the author is quite clear:

> "Diazepam (0.1–0.3mg/kg) given by slow intravenous
> injection, repeated as necessary, is effective at control-
> ling convulsions. In addition, **diazepam at approxi-
> mately 10 times higher doses has been reported to
> have a specific cardio-protective action in severe
> chloroquine poisoning.**"[96]

Brent (above) goes into considerable detail and with considerable supporting evidence over the cardioprotective effect of
diazepam and writing some fifteen years later than the journal
studies quoted by Wozz. This suggests that Wozz's claim that,
"Diazepam and the other benzodiazepines . . . are not an
antidote to the lethal effect of chloroquine on the heart,"[97]
must be viewed with considerable scepticism.

These studies querying the effect of diazepam on chloroquine
toxicity have been well-known for many years, but the majority
of modern authorities, like Brent, while admitting that the
action is not completely understood, come down clearly on the
side of the mainstream that concludes the opposite of the
Wozz authors. As *Olson* states:

> ". . . diazepam has been reported to antagonise the
> cardiotoxic effect of chloroquine (the mechanism is
> unknown, but **diazepam may compete with
> chloroquine for fixation sites on cardiac cells**)."[98]

---

[96] Ibid.

[97] Wozz, p.57.

[98] Olson K (ed), Poisoning & Drug Overdose, McGraw Hill 2007, pp.419-421.

Similarly a paper from Hammersmith Hospital and published in the British Medical Journal[99] had cited studies that diazepam increases the urinary excretion of chloroquine and went on to explain the effect as far as it is understood:

> "The action of diazepam at central nervous system receptors may contribute to its beneficial effects in chloroquine poisoning, but there is increasing evidence that a specific action of diazepam at binding sites on heart muscle is important. These putative receptors on cardiac myocytes are quite distinct from diazepam receptors in the central nervous system, being y-aminobutyric acid independent, and until recently had no known function. Benzodiazepine analogues at these receptors have been shown to shorten the duration of intracellular action potential in animal myocardium and may have anti-arrhythmic properties. Moreover, diazepam has been reported to reduce the concentration of chloroquine in rat cardiac muscle despite increasing blood concentrations."

On the basis of leading theoretical analysis, practical results, current clinical practice, and combined weight of opinion, it would seem likely that the Wozz authors simply failed properly to understand the action of diazepam in chloroquine overdose.

On the risk of PVS from using the compression method without a plastic bag:
Pieter Admiraal, a Dutch anaesthetist, posted on the Right-to-die Digest[100] that the compression method was dangerous

---

[99] Meeran K, Jacobs M, Scott J; Mcneil N, Lynn W, Cohen J, Pusey C, Phillips J, et al., *Grand Rounds - Hammersmith-Hospital - Chloroquine Poisoning.* BMJ 1993, 307:49-50.

[100] An online news digest managed by Derek Humphry.

since the brain stem has its own blood supply and hence persistent vegetative state might result (a condition possible when brain death but not brain stem death has occurred) even when the brain had died from lack of oxygenated blood.

Response:

This has been documented in exceptional cases of *manual* strangulation, or the 'choking game' played by some children.[101] None of the cases that I have been able to find in the literature that involve *ligature* strangulation involved PVS however, and it is necessary to ask the possible reasons for this while at the same time including all possible safety measures for persons using the method for self-deliverance. But the idea that the brainstem would simply carry on since it has its own blood supply is seriously flawed. As pointed out by one of the world's leading neurologists,[102] with carotid occlusion alone death usually results from brain swelling and herniation that destroys the brainstem (rather than the idea of brain death leaving the brainstem intact). Manual strangulation, for instance, often involves transient pressure on the neck, whereas pressure from a ligature would normally remain in place. This might suggest both a greater chance of serious oedema that would damage the brain stem, possible asphyxiation which would involve death of the brainstem, and continued obstruction of the venous return that would cause passive congestion of blood in the vessels within the brain.[103]

---

[101] See the chapter on Compression in this volume for an explanation of the choking game.

[102] Posner J, private correspondence, September 2010.

[103] Hawley D, McClane G, Strack G, Violence: Recognition, Management, and Prevention, A Review of 300 Attempted Strangulation Cases - Part III: Injuries In Fatal Cases, Journal of Emergency Medicine 21(3), pp. 317–322, 2001.

Hawley et al list the mechanisms, the first three of which apply to ligature compression, as described in this manual:

"1. Cardiac dysrhythmia may be provoked by pressure on the carotid artery nerve ganglion (carotid body reflex) causing cardiac arrest.
2. Pressure obstruction of the carotid arteries prevents blood flow to the brain.
3. Pressure on the jugular veins prevents venous blood return from the brain, gradually backing up blood in the brain resulting in unconsciousness, depressed respiration, and asphyxia.
4. Pressure obstruction of the larynx cuts off air flow to the lungs, producing asphyxia."[104]

Hawley *et al* reassuringly point out that, "the overall process is completely painless."

The theoretical possibility of the brain stem surviving however should not be completely discounted until there is more evidence, even if it would seem that, however rare, it is more likely to occur in cases where a person has been 'saved' or the pressure on the neck has only been applied for a short time. For this reason, I have strengthened the recommendation to use a small plastic bag with the compression method. Workshops have indicated this causes no practical problem.

---

[104] Ibid. p.320

Quote/Unquote

Is there a place for a few quotations? Small soundbites of verse, philosophy or poetry can be a way to focus or inspire – but they are so personal! What one person enjoys as profound, another may find trite. Here are a few favourites, but feel free to think of your own.

I've more come to an acceptance of the finiteness of life. I'm like a child whose play is not ruined by knowing that in an hour he'll have to go to bed. Further I identify with certain persons and groups who have chosen death with dignity rather than life without it. So, with the thinking and planning I have done, I feel my parachute is tested and packed, and I can turn my thinking to how to live creatively.

Morris Friedell

Death is not extinguishing the light: it is putting out the lamp because the dawn has come.

Anon

What separates a chosen 'good death' from a bad one almost always comes down, upon analysis, to the amount of planning, attention to detail, and the quality of the assistance, all of which are vital to decent termination of life.

Derek Humphry, Final Exit

It appears that often the suicidal older patient receives more sympathy than their teenage equivalents. Older people rarely have to confront the 'attention-seeking' or 'manipulative' labels that are frequently applied to their more youthful counterparts....Perhaps some nurses support the idea that an older person's suicide attempt is a sane response to an insane or harsh reality.

Lindsay Bowles, Nursing Times(1993) 89(31):32-34. p.32

While most drugs have side-effects (effects other than the purpose for which they are designed), and most side-effects are more pronounced when a drug is misused or taken in overdose, a side-effect like death is always going to be a serious problem for a drug manufacturer. The company responsible for manufacturing a drug that will cause death in overdose will always be nervous about such a product and there will be a search to develop safer alternatives. So, while there are some drugs that do reliably cause death if taken in this way, this number is small and decreasing.

Philip Nitshcke & Fiona Stewart, The Peaceful Pill Handbook

Doubt and confusion could be avoided if the uncertainties of case law were replaced by statute. We suggest that this could be achieved relatively easily by adding to the Suicide Act 1961 a section that excluded from the provisions of section 2 a registered medical practitioner who, given the existence of a competent directive, is providing assistance to a patient who is suffering from a progressive and irremediable condition and who is prevented, or will be prevented, by physical disability from ending his or her own life without assistance.

Ken Mason and Deidre Mulligan, Euthanasia by stages. Lancet
(1996) 347:810-811

The plastic bag is getting the same sort of public-relations reputation as the wire coat hanger did in the abortion debate, except the bag is 100 per cent effective.

Derek Humphry, Suicide by asphyxiation after the publication of
Final Exit, NEJM (Letters, Replies) 1994, 330(14):1017. p.1017

You speak to me of narcissism but I reply that it is a matter of my life.

Antonin Artaud, as quoted by Anne Sexton at the beginning of her poem, 'Suicide Note'

In the event a person is definitely going to die and he is either in great pain or has virtually become a vegetable, and prolonging his existence is only going to cause difficulties and suffering for others, the termination of his life may be permitted according to Mahayana Buddhist ethics.
The Dalai Lama, quoted by Roy Perrett in: Buddhism, euthanasia and the sanctity of life. JME (1996) 22:309-313.

Medical advances, without which Tony Bland could never in any event have been kept alive, are not unalloyed bonuses, nor is practice value-free. Doctors, lawyers, ethicists and others recognise that this is the case. But nothing will be solved simply by changing the way in which decisions are made – say, by removing them from the courts and bringing them within a legislative structure – unless other principles, cherished by all jurisdictions form the basis of the decision-making criteria. Legislation provides the opportunity to create a framework which does not rely on sophistry, and which also takes account of wider matters. Principles such as transparency and accountability of decision-making, formal justice and compassion will not inevitably form any more part of a legislative than a court-based framework, but they could.
Sheila McLean, Human Rights and the Patient in a Persistent Vegetative State. International Legal Practitioner 1994; 19(1):19-20.

It is sometimes argued that physician assistance in a patient's suicide would violate the Hippocratic Oath. It is true that the Oath, in its original form, does contain an explicit injunction that the physician shall not give a lethal potion to a patient who requests it, nor make a suggestion to that effect. (To do so was apparently common Greek medical practice at the time.) But the Oath in its original form also contains explicit prohibitions of the physicians accepting fees for teaching medicine, and of performing surgery - even on gall stones. These latter prohibitions are not retained in modern reformulations of the Oath, and I see no reason why the provision against giving lethal potions to patients who request it should be. What is central to the Oath and cannot be deleted without altering its essential character is the requirement that the physician shall come "for the benefit of the sick." Under the argument advanced here, physician assistance in patient suicide may indeed be for the benefit of the patient. What the Oath would continue to prohibit is physician assistance in the suicide for the physician's own gain or to serve other institutional or societal ends.

Peggy Battin, The Least Worse Death, 1994 OUP p128-129

Lay down

your sweet and weary head

Night is falling

You have come to journey's end

Sleep now, and dream

of the ones who came before

They are calling

from across the distant shore . . .

From Into the West *by Annie Lennox*

Index

(With apologies to readers: this index is far from complete or even systematic due to time pressures. Readers are urged to make their own index additions for private use during the course of studying the complete book.)

A

B

C

D

About the author

Chris Docker is an established writer in Law and Ethics in Medicine, producing key works for the professions, academics and the public on topics that include living wills, death & dying, and human transplants. For over 15 years he has been one of the world's leading researchers into the reality of 'self-deliverance' – the methods to accomplish one's own easy, peaceful and dignified death – when all other measures to relieve suffering and indignity have failed. He is Director of Exit and has led the interactive workshops run for many years across the UK. Five Last Acts is his third book on self-deliverance.

Short bibliography

- Collected Living Wills, 1992.

- Departing Drugs (principal author) 1993

- Beyond Final Exit (co-author) 1995

- Advance Directive / Living Wills, *in:* Contemporary Issues in Law, Medicine and Ethics (ed. S.A.M. McLean) 1996

- The Way Forward, *in:* Death, Dying and the Law (ed. S.A.M.McLean) 1996

- Living Wills, *in:* Finance and Law for the Older Client (Society of Trust and Estate Practitioners, Gen.Ed. C.Whitehouse) 2000 (updated 2003)

- Ethical and Legal Dilemmas with Organ Transplants, *in:* Health Services Law and Practice (eds: M.Bloom, A.Harris,S.Waddington) 2001.

- End of Life, *in:* Health Services Law and Practice (eds: M.Bloom, A.Harris,S.Waddington) 2001.

- Five Last Acts 2007 (2nd edition, 2010)